Visibility and Control

Visibility and Control

Cameras and Certainty in Governing

Jeff Heydon

LEXINGTON BOOKS
Lanham • Boulder • New York • London

Published by Lexington Books
An imprint of The Rowman & Littlefield Publishing Group, Inc.
4501 Forbes Boulevard, Suite 200, Lanham, Maryland 20706
www.rowman.com

6 Tinworth Street, London SE11 5AL, United Kingdom

British Library Cataloguing in Publication Information Available

Library of Congress Cataloging-in-Publication Data on File

ISBN 978-1-7936-1817-7 (cloth)
ISBN 978-1-7936-1818-4 (electronic)

For Katie

Contents

Acknowledgments

I owe a great deal of thanks to a number of people for their help on this project. First and foremost, I would like to acknowledge the patience and support of my wife and of my family. Without their understanding, there is very little chance this book could have been written.

I would also like to thank those at Goldsmiths who were kind enough to look at my work and offer their impressions and suggest the changes that mattered: Luciana Parisi, Goetz Bachman, Peter Koepping, Gregor Claude, and all fellow members of the Centre for Cultural Studies PhD program who listened to me during seminars and offered considered and informed responses to my thinking. Scott Lash and Michael Richardson deserve an enormous amount of appreciation and recognition for their patience and guidance in the final stages.

There are myriad others who have helped me without realizing it during the writing of this text. You are too many to name, but I will try to thank all of you as we meet again.

Part I

THE IMAGE AS EVIDENCE

Introduction

The "I," the Eye, and the Screen

A great deal of work has been done and is currently being done on the efficacy of surveillance technologies in the digital age. Much of this work involves an appreciation of the contemporary culture's reliance on technological systems for communication—social media, cellular connectivity, Global Positioning Service (GPS) technologies, and so on—and the emergence of data-driven methods of tracking people. The inclusion of cameras and GPS technology in mobile phone design has increased the certainty with which large corporations or states are able to actively track and produce evidence of a person's whereabouts and activities. There are even early indications of a shift in agency: Repeated releases of video footage depicting police misconduct and malfeasance appears to indicate a shift from domination to resistance. The lens may now be pointed toward those who are in positions of power. The technological means for private citizens to record and display the behavior of police in defense of claims of abuse is significant and will be taken up in more detail in the conclusion of this text. This does add to the overall impression that contemporary Western culture is characterized by a constant transmission and filtering of data. The current literature is rife with accounts and analyses of the collection of data and what that means on theoretical and practical levels. Intelligence leaks by Edward Snowden and Chelsea Manning provide a framework for an understanding of visibility under contemporary surveillance regimes. The sheer scope of networked data surveillance and the degree of intrusion it represents are astonishing, but an understanding of the scope of available information and the tools that are in use to monitor that information only tells part of the story. What normally gets left out of analyses that address this issue is how that data is used and what that indicates about the certainty felt toward systems that use technological means to capture and record information.

For the most part, there is a reflexive trust in machines. The collection of information via algorithms appears to follow natural laws rather than man-made ones. The positioning of a CCTV camera doesn't appear to indicate a position of bias or unconscious editing and a video file of an event has the same credibility whether it was filmed with a CCTV camera or a mobile phone. This book will use CCTV as a means of illustrating the social and cultural importance of the faith in communications technologies and, more specifically, images. The event of someone filming something and that filmed image being taken as self-evidence is as old as Vertov's *Man with a Movie Camera*. This text, however, will address networked video footage—namely, footage that is produced by and transmitted across a network—and how it functions in policing and prosecutions. Separating the two is crucial here; as will be argued later, part of the intrinsic validity of the CCTV image is the knowledge that the image is produced for the purposes of maintaining security and that this security is ensured by an apparatus that includes personnel as well as cameras. Its acceptability is rooted in the knowledge that the police and the courts have validated the technology by installing the camera in the first place and then accepting it as evidence in court. Whereas footage produced by an individual is often treated with a degree of skepticism by media and the courts—as was the case of the footage of LAPD officers beating motorist Rodney King in 1991[1]—the same degree of critical evaluation is rarely given to CCTV footage.

Typically, evaluations of the importance of the image are rooted either in case studies involving popular culture or theoretical analyses addressing the existing theory. This text will address these issues, but with also attempt to provide a new perspective in addition to the traditional elements; examples of legal decisions arrived at with the help of CCTV footage will be added to the argument. This will improve the technical understanding of how images can exert power or be used as mechanisms of power in Canadian and British culture.

The text will begin with a short historical overview of the use of CCTV in the United Kingdom and Canada. Next, different case studies taken from the Canadian and British court systems will be examined to illustrate the impact of CCTV on the prosecution of cases and court judgments. After an examination of relevant theoretical elements related to CCTV (including Marshall McLuhan, Jean Baudrillard and others) as a media format, the use of speed cameras and the implementation of CCTV systems as a means of testifying in court will be examined. The question of governmentality and the theoretical work of Michel Foucault will then be employed as a means of evaluating the importance of visibility in contemporary state policing and security practices. The G20 summits in London and Toronto will be evaluated as examples of the use of CCTV in anticipated moments of conflict and as a means of demarcating physical space as belonging to the state. Examples from popular culture will also be used to illustrate the degree to which faith in the veracity of images and other electronic data is taken for granted.

The earliest recorded link between a technological method of viewing someone without their knowledge and police surveillance occurred in Glasgow in 1824 when a camera obscura was used to watch a pickpocket at work.[2] The use of the captured image in policing, however, came into prominence around twenty years later when French police started taking daguerreotype images of convicted criminals. Police in the United States began keeping daguerreo-type images of prisoners in San Francisco, New York, Cleveland, and Chicago between 1854 and 1870. Canadian police followed suit in 1874.[3] These images were matched with textual descriptions of the subject and details of their crimes. The resulting pages were bound together in albums dubbed "rogues galleries" and were collected by police departments around the globe.[4]

These collections of sordid faces invariably complimented a belief that the criminality of a person could be predicted by measuring dominant facial features. Physiognomy, the technique of determining someone's character according to physical characteristics was accepted up to around the same time as the development of the rogues' galleries. The psychiatrist Hugh Welch Diamond employed photography in determining what he believed were the facial indicators of insanity and eugenicist Francis Galton created a form of composite photography that he claimed demonstrated different criminal facial types.[5] The result was that the collection of images of criminals took on two distinct purposes: the demonstration of repeat offenses and the indication of the features that made it obvious that they were doomed to offend in the first place.

Physiognomy eventually lost its credibility, but the use of photography in the process of policing and the compilation of data for security purposes was too useful to disappear altogether. The rogues' galleries were helpful in determining whether someone was a repeat offender using another name and the distribution of them to other jurisdictions allowed police and courts to demonstrate that someone was carrying out the familiar bad acts in new places and, therefore, should not be granted leniency as a first-time offender. The development of fingerprint identification cemented the link between the camera and policing as, to quote Jonathan Finn,

> The photograph is central to fingerprint identification. The camera is present from the crime scene to the courtroom. It is a central means through which prints are collected, examined, identified, and shared. The individual, physical print holds little value in comparison to its photographic representation, which

can traverse physical barriers and can be at work in any number of locations and context simultaneously.[6]

Most importantly, the fingerprint and the photograph of the print are almost never separated in practice. The photograph of the fingerprint is treated as the fingerprint itself and its introduction as evidence is rarely questioned. The camera is trusted implicitly and it is the details of the image rather than the reliability of the image itself that are the points of argument during the investigation and at trial.[7]

These previous uses of photographs in policing and in prosecutions dealt with managing existing problems rather than anticipating or capturing new ones. The camera's use was in its ability to be pointed at something that was worth capturing and capturing it. The fingerprint or the criminal had to already be known to the police in order for them to be captured. The major shift that occurred with CCTV was that the lens would be pointed at something that *had the potential* to be of importance rather than already being important.

Governments across the world present camera surveillance as though it is an intrinsic component of the policing of contemporary cities. For instance, an extensive system of CCTV cameras that were erected for the 2009 G20 summit remain in downtown Toronto despite prior assurances that they would be removed immediately after the event had concluded.[8] In Redbridge, United Kingdom, motorists' complaints regarding violations of their privacy and a lack of flexibility applied in assessing fines generated by CCTV cameras were countered by the local council's arguments that the cameras increased "safety."[9] The prosecutions that resulted from the captured footage all resulted in guilty verdicts since it was found to be impossible to challenge the video evidence—a camera cannot be cross-examined and no one would suggest that a machine only remembers certain things or has some intrinsic bias. The evidence given in these cases was therefore accepted as the testimony of unimpeachable witnesses. The subtext is always that the collection of information is benign rather than some sinister property inherent to the surveillance apparatus, but is this an assumption anyone should be making? If anyone raises questions about the efficacy or morality of the technology's operation, then the only response they are likely to receive is that they must have something to hide. The purpose of this book, therefore, is to challenge the assumptions made with respect to technology. Though this is not the first time this question has been asked, the approach, I would argue, is unique in that it attempts to include the active application of images in the judicial process (CCTV footage, speed cameras, etc.) to the interpretive question of how images function as a source of and justification for power in contemporary Western culture.

The majority of work on camera surveillance deals with one of two aspects of the problem. Either the study conducted deals with the media theory elements of the problem—how it is that interaction with the televised image influences further interactions and the way people navigate the world—or it evaluates the statistical data produced—how many cameras in how many cities capturing however many hours of footage for private or public organizations. This split between two possible modes of inquiry or possible perspectives for investigation means that one side of the equation will always be sidelined. This book is an attempt to work with both arguments in order to develop a combined perspective on the use of Closed Circuit Television in contemporary government and criminal prosecution.

Normally, media analyses of security technologies involve the use of media theory, historical examples gleaned from traditional and online news sources, and perhaps some of the industry literature related to the specific technology in question. There has been a focus on the importance of biopower in contemporary systems of government. In the interest of breaking new ground, the theoretical flow of the argument will apply the media-theoretical work of Marshall McLuhan and Jean Baudrillard to the theories on power and social organization produced by Michel Foucault. This book will not move away from the importance of biopower, but it will address the juridico-discursive power in the procedures of power as well and its connection with the public's understanding of and relationship with media formats.

The specific focus of this text allows for the introduction of a type of data that is normally left out of contemporary analyses of state power structures: the legal case history. The installation of CCTV networks is normally justified by pointing out that the footage produced can be used as evidence in criminal proceedings. Decisions from the court system in Canada and the United Kingdom will be used to illustrate the application of CCTV footage to court decisions in two related but demonstrably separate legal systems.

Actually, that is another key element of this book. The evaluation of the use of cameras in contemporary culture usually concerns anecdotal and historical cases, as in the case of theorists like Paul Virilio, or it involves highly technical evaluations that deal with emergent technologies and the saturation of technologies that exist and, as is evident in the work of researchers like Kelly Gates, the probability of the development of technologies that, as of yet, do not. There is a missing element in both of those approaches and it is the moment of the application of surveillance footage in the exercise of power. This moment can be located in the court system where the footage is being used as demonstrative proof of something. This instance where the footage is accepted as proof is the one that ties those two approaches together; the yearning for technologies that turn ambiguities into undeniable proof is exhibited by the indulgence of CCTV footage by the courts, and the culture's relationship with the televised image is explained in the willingness of the court system to accept an intrinsic veracity in what is displayed on screen.

The police and the courts are the lynchpin of all of this. A powerful temptation in media analysis is to focus on entertainment-related texts, and, for rhetorical reasons, there is use of popular film and other popular media as a metaphorical device in this analysis. That having been said, the point at which abstraction melts into the background and the tangible application of the West's passive acceptance of the accuracy and believability of the televised image becomes measurable is in processes of policing and the decisions of the courts. It is reasonable to say that the CCTV image is taken as self-evident in Canadian law because there are Supreme Court decisions that prove this. It is also reasonable to say that the determinations made by police after viewing CCTV footage of crimes are defensible because that is what British courts have stated in their decisions after the case was decided at trial. The courts are where rhetoric regarding processes of government and theories regarding the use of and the interaction with media formats come together. The subsequent decisions literally become precedent for how the practice of installing cameras and gathering footage is treated going forward.

NOTES

1. The King trial remains a fascinating moment in the history of interpretations of surveillance footage. Charles Goodwin pointed out in his article, "Professional Vision" (*American Antrhopologist* 96, no. 3: 615, 616, 619–620) that the footage of King's beating paradoxically formed the means through which the police officer's lawyers sought to get a not guilty verdict. The presentation and representation of the footage at trial "had the effect of filtering the events through a police coding scheme, as articulated by an expert who instructed the jury how to see the body movements of the victim in terms of that system." The data indicated in the video footage is not malleable, but the context and the potential interpretations of CCTV footage certainly are.
2. P. Fussey, "Beyond Liberty, Beyond Security: The Politics of Public Surveillance." *British Politics* 3, no. 1 (2008), 121.
3. J. Finn, *Capturing the Criminal Image: From Mug Shot to Surveillance Society* (Minneapolis: University of Minnesota Press, 2009), 6.
4. Ibid., 6.
5. K. Gates, *Our Biometric Future: Facial Recognition Technology and the Culture of Surveillance* (New York: New York University Press, 2011), 18–19.
6. J. Finn, *Capturing the Criminal Image: From Mug Shot to Surveillance Society* (Minneapolis: University of Minnesota Press, 2009), 33.
7. Ibid., 40.
8. "Toronto Police Want to Keep Most G20 Security Cameras." *toronto.ctvnews.ca*. Bell Media. November 15, 2010. Web. February 20, 2014.
9. Douglas Patient, "AA and RAC Raised Concerns Over Use of Cameras Which Automatically Issue Fines." *guardian-series.co.uk*. Newsquest. February 19, 2014. Web. February 20, 2014.

Chapter 1

The History of CCTV in Great Britain and Canada

GREAT BRITAIN

Technological surveillance of the public in Britain goes back much further than one might think. The common perception of British police's active use of technology is that it started around the end of the twentieth century. The contemporary use of dashboard cameras in police vehicles, GPS/SatNav systems in vehicles and on the persons of police officers, and cellular communications technologies that keep the entire force in communication with itself seem like the first truly innovative technology in policing since motorized transportation or the fingerprint. This is not, however, true. A camera obscura was used in Glasgow in 1824 to apprehend a pickpocket. Cameras were also used to observe public spaces during the coronation of Elizabeth II in 1953.[1] These surveillance systems were ancestors to the installed, stable apparatus that is the Closed Circuit Television Camera (CCTV), but they point to British authorities' enthusiasm for technology that assists in the monitoring of the domestic population. They were used for a specific situation in each instance, but they indicate a willingness on the part of British police services to use technical means in order to monitor civilian populations. The trend over the recent history of the country also indicates an enthusiasm for the use of technical tools in the practice of policing. The use of technical means to assist policing practices would have an obvious appeal, and the widespread application of the technology is a result of the enthusiasm linked to it.

CCTV cameras were introduced to the domestic population of the United Kingdom by a company called Photoscan in 1967.[2] The ability to capture video images on tape and replay them was immediately appealing in terms of loss prevention. The possibility of identifying and prosecuting shoplifters had an obvious appeal to independent businesses as well as to the insurance companies they depended on, providing a visible deterrent to theft. Whereas previously a prosecution for the theft of property would normally have had to rely on firsthand accounts delivered by multiple witnesses or in some cases only that of the shopkeeper whose word the accused could challenge, the installation of cameras and the possibility of presenting photographic evidence of a theft offered a natural appeal to beleaguered shopkeepers fed up with petty crime. The transformation that would take place in British retail was, therefore, entirely down to the interest of private businesses at the beginning. The motivation was the protection of private property and the prevention of theft.

From the 1960s up to the 1990s, this was the primary use for the technology in the United Kingdom. For a long time, the notion of using it in an active policing context surprisingly does not seem to have been considered, although its appeal in monitoring areas under scrutiny by police services should have been obvious. Whatever the reason for this neglect, there is no indication that an expansion of electronic surveillance into public space was even contemplated for the first thirty-five years of CCTVs presence in the United Kingdom. It was very much a tool that businesses could use as evidence of theft in the courts. It was strictly a benefit for commerce and a mechanism for securing the safety of property and the financial health of retailers.

It could not remain that way forever. The clear benefits of the technology must have been evident after its use was accepted in the courts and, when the police were able to use the footage taken on private property, the free-for-all of public space would have seemed like a massive void begging for application of the technology. As a gradual but deliberate step forward, then, the next location to be covered was semipublic: In 1975, London Transport installed cameras in stations on the Northern Line of the London Underground rail network. Over the next five years, the camera system expanded to include stations on the eastern end of the Central Line and at Oxford Circus station. The explanation given was that the cameras would aid in deterring, and/or providing evidence for the prosecution of, robbery and assault on members of staff.[3] Whether or not this served these purposes, it certainly changed the physical properties of the stations. The physical area scores of commuters would need to move through on a normal working day was now being watched from afar. This one space, one small area that was deemed to be both volatile and important, was now part of a larger apparatus dedicated to security and the linkage of defined areas with the act of policing.

In 1974, 145 cameras were installed to monitor the major roads around London. The stated purpose was to calm, or at the very least measure, traffic in the capital. The project was named the Central Integrated Traffic Control system[4] and marked a movement from the surveillance of persons for the purposes of determining criminality to the measuring and monitoring of movement. The issue was no longer the monitoring of criminal activity in darkened areas of the transport system or making use of the footage in criminal proceedings. The way in which people use public space, the ease of their flow along public roadways was the new rationale for surveillance by camera. London roadways were notorious for traffic jams and general congestion. The task of monitoring which areas were jammed and why was an enormous job that could swallow up significant amounts of the man hours available to the Service. Positioning a camera in areas where it was known that there were regular disruptions, however, had the advantage of eliminating the demands on a physical presence as well as establishing a measurable feed of data that could be used in urban planning as well as in establishing roadwork schedules.

Still, it was inevitable that eventually security services would want to make use of a mechanical system that, at least in an abstract sense, was carrying out one of their primary duties. The perceived need for so-called public order policing was the rationale for the development of the Lynx system and the expansion of CCTV capability into public areas. This came into effect in particular with the monitoring of pickets during the miners' strike of 1984–1985, at the usual rallying points for other public protests and demonstrations, and for keeping tabs on "football hooligans" provided the rationale for the increased presence of cameras in public or semipublic areas (such as football stadiums). The monitoring was limited in terms of the overall time frame, however, each of these expansions was permitted during the events used to justify their use. Once the protest, strike, or match was over, the cameras were no longer recording.[5] None of these rationales for surveillance allowed for the same sort of permanence that accompanied either the protection of public transportation personnel or the management of automobile traffic.

It doesn't appear to have been noticed at the time, but in 1985 this temporariness started to become permanent. The seaside municipality of Bournemouth began a locally funded CCTV program that would permanently monitor the town's promenade. By the end of the decade, a handful of other municipalities (King's Lynn, Coventry, Wolverhampton, and Plymouth among them) would implement their own CCTV surveillance systems in public areas. Even by 1991, there were only ten high-street or city center systems operating in the entirety of the United Kingdom and all were paid for by local authorities.[6] The normal procedure was to partially fund the systems with money from local businesses as well as to take funds from the budget of local police services. The partial sourcing of funds from residents resulted in the creation of a CCTV monitoring project that came from the local population via their council tax rather than from the centralized government office or division. From this it might be concluded that the absence of CCTV in other municipalities could have been the result of ideological concerns relating to privacy rather than being due to financial constraints.

This is a point at which the research of CCTV gets complicated. Those who write on the subject, whether it is for the purposes of promotion in governmental or private sectors or for academic analysis, as in the case of this text, normally have a preexisting ideological position on the matter. Those in favor of CCTV cameras routinely cite opinion polls that demonstrate widespread public support for their installation. Those who claim that there is no operational benefit to their implementation will often do so with polling data that demonstrates public concerns over privacy to buttress their argument. In 1997, in the West Yorkshire town of Shipley, the local constabulary sought public input regarding a proposal to install video surveillance systems in the town center. According to their data, "only 1 out of 50 respondents had a 'concern' about privacy, all others being enthusiastic about the project." During the same period, the Bradford City Council conducted a poll, which indicated that 40 percent of the 4,000 respondents had "strong opposition" to the plans.[7]

The need for some form of public consent is instructive, however. A recurring justification added to the installation of CCTV systems is that they provide citizens with a feeling of security regardless of the operational benefits of the technology. This, apparently, was not the case in Glasgow where the cameras were blamed for increasing the local population's perception of the threat of crime in the area.[8] What is needed to prevent this sense of vulnerability is an event—some sort of real-world catalyst that encourages people to fear the amorphous, unidentified "other" more than they do the power of an overreaching state.

The likely catalyst for the exponential expansion of CCTV networks in Britain during the mid-to-late 1990s is traceable to one such horrible event: the abduction and murder of James Bulger in 1993.[9,10] Bulger, a two-year-old child, was abducted from a shopping center by two ten-year-old boys. Having seen the child in Manchester city center, the two older boys led him away to some railroad sidings, where they tortured and eventually killed him. His body was left on the tracks and discovered two days later.[11] The senselessness of the crime, the horror at discovering that his killers were children themselves, and the realization that the small boy had been led crying through public areas without being stopped or questioned by any adults beggared belief. There was one significant detail that captured the media and the public's attention: his abduction had been recorded on camera.

The killers were filmed by CCTV cameras leading James Bulger away from the shopping center and it was generally accepted after the event that the footage had been instrumental in tracking the assailants down. The horror of the case coupled with the introduction of a relatively new modality of evidence resulted in a groundswell of support for the establishment of CCTV monitoring systems across the country.[12] The Home Office announced that it was now earmarking £2 million in funds for the development or expansion of CCTV programs that would be awarded through a City Challenge Competition.[13] Bids were to be made in conjunction with local businesses, local authorities, or police and government agencies (arguably as a method of demonstrating that the cameras were invited by local citizens rather than inflicted on them by distant authoritative organizations). According to Goold et al., "by the end of the mid-1990s, the question for local authorities was not, 'why should we have CCTV?,' but rather 'why wouldn't we have CCTV'?"[14]

By all accounts, the subsequent expansion was exponential. McCahill and Norris write that "By 1994 the Home Office reported that 79 towns or cities had some form of open street CCTV systems."[15] The increase in interest and the subsequent increase in expenditure were massive. Between 1994 and 2002, more than 800 bids were made to establish public CCTV systems and at least £3 billion was spent on the installation and maintenance of CCTV camera systems across Britain.[16] According to Pete Fussey, this expenditure accounted for 75 percent of the Home Office crime prevention budget between 1996 and 1998 and, in 1999, that percentage rose to 80 percent.[17] Both Conservative and New Labour governments would loudly espouse the virtues of CCTV cameras, making it a central component of their crime policies.[18] The open and unapologetic use of CCTV in public areas in Britain continues to this day and there is very little public opposition to the presence of the cameras. Closed Circuit Television, it seems, is simply a typical feature of British urban life.

CANADA

Canada, on the other hand, has had a much more nuanced relationship with CCTV. The city of Hull in Quebec is an interesting case in point. Hull is situated directly across the Ottawa River from Ottawa, Ontario. In the culturally determined tradition of Canadian governmental organization, the city is governed by Quebec legal code (which is technically rooted in the Napoleonic code of laws) and sets a legal drinking age of eighteen. Across the river, in Ottawa, the minimum age for legal consumption of alcohol is nineteen. Quebec also allows its bars to close two hours later than they do on the other side of the river.[19] Naturally, this results in a flood of newly legal Ontarians heading across the river to take advantage of the nightlife one year earlier than they would be able to at home. Add to this the normal cultural, ethnic, and nationalistic frictions between Francophones and Anglophones and the potential for closing-time skirmishes between bar patrons in Hull could reasonably be labeled a certainty.

A very limited CCTV system was installed in Hull in 1993 and was used until 1999. The cameras focused on a stretch of the downtown area where twenty-four bars and nightclubs were located.[20] There was significant media coverage of the installation of the system that cited concerns over the effect on civil liberties for the local population. The use of the system, however, received little active interpretation as,

> The Hull police department showed no interest in conducting an evaluation of the technology, simply because the system was perceived to be essentially a *dispatching* tool. According to the Department [. . .], monitoring was used essentially to prioritize calls, to alleviate the need for additional foot patrols and to help officers arriving on site to identify trouble makers [*sic*].[21]

The deviant behavior that generated the desire for the cameras only dissipated when a local bylaw required Hull drinking establishments to close at the same time as their counterparts on the Ontario side of the river. According to Stéphane Leman-Langlois, the signage that accompanied the cameras—the typical alerts that inform citizens that they are in an area that is monitored by cameras—remains even though the cameras themselves were removed as soon as the deviant behavior disappeared.

The most successful CCTV implementation project in Canada took place in London, Ontario.[22]A city with a population of 430,000, it resides halfway between Windsor and Toronto along the McDonald Cartier Freeway (otherwise known as the "401"), the main highway that runs from Windsor/Detroit border to the Quebec border. London's CCTV system was a response to the same sort of public outrage that characterized the James Bulger story in the United Kingdom. The story was less collectively traumatic—the victim, Michael Goldie-Ryder, was twenty years old rather than two and was stabbed rather than being tortured and beaten mercilessly—but still involved the violent death of a person and the subsequent horror and shock of a community. Once again, the catalyst for trading freedom from surveillance for assurances of security began with a tragic and ultimately pointless act of violence. A grassroots campaign emerged in the aftermath of the murder and resulted in the installation of sixteen permanent cameras in the downtown core of the city in November 2001.[23]

The London example is noteworthy because, in response, the public demanded the installation of the cameras. It was not a matter of the government deciding to try the practice out. Local businesses were complicit, but they were not the driving force behind the proposal. Individual citizens were certain that the murder could have been prevented or, at least it would have been easier to catch the murderer, if there were an established surveillance system in place at the time. In contrast to the Jamie Bulger murder where CCTV was legitimized by the event, the killing of Michael Goldie-Ryder prompted the demand for cameras where there had been none before.

In a similar vein, the mugging of a local celebrity in the downtown area of Hamilton, Ontario, generated a media blitz decrying the lack of public safety in the area and promoting CCTV as a solution to the problem. The typical benefits of the technology were espoused regularly in the pages of the *Hamilton Spectator*: "intervention in '[. . .] drug use/trafficking, prostitution, public intoxication and panhandling.'" Hamilton was a steel town that has suffered under the forced restructuring of the North American Free Trade Agreement (NAFTA) and the subsequent decline in manufacturing work available in Ontario. The city has a population of about 520,000 and is situated on the western shores of Lake Ontario. A dilapidated city center was decried as a waste of prime real estate and a drag on the local economy. The push to promote business and sponsor a rejuvenation in the area required a reframing of downtown and the first step in that process was determined to be a reduction in crime. Rather than hiring more police officers or offering greater access to community programs for drug addicts or the homeless, the uncomplicated solution of monitoring people and punishing them for bad behavior was adopted with the aim of fixing all of the problems listed in the newspapers. The added benefit of being able to identify lost children was also mentioned, possibly as a nod to the abduction of James Bulger.[24]

The Hamilton process is continuing, but it is noteworthy in the sense that it appears to provide some context regarding the Canadian attitude toward surveillance. The country is a big one with a relatively sparsely distributed population. Even the country's largest city, Toronto, with a population of 2.6 million, does not compare to the population density experienced in major cities in Europe and elsewhere. Row houses are becoming more prominent, but detached homes are still the norm. Giant glass towers full of condominiums are a normal part of the skyline in most cities, but the walls are thick—it is difficult to hear your neighbors even if you are physically close to them. People, in short, are accustomed to a bit more elbow room. The need to identify an area that is problematic, or dangerous, and to provide specific examples as to why it is regarded as dangerous, therefore, appears to be less a fundamental requirement but more to suggest a proposal to chip away at the population's privacy. For people who are accustomed to a certain intrinsic privacy, any suggestion that they should surrender it must provide compelling reasons.

Equally, Canadians in general don't have the same instinctive fear of government that is common in the United States. The continued symbolic relationship with the British Crown and the lack of a revolutionary past is probably a significant part of the reason why. It is in line with this, perhaps, that a traumatic event like the murder of a young man in a busy area of town or the demarcation of an area of the city as "unsafe" is enough to cause citizens to weigh the importance of their anonymity versus their safety. The case still has to be made, however, and without a catalyst, it seems to be more difficult than people think.

In Brockville, which is south of Ottawa along the St. Lawrence River and east of London, a proposal to install and maintain a significant number of CCTV cameras in the downtown core was defeated by public initiative.[25] Between a relentless campaign carried out by the local newspaper and a subsequent series of letters to the editor,[26] the Safe Community Coalition retracted the proposal and the plans to install the cameras were scrapped.[27] In this case, there was no event or catalyst—just concern raised by a member of the local police force who thought it would be a good idea and started a campaign to convince the local government and citizenry to set it up. A tidal wave of opposition resulted and, without a murder or a robbery or, really, a significant crime rate to point to, the citizens of Brockville decided that their privacy was worth more than a promise of safety.

In Peterborough, a small city in central Ontario (pop. 78,000), a public CCTV system was initiated in 2001. Twelve cameras were put in place that monitored a variety of public locations around town (marina, museum, library, etc.). The feed was not monitored live nor were the cameras manually controlled. Still, the province's Privacy and Information Commissioner was forced to review the legality of the city's surveillance practices when twenty registered complaints were filed in 2004.[28]

The original push for the cameras appears to have come from the business community. Impeding panhandlers and drink-related violence or property damage was the motivation. However, a number of civil rights and community activist organizations vocally opposed the policy and, on June 17, 2004, the lead proponent of the program was pushed to disclose data regarding the correlation between CCTV and crime reduction, the members of the committee that had originally proposed the installation of the cameras and the long-term cost of maintaining the network at a public meeting. Whatever his answers were, they weren't enough to stem the rising tide of opposition to the policy.[29] The business community countered waning government and public support by suggesting they set up their own surveillance system and assume the cost. The Privacy Commissioner of Ontario (understandably) took issue with the proposal and declared opposition to the scheme. No CCTV system has been installed in the area since the public debate terminated in 2004.[30]

PRIVACY

Actually, the mention of the privacy commissioner highlights an interesting discrepancy between Canadian and British political history: Canada has had a federal privacy commissioner since 1977[31] and the province of Ontario has had their own since 1987,[32] but no specific legal right to privacy existed in the United Kingdom prior to the passing of the Human Rights Act in 1997.[33] The reasons for this are complex and beyond the scope of this text. It could, however, be surmised that the different reactions to the establishment or proposed establishment of CCTV systems in the two countries are rooted in the presence or absence of a legal right to privacy itself.

That the Privacy Commissioner of Ontario responded to a plan to establish a privately owned and operated CCTV system in a public space is not entirely surprising—that is his or her job. What is significant is that the creation of the position in the abstract enshrines a certain agency on the part of the population with regard to their own exposure. It establishes a subtext for all subsequent debates regarding the right of privacy for citizens. A policy that would intrinsically take that away should be debated and the merits must benefit the population as a whole rather than one group over another.

The absence of an official charged with overseeing surveillance and privacy matters in a country like the United Kingdom, on the other hand, raises a question as to whether the public has the right to make demands for their own privacy at all. Prior to 1997, if the British Parliament determined that a camera was necessary in order to ensure the safety of the public, the only valid question would have been whether the camera would actually accomplish the goals the state claimed it could. The significance of this cannot be overstated: it is the equipment and not the practice that can be challenged. Unlike in Peterborough, Ontario, where the simple act of challenging the legitimacy of the practice was enough to threaten the CCTV network, people in a municipality that have no right to challenge an invasion of their privacy can only oppose the use of CCTV by demonstrating that it is not serving the purpose of preventing crime. Even then, those who defend the cameras need only point out that there is very little crime because of the cameras and there would be a great deal more if they weren't there.

Later in this text some of the implications of this will be looked at in more detail by considering the use of CCTV at the G20 summits in London, England, in 2009 and Toronto in 2010. In both cases, the use of CCTV was a significant component but it functioned very differently in the different countries.

NOTES

1. P. Fussey, "Beyond Liberty, Beyond Security: The Politics of Public Surveillance." *British Politics* 3, no. 1 (2008), 121.

2. M. McCahill & C. Norris, *Working Paper No. 3: CCTV in Britain.* Hull: Centre for Criminology and Criminal Justice, School of Comparative and Applied Social Sciences (2002), 8.

3. Ibid.

4. Ibid.

5. M. McCahill & C. Norris, *Working Paper No. 3: CCTV in Britain.* Hull: Centre for Criminology and Criminal Justice, School of Comparative and Applied Social Sciences (2002), 8–9.

6. Ibid., 9.

7. S. Leman-Langlois, "The Myopic Panopticon: The Social Consequences of Policing Through the Lens." *Policing and Society* 13, no. 1 (2002), 48.

8. Ibid.

9. D. Lyon, "Globalizing Surveillance: Comparative and Sociological Perspectives." *International Sociology* 19, no. 2 (2004), 142.

10. A. James & C. Jenks, "Public Perceptions of Childhood Criminality." *British Journal of Sociology* 47, no. 2 (1996), 320, 322–323.

11. E. Ferguson, "Ten Years On." *The Guardian Online.* February 9, 2003. Web. December 16, 2014.

12. B. Goold, I. Loader & A. Thumala, "The Banality of Security." *British Journal of Criminology* 53 (2013), 981.

13. M. McCahill & C. Norris, *Working Paper No. 3: CCTV in Britain.* Hull: Centre for Criminology and Criminal Justice, School of Comparative and Applied Social Sciences (2002), 12.

14. B. Goold, I. Loader & A. Thumala, "The Banality of Security." *British Journal of Criminology* 53 (2013), 981.

15. M. McCahill & C. Norris, *Working Paper No. 3: CCTV in Britain.* Hull: Centre for Criminology and Criminal Justice, School of Comparative and Applied Social Sciences (2002), 9.

16. Ibid., 14.

17. P. Fussey, "Beyond Liberty, Beyond Security: The Politics of Public Surveillance." *British Politics* 3, no. 1 (2008), 121–122.

18. R. Coleman, "Images From a Neoliberal City: The State, Surveillance and Social Control." *Critical Criminology* 12, no. 1 (2003), 29.

19. S. Leman-Langlois, "The Myopic Panopticon: The Social Consequences of Policing Through the Lens." *Policing and Society* 13, no. 1 (2002), 48.

20. Ibid.

21. Ibid., 49.

22. S. P. Hier, J. Greenberg, K. Walby & D. Lett, "Media, Communication and the Establishment of Public Camera Surveillance Programmes in Canada." *Media, Culture & Society* 29, no. 5 (2007), 734.

23. Ibid., 549.

24. Ibid., 550–551.

25. Ibid., 738.

26. Ibid., 739.

27. Ibid., 741.

28. Ibid., 741.
29. Ibid., 743.
30. Ibid., 744.
31. "Officers of Parliament—Privacy Commissioners 1977 to Date." *Parliament of Canada*. June 6, 2014. Web. December 17, 2014.
32. "IPC History." *Information and Privacy Commissioner of Ontario*. Web. December 17, 2014.
33. B. Goold, I. Loader, & A. Thumala, "The Banality of Security." *British Journal of Criminology* 53 (2013), 982.

Chapter 2

Theoretical Elements of Government Surveillance

LEGITIMACY

In the interest of understanding what is behind the implementation of these procedures and tactics, it is useful to begin with Jürgen Habermas. When unpacking Max Weber's work on legitimacy in the process of governing, Habermas highlighted the importance of its psychological impression.[1] In discussing Weber's assessment of legitimacy and its legal roots, he noted, "Legality can create legitimation when, and only when grounds can be provided to show that certain formal procedures fulfill material claims to justice under certain institutional boundary conditions."[2] While this statement is pulled from a conversation about faith in the law and its contribution to the stability of a polity, it does highlight the need for a population to believe in the fairness and equanimity of the system that claims dominion in it. This is fundamental to the system's perpetuation. Where previous incarnations of social control in the West based their legitimacy on a claim of divine right or a simply upon an overwhelming capability to inflict violence, the supposed motivational inertia of technology allows for a permanent appearance of fairness. In periods of absolutism, in contrast, the justness of the punishment was embodied in the very fact of its enactment. As Michel Foucault argued, "A successful public execution justified justice, in that it published the truth of the crime in the very body of the man to be executed."[3] Foucault was speaking specifically about executions that took place under monarchical forms of government, of course, and his observation was linked to the legitimacy or validity of the use of violence in the preservation of those regimes. The validity of the action and of the condemnation was rooted in the authority of the structure that exerted power on the body of the condemned. The reason, the justification, was based on an existing authority and the validity of that authority was rooted in the existence of the authority itself.

CCTV played an important part in undermining such a concept of authority. The apparatus is a machine; it functions according to electronic impulses and cold mechanisms comprised of glass, wire, and metal. It has no capacity for bias. It is impartial, simply recording data so long as it is connected to an electrical power source. The lack of agency on the part of the CCTV camera seems to turn it into part of the landscape—something that has an anecdotal presence functioning as part of the background and has no intrinsic agency. It can only capture what happens in front of it.

As such, that seemingly passive act of looking out of a window described by Henri Lefebvre, and hearing "rhythms responding to one another,"[4] and allowing for "a bit of time, a sort of meditation on time"[5] that is required to take in the aural information coming from outside is not permitted here. Instead, the image as delivered by CCTV requires focused attention. It does not pause. It does not move from the stable position of the camera. The image as transmitted requires participation and attention in order for it to make sense. If it is a live feed, it cannot even be recognized that there is a moment on display that it would be useful to return to unless it was watched contemporaneously through the camera. In short, if the desire is to understand it, it must be engaged with if the environment in question is saturated with these cameras.

Inanimate objects are inert, after all. There is a neutrality to anything that is not physically connected to a living breathing body. The mechanism does not prejudge, it does not have ulterior motives. In terms of motive, it is inert. This "inertness" is a primary area of interest in this research. The use of technology only suppresses resistance toward the actions of government as long as the faith in the banality of the technological apparatus remains unshakable. Questions regarding the inherent subjectivity of the experience of electronic media, or the ways in which its function cannot be separated from the motives behind its use, are often overlooked. We tend to see the world of electronic media as an appendage—as something that can either be attached or removed as the circumstances warrant. Things may not be so simple, however and this is why this text seeks to evaluate this relationship between the body and electronic media within the defined limits of camera surveillance.

CCTV is, at a basic level, an appropriation of what is generally referred to as "television." It is an image that is captured by a camera and transmitted to a screen in another location. Admittedly, the comparisons are easier to make with earlier incarnations of television: From the 1950s through to the early 1980s, the practice of consuming television necessarily involved viewing programs as and when they were broadcast. The viewer had no possibility of seeing the program again at another time as video recorders had not yet been invented and, once they were, for many years the cost was prohibitive for the average consumer. The contemporary DVR- and video-on-demand version of domestic television consumption involves a looseness when it comes to the temporal restrictions or specifications of the audience's consumption of television.

Discussions surrounding television's social value, or lack thereof, are normally limited to the social or moral quality of television presentations. It is typically a question of the impact of the televised image as it is *broadcast*. Naturally, much of this discourse revolves around notions of the effect of television on the viewer. The content of entertainment programs, predominantly sex and violence, is often the principal area of concern, whereas the way in which the medium delivers its information is frequently overlooked.

When looking at the use of the medium as a component of governing, as something that exists in a closed circuit between the camera and a single, if not limited, number of recipients, however, certain properties become more important. The ways in which video alters the visual field, the way the body and the signal interact with each other, the conversion of the subject into a surveillance object, pull both the viewing subject and the imaged subject in different directions that make the process a lot more complicated than what happens in simple entertainment programming. With this in mind, then, much of the media analysis of television has been concerned with how it is consumed in a commercial, domestic capacity—as entertainment delivered directly to consumers, and this has typically been dominated by the need to deliver audiences to advertisers. The motive is entirely different, even though the surveillance image can sometimes appear in entertainment programs that repurpose CCTV and police surveillance footage (*America's Dumbest Criminals*, *World's Wildest Police Chases*, etc.). Even in extreme cases, the addition of subtitles, an accompanying audio track, or some sort of opening contextual information as is the case in Sunshine Press' YouTube post entitled, *Collateral Murder—Wikileaks—Iraq*,[6] which depicted the killing of two Reuters photographers in New Baghdad by a US Apache Helicopter crew in 2007, there is a sense that the impact of the original text has been softened. Before the original surveillance image is edited, voiced-over and delivered in between commercial breaks, it behaves very differently for the viewer. There is an immediacy present in it. The inability to predict what will come next, the banality of the streaming image absent the dramatic changes in perspective normally associated with visual entertainment modifies the viewer's response to the surveillance image.

Precisely where, then, does CCTV fit into the process of governing and the social reality it is added to? How does the use of a camera to record physical space with the expressed purpose of using the resulting footage in the determination of guilt and the possible suspension of an individual's freedom affect the normal procedures of that governing system? How does it modify the subject's experience of the physical world around them?

As much as populations are subject to systems of control—social, religious, economic, and so on—those systems rarely announce themselves. Police officers, in the sense that they are able to carry out what would otherwise be assaults and kidnappings on behalf of the state, announce themselves overtly, but that signification is still framed upon a body—a corporeal form. Insofar as that power is declared, it is still rooted in the representation, the badge or the uniform rather than the person waving the badge or wearing the uniform.

The camera stands in the same way as a representation of the state but one that is disembodied. The police officer, the vulnerable human draped a uniform, in the representation of the state, disappears. When it comes to a police officer, the appearance of the human form has to be modified in order to match the power it is granted by the state—the uniform accomplishes this. The visual impression added to the police officer's body becomes the preemptive response to questions of the validity of that body's actions (ordering others to "move along," issuing fines, arresting people, etc.). Though it is the basic human body that will carry out these actions on the part of the state and, subsequently, would appear to be the only strictly necessary element in policing, the representation allows for a presumption and resulting impression of legitimacy in relation to the actions the officer carries out.

By contrast, the camera, in its nonhuman and irregular form, represents an omnipresent and recognizable power that passively captures everything taking place before it. The recording captures actions over a great expanse of time and space and allows the police the luxury of reviewing and evaluating all of this activity at their leisure. The majority of video evidence captured is not really evidence of anything at all—at least nothing of interest to security services—but it usually is captured and filed nonetheless. A general public awareness of this modifies the impression of the scope of police knowledge. At first glance, the CCTV camera encourages subjects to believe that the power structure is ever-present; that it has managed to conquer space and even time.

This is, from the analytical perspective of this book, the most notable thing about the death of Ian Tomlinson. Mr. Tomlinson was murdered by Police Constable Simon Harwood during the 2009 G20 summit in London, England. The key moment, for the purposes of this analysis, took place when the Independent Police Complaints Commission denied that there had been cameras positioned in the area where Mr. Tomlinson was killed. Mr. Tomlinson had been moving through the financial district in central London, near the Bank of England, when he was attacked. The reaction to the claim that no cameras had caught what had happened from those who had petitioned the government to investigate it could best be described as incredulous.[7] It was simply impossible for people who live in London and were familiar with the area in question to believe that there was no CCTV footage of the event. The belief in total exposure was so total that the suggestion that an event could take place in that area without being captured was interpreted as either an indication of overwhelming incompetence or a blatant lie. For the first time, the Metropolitan Police were dealing with the condition of total exposure from the other side of the lens.

What, then, does this mean for those who simply move through an urban environment and, whether they like it or not, become part of this mechanism of surveillance? How does the public's involuntary inclusion into the fabric of police surveillance modify or rupture their relationship with the power structure? Does it bring them closer to the state or push them further away?

THE MEDIATIZATION OF SECURITY

As noted earlier, the roots of camera surveillance go back much further than current incarnations like CCTV and photo radar and it is worth considering how it is that the camera became a component of security. It is surprising to discover that a technology as archaic as fingerprints is intrinsically linked to the technology of photography. Yet, as Jonathan Finn has pointed out,

> The photograph is central in fingerprint identification. The camera is present from the crime scene to the courtroom. It is a central means through which prints are collected, examined, identified, and shared. The individual, physical print holds little value in comparison to its photographic representation, which can traverse physical barriers and can be at work in any number of locations and contexts simultaneously. The collaboration between the theory of fingerprint identification and photographic technology produced coherent, unified, and highly effective inscriptions that were both immutable and mobile. The unique collaboration marked an essential transformation in law enforcement and criminal identification practices.[8]

What Finn is talking about here is the development of a new technology in the nineteenth century that (supposedly) provided a means of confirming the presence of a person in a physical space simply by virtue of its existence and a subsequent use of a technology that would allow the evidence in confirmation to be preserved, moved, and duplicated with virtually no limitations. For a culture of law enforcement that would have needed to rely entirely on human witnesses or material evidence (bloody knives found in the suspects' closet, the stolen items traced back to a person who would logically be the thief, etc.), the apparent immutability of the fingerprint must have seemed like manna from heaven.

The indexicality of the fingerprint is the primary reason for its popularity—while similarities between different persons' appearances may cause an erroneous identification, the fingerprint is a seemingly clean forensic artifact that does not immediately declare its ethnicity, sex, or age and allows for the kind of clinical determination of a connection between the artifact and the human being who has been present at a particular place that is often disputed in eyewitness identification. The main reason for this, I think, is the link between the print itself and the method of delivering it to investigators: the print is the result of a supposedly objective evaluation of a relic of human contact with the physical environment and the culturally accepted indexicality of photography.

The industrial revolution taught humanity to rely on mechanical processes that took over from flawed, subjective human capabilities. In the process of gathering evidence, of determining the criminal culpability of a person, the appeal of adopting or applying new, more technical approaches to the process of investigation can be easily understood—any system that honestly wants more effectively to capture and punish the guilty would naturally welcome any tool that would facilitate this. By all accounts, then, the only limitation to the adoption of fingerprint evidence once its efficacy had been demonstrated was the chance it gave for police departments to centralize the exchange of information between different bureaus. In Europe, where police departments were already more effectively centralized, the process went smoothly. In the United States and to a lesser extent in Canada (where the Royal Canadian Mounted Police already comprised a fairly comprehensive national police service), the process was slower as the lack of centralization resulted in institutional barriers and technical holdups providing obstacles to its general adoption but there was the same enthusiasm about its viability.[9]

And this is key to the adoption of fingerprint technology as a means of identification in criminal investigations; it is transportable, reasonably cheap (the only costs were those of dusting the surfaces at the crime scene, photographing the revealed print, and then developing the photographic negative), and it has that wonderful aura of objectivity that accompanies most technological developments. To quote Jonathan Finn again, "Allied with photography, fingerprinting produced identification information that was concise, compact, and readily transferrable. The resultant documents served the communication and records-keeping needs of law enforcement."[10] And this record keeping allowed for easier identification of repeat offenders by preserving the captured prints for use both in future cases and past ones that still remain unsolved. The emergence of the fingerprint as a means of comparative information sharing allowed crime investigation to be conducted on a network. It moved information from what was limited by the actual physical body of the suspect and the geographic location in which the crime took place to the photograph and the filing cabinet.

To quote Paul Virilio, "The introduction of fingerprints as proof of criminal law marks the decline of the story, of the eye-witness account and the descriptive model, once the basis of every investigation and crucial to writers of previous centuries."[11] This movement to something that is benign, supposedly untainted by prejudice or unintentional error makes a lot of sense from the perspective of those who carry out investigations. The overwhelming majority of criminal investigators genuinely want to catch the perpetrators of crime and, it follows, fear discovering that they've imprisoned the wrong person and allowed the actual perpetrator to go free. The introduction of a system of identification that appears to use only unimpeachable data linked to specific human beings carries an obvious appeal. The investigator can rely on data discovered due to a human body's direct interaction with the physical environment.

This appears to be the rationale for the adoption of technology in police practices—in one sense it makes the process of investigating crime simpler and in the other sense, it reduces the likelihood that errors will be made and innocent people will be sent to prison. The mechanism appears to eliminate the risk of human error. The technology is clean; it harbors no prejudice and has no interest in the outcome of an investigation. It appears to be the perfect antidote to dishonest or mistaken witnesses and overzealous police officers. It eliminates the circumstantial concerns having to do with physical evidence, where the physical artifacts or proceeds of a criminal act might come to be in the possession of a person despite their lack of involvement in the actual event (fencing stolen goods is a good example of this), but the presence of the finger print is an indexical indication that the person connected to it must have been in that physical space. All that is left to demonstrate is the temporal connection to the crime.

This supposed impartiality is often used when justifying the use of technologies in police practices. The use of some abstract system of signification or capture has the effect of dampening doubts regarding procedure, even when the known end of the process of gathering information must involve a human actor. Fingerprint evidence is still a very good case in point here and the case of Brandon Mayfield, a military veteran and lawyer in Oregon on the West Coast of the continental United States, illustrates it perfectly.

TECHNOLOGY AND UNCERTAINTY

Brandon Mayfield's fingerprints were in the federal database due to his military service and because he had been arrested many years previously. When terrorists bombed commuter trains in Madrid, Spain, in 2004 killing nearly 200 people, Mr. Mayfield's name came up in the investigation. Spanish police had discovered a partial fingerprint on a plastic bag found in a car that had contained materials from the attack. The print was sent to cooperating police organizations and an official from the Federal Bureau of Investigation responded, declaring that a "100% identification" had been made with Mr. Mayfield. He was arrested and held for two weeks. It did not appear to matter that Mr. Mayfield was not in possession of a valid passport at the time of the attack and therefore could not have traveled to Spain. His assertion that he had not left the United States in a decade carried no weight. It also did not matter to the FBI that the Spanish authorities expressed significant misgivings about the conclusions the FBI had drawn. It was only when the Spanish investigators were able to definitively match the initial print to an Algerian man living in Spain at the time of the attacks that Mr. Mayfield was released.[12]

The question that emerges is obvious: if the evidence presented should link a specific body to a specific piece of evidence, how is it that two different law enforcement organizations can reach such different conclusions without introducing any other evidence into the analysis? A possible explanation might have something to do with the certainty applied to technical practices. David A. Harris points out that "Months after the humiliating exposure of the Mayfield debacle, some of those involved continued to insist that the matching of prints to identify unknown perpetrators could not produce mistakes—*ever*" [italics author's]. Months after the FBI's findings had been proven wrong, one of the agents responsible for identifying Mayfield from the fingerprint found in Spain told the *Chicago Tribune* that he would continue to "preach fingerprints until the day [he died]. They're infallible."[13] This absolute certainty in the efficacy of the practice, of the proposition of validity that is tied to the technical practice of gathering the evidence from which the specter of human error has been exorcized as a result, is probably the most compelling argument in favor of the mechanization of security or policing. Even in the face of conclusive evidence indicating human error in the process and the pitfalls that come from blind faith in the accuracy of the reading, those who use the technology can develop a quasi-religious appreciation for the veracity of results delivered by technical means.

The main issue here, I think, is the belief that practice cannot interfere with data. To continue considering the use of fingerprint evidence as an example, it is worth looking at the process of comparing two fingerprints in order to declare a match. Or, at least, it would be useful were there a single approach that was used in all instances. David A. Harris explains:

> There exists no consensus among fingerprint examination experts on the number of characteristics that the known and unknown prints must have in common in

> order for an examiner to declare a match. Rather, "considerable disagreement" remains, and different countries have adopted varying standards on this crucial point. For example, France and Italy both require sixteen matching characteristics; Australia requires twelve; Brazil and Argentina require thirty. But in the United States, fingerprint experts operate under a different standard: there is no minimum number of corresponding points of identification necessary for an identification. Both the FBI and the International Association for Identification, the professional certifying organization of fingerprint examiners, have adopted this nonstandard, and it forms the basis for what every examiner in the United States does when making a determination of a match.[14]

Harris's interest is in practices that are used by American officials, but I think the point is generalizable to the overall concerns of what I am considering: namely that the use of seemingly complex and abstract methods of investigation purify anything to which they are applied. The danger, as Harris has pointed out, lies in the assumption that because technologies involve some sort of abstraction, then it follows the results they produce are scientific. Regarding the specific fallibility of fingerprint evidence practice he argues,

> What science and scholarship of the last fifteen years tells us is that, contrary to the usual claims its proponents make, it does not always work. It is, as practiced, fallible; mistakes get made, and we cannot even tell for certain how often this happens. It is not a science in any true sense of the word—certainly not compared to something like DNA identification.[15]

It might be reasonable to question whether DNA identification is really infallible either. However, what repeatedly becomes the focus of concern here is that, technologies or procedures are introduced in a desire to limit the potential pitfalls of human error and bias in any system of investigation. A developed strategy is often treated with the same reverence as the introduction of technical tools. The police procedure of interrogation, referred to as "The Reid Technique" in the United States, is an example of this. A prescribed series of steps allow the officer(s) conducting the interview to believe that they can spot a lie, can determine guilt, and are capable of demystifying the complexities of interpersonal communication as long as the steps are strictly followed.[16] Ambiguities and uncertainties inherent in police work, through a sort of Taylorist approach to assessing and interacting with the social world, can be smoothed over and hopefully eliminated altogether.

As another example, let's look at the 1931 *Manuel de police technique* used in French policing circles which confidently claimed that "One fingerprint taken at the scene of the crime is worth even more than the criminal's confession."[17] The mechanism begins to overshadow the human factor on both sides of the equation. Also, the uncertainties that come from personal interaction—the person may be confessing because of insanity, or may simply be an attention seeker, or protecting the person who is actually responsible, and so on—are hopefully eliminated with technical investigative and security techniques.

Peter K. Manning has argued that the tenets of "rationality" and "procedure" have formalized such areas of human endeavor as "music, art, literature, religion or public administration."[18] It follows logically, he claims, that the practice of policing would be rationalized according to the same historical forces probably best codified as "trial and error." That Manning is an apologist for the police is evident in his proposed definition of policing:

> Democratic police, constituted of many diverse agencies, are authoritatively coordinated, legitimate, and trusted organizations that stand ready to apply force, up to and including fatal force, in a legitimate territory to sustain political ordering. They accomplish their aims via surveillance, tracking, investigating, and monitoring incongruities.[19]

Given what has been learned about police behavior in recent years from the many cases of wrongful convictions, it seems reasonable to think that he is a fantasist when it comes to the practice of policing. He rationalizes this practice in this way:

> The state holds out violence as a means to coerce compliance only if habit and expediency fail. They are expected to use the level of force needed to control a situation, yet not escalate disorder. In practice, little violence is routinely administered (Mastrofski, Reisig, and McCluskey, 2002). While police are increasingly heavily armed in America, the absence of visible police coercion is a sign of legitimacy and of the effectiveness of informal controls. (Banton 1964; Black 1976)[20]

The publication date for Manning's book is 2015, so it is possible that he would not have been aware of the killing of Eric Garner by NYPD officers or the murder of Michael Brown by Ferguson, MO police or any of the comparable shootings that took place prior to or shortly after either of those events. It is remarkable that Manning, who researches policing and claims to have a direct relationship with numerous police departments, is unaware that the collection of data on police use of force in most countries and the United States in particular is negligible.[21] D. Brian Burghart, in an article he wrote for *Gawker*,[22] points out that there is no centralized database regarding use of firearms by police on the job in the United States. The overwhelming number of shootings by police are never reported outside of department or legal channels. Data is not collected and compared or evaluated. Manning therefore has no basis for his argument regarding performativity as a means of maintaining order. Most importantly, his assertion that the police generally do not use the widening array of lethal weapons available to them to kill suspects or other citizens is entirely without statistical support. The absence of research does not indicate that the research does not need to be done—only that someone has yet to do it. There is however ample evidence to show that coercion is a central part of policing.

Whatever the case, the assertion that there is a widening array of technological tools available to the police is a valid one. As mentioned above, the belief that technology will make police work simpler appears regularly in contemporary reviews and analyses of policing. Fingerprint evidence is one of the earliest attempts to marry science with the active element of police investigations, but the enthusiasm for CCTV cameras is easily understood once it is realized that the witness in an image and the footage produced will be treated with the same sort of acceptance as the photograph of a fingerprint. According to Manning,

> The idea of technology is more important than the materiality of technology because it is ideas that drive its installation, social shape, aesthetics and uses [. . .]. The technological infrastructure of policing, the speed and efficiency of information technologies, is in everyway a tertiary question with respect to the quality of police work because it does not foreordain what is done but creates a number of channels for rationalizing it.[23]

The practices come to form the way in which the technology is used as much as the technology might influence the way the job is done. Over the long term, it is likely that the technology will modify the day-to-day approach to the act of policing or of implementing security, but the absorption of technology into the practice of conducting security or policing will follow the established approach to the job rather than revolutionize it. This is evident in light of the initial enthusiasm for DNA testing in criminal cases due to the seeming infallibility of the test results and the subsequent ability to obtain a conviction, but the realization that the same breakthrough could allow defense attorneys to further complicate the lives of police and prosecutors by stringing out an endless sequence of appeals on existing convictions induces a collective unease.[24] Manning's confidence in the capacity security forces have to adapt to changing social situations or their potential as a progressive social force is very limited:

> Society is what it is, and changes little. Such lasting and troubling things as homelessness, mental illness, poverty, crime, and inequality are beyond the

> scope of policing, and beyond the understanding of the average police officer. This is not a hindrance but a logical necessity, given the demands of police work as now done.[25]

It's hardly surprising, then, that Manning's review of technology is rooted in a question of servicing existing police procedures and perspectives. The apparent inability of police to be an agent in social change or to push the tide back on homelessness, mental illness, poverty, crime, or inequality certainly streamlines the job description and limits any significant hopes there might be for the police to be a positive influence in the general culture. As such, it makes sense that technological advancements would do no more than simply augment security forces' mystical ability to preserve order without the use of violence or the supernatural event of social progress. Social progress is something that happens somewhere else because of the efforts of other people. The directive of the police is very often, as it was in my home town of London, Ontario Canada, emblazoned on the side of police cruisers; "To protect and serve." There is no progress implied in that statement—only the preservation of things as they are. Interpretation, considered modification of practices according to what might work better next time and the adjustment of those practices in following instances to continue improvement are beyond the scope of "protecting and serving."[26] The use of technology in the practice of policing is therefore legitimized by how well it allows police to do what they were already doing better. It is not to interpret or modify the job.

The logical conclusion, then, is that there are two possible approaches to evaluating the efficacy or even the popularity of technological processes and tools when they are introduced to the practice of policing or security. The first is the capability for an advance that would radically reform the normal methodology security forces use in doing their jobs.

There is also a possibility that the technology will entrench rather than modify existing prejudices and practices. In this light, certainty is a double-edged sword. The case of Brandon Mayfield mentioned above is a good example of this. Fingerprint evidence was evaluated poorly, but the belief in the intrinsic efficacy of the agencies involved as well as the personal skill of those who were tasked with making an identification through the prints overshot the scientific objectivity that was supposedly fundamental to the practice. The evidence still has to be evaluated and this can only be done by people and, for those who are involved in evaluating it, the technology seems to reinforce the belief that their positions as experts in the field precludes any possibility of human error being introduced.

Kelly Gates has pointed out that research into automated facial expression analysis and functional magnetic resonance imaging follows a belief that external or physiological measurements will one day allow surveillance systems to determine the thought processes of individuals without interviewing them, but that such faith in technology is unlikely to be rewarded.[27] The nuances of human thought and its individual expression make reductive models that would decode input from myriad variable sources into one usable filtration system all but laughable. This does not prevent those who are interested in selling the technology from espousing its inevitability.

In the spring of 2015, Microsoft unveiled a website called "how-old.net." The site encouraged visitors to upload digital photographs so that it could guess the age of individual faces displayed. Somewhat surprisingly, rather than uploading photographs discovered from the Internet, a significant number of users uploaded pictures of themselves. The obvious overtures to concerns about privacy were raised,[28,29] but in a culture where every minute detail of the personal lives of millions of people are voluntarily uploaded to Facebook, Twitter, TikTok, and Instagram, the argument bears an uncomfortable similarity with slamming the barn door after the horse has already bolted.

Gates argues, "Simply by nature of being computerized, facial recognition systems are deemed more accurate and objective and less subject to the prejudices and apparent inadequacies of human perception." This fits into the argument for finger printing brought up at the beginning of this section. That a technology is introduced often functions as a sort of caulk for the cracks perceived in human perception or communicative practices. The use of a machine makes the transmission of information more accurate or the understanding of what has been more faithful to the objective reality of the event. Further, "The claim is that these technologies will create accurate, precision-guided, objective, all-seeing machines that function much better, more efficiently, and more powerfully than human perception alone."[30] This is not intrinsic to electronic technology as evidenced by the faith in fingerprinting, but electronic technology is certainly augmented by it. The immediacy of the information, the collapse of geography-linked-to-time barriers would appear to solidify the gaps in communication and preserve the purity of the image or the sound recording, and so on.

Catherine Zimmer points out that "As video surveillance has diversified and multiplied in form and use throughout personal and social worlds, its incorporation into film as trope and technique has become commonplace."[31] This makes sense, she argues, as film is an intrinsically visual medium and the technology of film is, at a basic level, about the production of knowledge and the exchange of information through visibility and, in a literal sense, surveillance.[32] The indexicality of the images produced by the camera, whether the purpose of the shot be outright surveillance or part of a fictional project, grants the image an instant credibility.[33] This is, of course, not limited strictly to video surveillance—the texts created around the Watergate scandal in the United States in the 1970s and the HBO series *The Wire* are immediate examples of this[34]—but as far as directly transferrable formats of information are concerned, the emphasis on visibility as a means of establishing fact is understandable since film is a medium that demands it be *watched.*

Zimmer argues that the use of surveillance is "normalized" in the plot of contemporary films. At first glance *The Cabin in the Woods* (Goddard 2012) seems to support this. A comedy horror plotline involving a group of university students who are lured to a rustic site where some paramilitary/intelligence spooks have set up an elaborate trap to trick them into sacrificing themselves to an unspecified pantheon of ancient gods, the film revolves almost entirely around an elaborate surveillance dynamic. The more interesting interpretation is that the film uses the "normalized" tropes of supernatural beings and ancient deities (at least within the confines of the horror film genre) and that of technological ubiquity (in terms of the accepted contours of the lived experience in the twenty-first century) to bring the two genres of comedy and horror together. The destruction of a total surveillance environment can only be achieved by supernatural powers. This is demonstrated by the fact that any attempt at escape made by the protagonists is thwarted by their pseudo-military captors. Only the gods and the demons can cross the border in the end.

The old argument that life imitates art and art imitates life comes into focus here. The horror genre is normally one that uses exaggeration as an intrinsic component of telling the story. The films Zimmer covers in the first chapter of *Surveillance Cinema*—so-called torture porn films like the *Saw* series or *Hostel*—use surveillance technology as a means of grounding the outlandish plotlines in some sort of believable technological framework. The degree to which surveillance and the specter of massive technological infrastructures normalize other, seemingly more fantastic elements of a fictional plot brings this narrative back to the topic at the top of this section—that the use of new technologies in the practice of surveillance or identification is something that feels natural after it is normalized in the culture.

This quality of naturalization or normalization is a major concern in this book. Once the public stops interpreting or second-guessing the information read in technology's output, the public permits others to make the interpretations for them and, in doing so, establish what a "correct interpretation" is. This can be seen from the very first: once the idea of the fingerprint had been naturalized in the court system, it was a small leap for the experts to acquire a seemingly religious faith in the efficacy of their interpretations and this explains the fact that they would hold Brandon Mayfield in prison for two weeks despite the ambiguity of the data. Those who invariably see infallibility in human institutions, as exemplified by Peter K. Manning's reverence for the police, would undoubtedly recoil at the suggestion that the mechanism used for delivering information to those institutions might influence the way the information is interpreted. Those who continue to dream of developing even more intricate systems capable of reading the mind of someone from a distance without their awareness or consent as is the case with gait scrutiny or automated facial expression analysis must still believe in this irreducible and as-of-yet undiscovered vein of truth that is available through mastery of reading the human body.

It always seems to begin with a technology. Some tool that expands, focuses or augments an existing system of perception is the key that will unlock the unknowable properties of the other and allow institutions to manage human beings across time and space. For adherents of this strategy, the current apparatus is always just a step away from absolute certainty and it is through the augmentation of existing media tools and experiences, and through the naturalization of that progress, no matter how invasive it becomes, that certainty will one day be achieved.

Underlying all of this is the question of who is doing the watching and under what circumstances. This will be dealt with more closely in the second section of the book, but broadly speaking video captured by CCTV cameras is reviewed either by police or by private security forces after knowledge emerges that a crime has been committed. In a limited number of cases, like the Toronto G20 summit, police or security forces may view the feed live, but the typical use of CCTV video is as a means of review.

This modification by which Closed Circuit Television changes the mechanics of contemporary government functions in two directions: how the government approaches the management of its population, and how that population relates to the space around it. For example, CCTV cameras are so ubiquitous in London that they blend into the background—one need only step into Waterloo station to experience this. The overwhelming presence of the cameras and the forced exposure of anyone who must take public transportation at any point make this exposure appear natural. On the other side of the Atlantic, the cameras erected to handle increased demands for security in Toronto during the G20 summit are still there—as noted earlier, they were supposed to be removed at the conclusion of the summit and, for the most part, were not.[35] The fact that their installation drew relatively little public attention or complaint could have something to do with why the cameras are still there. Whatever the case, this second example attests to the speed with which a government can come to rely on the data produced by those cameras. The first demonstrates how easily a population can learn to see them as part of the landscape.

MEDIA

Electronic media develop their own position. Or, more accurately, electronic media create and occupy their own position. The world experienced through an electronic apparatus like a monitor is different from the world simply viewed through a window. McLuhan argued that "with the arrival of electric technology, man extended or set outside himself a live model of the central nervous system itself."[36] Put into the specific context of this argument, the viewer comes to grips with the image by attempting to place themselves in it. The image is comprehended by ignoring the fact that it is an image. In the case of CCTV, the sense of place, of stability of position, is adjusted in order to reconcile the fact that the viewer is in a different place from the source of the image displayed before them.

The position is established through both the production and the recognition of a signal. The camera is still in the window and the observer is still in another location. The event that forces the observer to recognize the image as a reality that is happening somewhere else is the capturing of the image of that street by the camera and its subsequent transmission of that information to them in another physical space. This, in a nutshell, is CCTV. It is the linking of that real-world event with an observer who is beyond the reach of that event. In that moment, the image produced is both the expansion of a particular determination of agency and a consequent dissociation with an immediate physical reality on the part of the recipient.

In *Understanding Media*, Marshall McLuhan begins with a discussion about electricity. He points out that the fundamental social result of the introduction of electricity is "decentralization."[37] That this decentralization functions across temporal and physical barriers and comprises the essential relationship we have with reality is but one of the fundamental results of the presence of electronic media.[38] Returning to the window, though the street would appear roughly the same if the observer were viewing it personally or retranslating the image on the screen transmitted to them by the camera, the experience of the scene is different from one instance to the other. The observer is keenly aware that the image displayed by the camera is nowhere near them. The perspective belongs to the machine they have placed in the window to capture the image for them. They do, however, experience the image on the screen as though it were immediate. If someone witnesses a train pull into a station on a monitor, they compress the slight delay in the signal and the distance between themselves and the life-world event as they are witnessing it. As such, the observer is split between two places at the same time. In line with McLuhan's thinking, the properties of electronic communication require a recognition of immediacy that cannot be reconciled with the location in which the signal is experienced.

What this means is that the body itself breaches its own physical limits through the introduction of the signal. This "decentralization" is not so much one of the mental production of understanding linked to the communicative ability of the organism as much as it is about that initial recognition of the outside world—that *unprocessed* recognition that would be best assigned to the acuity or the immediacy of the central nervous system. The view from the window, whether mediated by the camera or not, captures the same basic information; the number of cars on the street, the number of people walking down that street, the names of the shops, the number of doors, and so on. Yet a rupture occurs because of the subject's inability to anchor their experience of the camera's view from the window without use of their other senses. They may recognize a Subway sandwich shop façade in the street image they see on a monitor, but the overwhelming odor of salt and baking bread is not present. Nor can they hear the door opening and closing as the customers enter and exit the shop. In terms of their own personal experiences, they might know what all of these things sound like or smell like, but the immediate information available to them begins and ends with the visual. There is a spontaneity necessary to the sudden image that puts the subject off-balance and requires an adjustment to enable them to come to terms with it. This push toward adjustment requires an elevation of certain senses at the expense of a total disconnect with others and this is at the root of McLuhan's idea of decentralization.

For McLuhan, this decentralization of the body occurs when the apparatus that allows the body to navigate the world beyond it is extended. It is not necessarily that the mind is unable to reconcile the place of the body with the introduction of electronic media. The difficulty encountered as specific to the window example lies in the division between what is immediate and what is present (the image taken from the camera and the window view itself). The result is that, through extension of the sensory apparatus, access is gained to areas that are outside of the normal physical limits of the senses. For McLuhan and for the view we have out the window, this means that the body is now incidental to the comprehensive capabilities of the mind.

This presence, this connection to other people via artificial or manufactured means,[39] establishes a connection with the rest of the world that has no physical or temporal root but operates in a more immediate way on the subject than is the case for the products of earlier means of communication, whether it be the printing press or smoke signals. The recipient is always aware of the latter's status as representations and so their distance from what is being represented is maintained. What this means is that the relationship between the body and the rest of the world, and the way it divides impulses coming from outside and the reactions generated inside of the frame, is complicated at a fundamental level.[40]

DUPLICATION

The televised image is a representation of a life-world event. What is seen on the monitor is understood to be an accurate representation of what has happened in the physical location of the camera. The viewer interprets it as a duplication of the actual event depicted on the screen. Baudrillard pointed out that "To dissimulate is to feign not to have what one has. To simulate is to feign to have what one hasn't. One implies a presence, the other an absence."[41] In the instance of televised surveillance, the camera is the production of simulation. The production of the image is the expressed attempt to capture what cannot immediately be obtained. There is an interest in that physical space, in what may happen in that location, but the idea of putting a human pair of eyes there to capture the events taking place is simply impractical. This, in a nutshell, is the technological purpose behind the adoption of CCTV in every instance; the desire to produce an interminable, (ostensibly) intractable record, a record that defies the limits of the human attention span and avoids muddy questions having to do with prejudice and perception.

The personalization of the viewer's reaction to CCTV relies on the application of previous knowledge to the unknown or the unfamiliar images presented on the screen. When viewing something presented to her/him on a monitor, the viewer will apply previous experiences in order to make sense of the new data. The camera at the window presents the viewer with an image that must be decoded. Unlike the model proposed by Stuart Hall, however, this decoding apparently occurs without any prior encoding, at least at the level of human agency.[42] The image, produced by the camera, as a representation of reality, must be infused with the viewer's previous experiences of reality in order to mean anything.

The image is used as an indication of a reality. The reality itself takes shape when the observer recalls comparable items depicted by the image from their previous experiences. The image makes sense to them as a composite of recognizable elements brought forward from their memory. And so, when a long strip of tarmac running between objects that look like domiciles is displayed, the observer assumes it must be a road. That the ultimate function of comprehension is a marriage between memory and the weighing of memory against similarity is an obvious precursor to the very idea of communication. In order for a message to be comprehended at all, some common ground must be identified. This is also why, for instance, students being introduced to a new language are first given a list of common and unproblematic phrases—telling the time, introducing themselves, and so on—because establishing a line of comparison is the basic element in a process of comprehension. The new is experienced through recollection of and comparison with the familiar. This argument falls in line with Baudrillard's conception of *Integral Reality*.[43]

In *Simulations*, Baudrillard wrote,

> Abstraction today is no longer that of the map, the double, the mirror or the concept. Simulation is no longer that of a territory, a referential being or a

substance. It is the generation by models of a real without origin or reality: a hyperreal. The territory no longer precedes the map, nor survives it.[44]

Baudrillard was, of course, writing on the general topic of mechanical reproduction and the sociocultural result of media and communication in the abstract. If, for the specific purposes of this book, this passage is applied to CCTV, it sharpens the argument that CCTV involves a conceptual obliteration of the separation between the life-world event as captured by the camera and the image on the monitor as delivered by the camera. For Baudrillard, the development of media emphasizes the primacy of the text. This is why the map now precedes the territory. It has more to do with the availability ofthe map (as text) than it does with any notion of accuracy or reliability.

The primary question is the nature of the introductory experience. For example, if I am planning to travel somewhere I have never previously been, I will normally consult a source ahead of the actual trip to familiarize myself with points of interest, tactical concerns—roads, hotel locations, travel between the airport and the hotel, and so forth—and determine my movements accordingly. Obviously, this research does not give me a preemptive experience of the actual terrain. What does happen, however, is that I now have prior experience of the area I am planning to discover by means of a text that represents it and each experience I have of that area once I've arrived will be colored by the initial research. It is not so much that the destination does not exist, but that I have generated previous knowledge of that destination as a result of the research. The destination now functions as a fully formed copy of the research I have conducted. There is no way to disregard the information I have gathered about the area I am traveling to once I am physically in the area itself. In attempting to form an understanding of something in advance, or in recognizing similarities in things that were experienced before and might be experienced again, the inevitable result is a prejudicing of future experiences. The same thing goes for the reading of flattened or poor-quality images delivered by electronic media—new and sometimes incomplete information is read through the prism of previous experiences or preformatted assumptions. It is the same for CCTV images.

The idea of the copy, of the reproduction, is merely a contemporary extension of this recognition of the necessity of identification on the basis of similarity. For those of us who live after the advent of mechanical reproduction, there is a new complication; the very real possibility that our first encounter may be with a duplicate or a reproduction of something. CCTV is, by definition, a representation of a life-world event happening elsewhere. It is a duplication. For Baudrillard, as explained in *Precession of Simulacra*, the argument that the duplication comes before the real in the order of authenticity fits with this example. The saturation of duplication or representations in contemporary life requires that a significant amount of the life world must be understood according to a faith in representations rather than evaluated and compared against an encounter with an original or "actual" referent. Over a long enough time line, representations rather than the original become the referential. The result is that those who are familiar with representation, who encounter it on a regular basis, will come to trust it over time. The level of familiarity the subject has with the image as transmitted by the CCTV camera and as displayed on the monitor is contingent on this faith in representation. It is rooted in their willingness to believe in the accuracy of a representation even though the limit of their direct experience ends with the duplication rather than the actual event.

DISTANCE

A procedural contention in this argument is that it is impossible to talk about media without addressing the notion of distance. The functional result of a media transmission, be it radio, television, or even print, is the creation of a specific space. In this area, the issue is the creation of a space. The purpose of media—from the Gutenberg bible to satellite radio—is the transmission of human thought and expression across vast distances. How does this create space? The linkage between the receiver of the message and the producer of the message resides in the imagined recipient or recipients and the imagined producer or producers. In other words, communication requires the author to address a phantom recipient. It also requires that the recipient address a phantom author.

This is perhaps the only angle on which this text can link the theories of Baudrillard and McLuhan. McLuhan saw the effect of electronic media as the extension of the body—the modification of the reach or the agency of the physical form through the properties of media. Baudriallard saw it as more of a contraction, a duplication to the point of ubiquity that resulted in the bringing-in of the world around the audience. Baudrillard is talking about ubiquity creating a vacuum in which duplication cannot be recognized and therefore cannot exist. That may sound like a contraction of space rather than an expansion of it, but it is important to bear in mind that this elimination of the possibility of determining authenticity expands the referential plane rather than contracting it. The copy is a referent back to another object and exists as a shadow of that object. The CCTV signal is, while supposedly a representation of a real happening, the point at which the happening becomes a representation and, necessarily creates its own referential space between the experience of its being viewed on the screen at the point of reception and the point of capture at the camera.

The result of this is the production of a copy. The signal itself, at the point of reception, must be understood as a copy or a direct and credible repetition of events taking place in a real-world space. The difficulty here, as mentioned above, is that the collapse of representation that occurs in Baudrillardian theory requires an appreciation of the degradation of the idea of "the original." To wit:

> This is how all the holdups, airplane hijackings, etc. are now in some sense simulation holdups in that they are already inscribed in the decoding and orchestration rituals of the media, anticipated in their presentation and their possible consequences. In short, where they function as a group of signs dedicated exclusively to their recurrence as signs, and no longer at all to their "real" end. But this does not make them harmless. On the contrary, it is as hyperreal events, no longer with a specific content or end, but indefinitely refracted by each other [. . .] it is in this sense that they cannot be controlled by an order that can only exert itself on the real and the rational, on causes and ends, a referential order that can only reign over the referential, a determined power that can only reign over a determined world, but that cannot do anything against this indefinite recurrence of simulation, against this nebula whose weight no longer obeys the laws of gravitation of the real, power itself ends by being dismantled in this space and becoming a simulation of power.[45]

It is this idea of a "simulation of power" that is directly applicable to the idea of media surveillance. The mistake here, obviously, would be to read Baudrillard's comments as though he is degrading the agency of the resulting simulation of power. The point of this comment is to illustrate that the presence of agency is no longer necessarily located in the "real." This space that is being dissected, this location that exists between the creation of the surveillance text and the reception of that text is governed by a system of power, but that power is more present where it is simulated—within the confines of the image and referential structure of the text—than it is in the subsequent reality that will govern the results of the image captured. In other words, Baudrillard's suggestion that the limits of violence are now confined to the order of simulacra is one that bears teasing out.

This leads to the question of how a message is constructed. A thought, or line of thinking is constructed with an intended audience in mind. Unlike when a subject thinks to themselves, or talks to themselves, the construction of a message for the purpose of an external audience will always involve at least a cursory consideration of the potential audience's preferences, biases, and capabilities. That projection of thought, of an idea, requires the inclusion of the idea of an audience into the construction of the text. In other words, you can't create a message without at least a cursory nod to those who will most likely be receiving it. In this sense, it is worth noting that, while many messages come into contact with people who are not the intended recipients of the signal—perhaps more so since the development of electronic media—the message at its inception always has an ideal recipient in mind at the point of its creation. In the case of CCTV, the intended recipient would normally be a member of the security system. As most CCTV footage is viewed after the fact, the desire is to provide a clear image of something that could be used to prove the alleged properties of an event. This will determine the area under scrutiny, the installation of lights in the area that will illuminate the desired space, and so on.

Intent is a curious element of this argument. This text is, at root, debating the characteristics of a surveillance medium—a machine that is used to keep an eye on the population. The popular understanding of media is that of a broadcast or a public social entity. In reality, of course, the use of media has had a private function since its inception. If the advent of electronic media is used as the starting point for the analysis, the telegraph was used to transmit private messages as often as it was used to convey information destined for the public.[46] Perhaps this is the dark side of McLuhan's projection suggestion.[47] The difficulty with this idea of the extension of the central nervous system is that there is more implicit in the interest of reception than there is in the act of transmission. The accurate dynamic might have more to do with a meeting of individuals over improbable distances than it would with the expansion of a consciousness out into the void. I think the main problem with this idea of extension is that it implies a "searching" action that is not necessarily compatible with the overall dynamic.

Granted, the searching does tend to get buried in the abstract construction of any message. A message must be transmitted. The thought must leave the author and arrive at a recipient. There is a tendency, however, to ascribe the act of communication to this "leaving" moment. This transmission implies an extension on the part of the producer of the message. Even in the case of CCTV, the message transmitted is the status of the space under surveillance, or that there is a space under surveillance and the status of that space is updated constantly. Just because there is often no specific event being depicted by the CCTV image, this does not mean that there is no "message." For the subject, the message is one of exposure. For the viewer, the message is surveillance. This surveillance is embodied in the constant anticipation of data. The event will be data, or a variation in the typical pattern of the data presented, but this anticipation is a direct by-product of the stability of the normal transmission. Regardless of the current shape or properties of the image on the monitor, the message transmitted is that there is a constant transmission of that message.

In that transmission is the requirement that a body must receive the message and be affected by it. The body is now conscious of what is happening beyond its normal limits via the input of signals carried via electronic media. The body is now also capable of sending impulses past its own physical limits via the carriage of electronic media. People can surf the Internet, make phone calls, determine what they want to watch on television—all of these events involve a mode of communication that extends the body. It would be going too far to suggest that this implied some sort of active connection between the user and the larger information matrix, and I think that "Integral Reality" is the best explanation of why this is.

"Integral Reality"[48] implies that reality has stretched past the simple original/copy dynamic. According to Baudrillard, the system of representation has flowed past the point of a recognizable original. Everything is now a copy of a copy—there is no original. However, to quote Baudrillard with respect to distance, "Let us be clear about this: when we say reality has disappeared, the point is not that it has disappeared physically but that it has disappeared metaphysically. Reality continues to exist; it is its principle that is dead."[49] Further, "just as verification puts an end to the workings of truth (for truth, if it exists, is something to be fought over, whereas verification transforms it into a *fait accompli*), so we have moved from reality as principle and as concept to the technical realization of the real and its performance."[50] It is this notion of the death of reality or, to be more accurate, the original, that requires the introduction of a secondary space. The movement of the text from the original source to the point of reception requires that the "real" be apprehended at a location separate from the text's creation. In the case of CCTV, it would be the requisite notion of immediacy and the impossibility of being in the same physical space that erupts this reality. In other words, enclosure of the "real" brought on by the exposure to electronic media requires an expansion and modification to the general understanding of what the "real" in fact is.

If I am now suggesting that the notion of the "real" is something that is all pervasive I have to admit that, in at least two major respects, this notion of proximity has evaporated. When talking about this thing that is "media," in light of the work of Baudrillard and McLuhan, it is necessary to assume at this point in theoretical understanding that the immanence of the electronic signal is now purely immediate—there is no distance between the mind and anything else as there is no such thing as duplication any longer and the distance between the subject and the rest of the world has evaporated. It is crucial to deal with this idea of proximity, however, and there is a definitive schism to the suggestion that the limits of the body have evaporated and the suggestion that all reality represents a limitless "real" as a result of the ubiquity of duplication. Baudrillard's theorem would appear to be at odds with McLuhan simply due to the location of the signal in relation to the mind comprehending the signal. The primary issue here is whether it is possible to suggest that there is a collapse of distance on the part of the individual while at the same time suggesting that the collapse is a social reality born of repetition.

From Baudrillard: “Reality has fallen prey to Virtual Reality, the final consequence of the process begun with the abstraction of objective reality—a process that ends in Integral Reality.”[51] Putting this in front of McLuhan’s observation that “with the arrival of electric technology, man extended, or set outside himself, a live model of the central nervous system itself”[52] colors the interpretation of the connectivity of the mind to the outside world. Further, “for it is now possible to program ratios among the senses that approach the condition of consciousness. Yet such a condition would necessarily be an extension of our own consciousness as much as wheel is an extension of feet in rotation.”[53] This is a recurring theme in McLuhan—this causal history of media and this connective relationship between the human body and technology. Baudrillard, by contrast, has a far less participatory understanding of the functions of media. For Baudrillard, the location of media is the area outside of the human—there is a tangible and demonstrable split between the body and the apparatus that alters the reality outside of the body. McLuhan argued emphatically that technology is inherently an extension of the properties of the body. His conception of the sovereignty of the body with the advent of technology was limited at best. In the case of CCTV, McLuhan would most likely have argued that the eyes of the security personnel viewing the image would have been dragged to the location of the camera whereas Baudrillard would probably have argued that the image transmitted by the camera would have replaced or eclipsed the reality of the events taking place in the physical “reality” of the area in front of the lens. In both interpretations, of course, each new advance in media has moved the human further toward a condition of total externality. The production of electricity and the harnessing of that power for various uses has resulted in the desolidification and scattering of the human body across time and space.

Working within the context of Closed Circuit Television surveillance, then, the question of where the surveillance is actually taking place is one that is complicated by McLuhan and Baudrillard’s thinking on media. Therefore, the main schism here is the difference between the two theorists’ understanding of the body’s relationship with externality. McLuhan has a self-contradictory schematic that involves total connectivity with a marginal amount of agency accompanying the arrangement. Baudrillard, conversely, comes primarily from a position of detachment coupled with a constant potential for agency. With respect to a conversation about “distance,” each theorist would locate the event of communication in a different place. For McLuhan, the event is an externality that is adjacent to the body no matter where it “really” occurs due to the body’s extension. For Baudrillard, the event takes place at the point of the internal system of interpretation’s adjustment to accept the external reality as it is. The media event that is simply looking at a video image is, for McLuhan, an extension of the eyes and the brain. For Baudrillard, it is the forced internal acceptance of reality in all its repetition and similarity with previous repetitions. This problematizes an interpretation of CCTV because it begs a choice between two theoretical positions: is CCTV the transportation of the viewer from one place to another (albeit with a corresponding limitation in sense perception) or simply a forced reappropriation of memory that is determined by the properties of the image on the screen?

There is also a value judgment here, and it's one that will need to be worked through if this text is going to fully explain the locations of the subject, the camera and the observer in the dynamic of CCTV. There is a point at which theoretical discussions, if they lean toward a postmodern perspective, tend to value the comprehension of the human brain outside of the impulses that bring about that comprehension. To look at the mediated reality the contemporary Westerner now lives in and agree with McLuhan's argument of the body's extension is to privilege the body's understanding of its new capabilities with respect to electronic media rather than the media that delivers those capabilities. To view the same event from Baudrillard's perspective is to assume that reality is a matter of negotiating between event and interpretation of the event without looking at the cold, physical elements that brought the event into being. With respect to McLuhan, he employed a method of reconciling this with a decidedly structuralistic impression of how the world works. Though there is a great deal to be said with respect to this metaphysical understanding of the impact of media on the corpus, the events that bring about that understanding still take place in a meat-and-potatoes style of cause and effect driven by the corpus and the brains connection to nerve endings riddled throughout that corpus. The body is the vehicle through which the brain experiences the external world. The reason that media is even worth writing about is that it expands the scope of that corpus' process of understanding and comprehension. The function of media for McLuhan, at root is largely about distance.

Baudrillard, from the other direction, appears to remove the body from the majority of the process of comprehension. The metaphysical here is sovereign and all impressions occur as a result of signals sent through the eyes (and occasionally, the ears). This element of the vanishing of reality, and the specific indication that it is duplication that makes it vanish, is something that happens as a result of this impossibility of direct interaction between the external world and the internal process that is comprehension. This idea that there no such thing as an original any longer and all entities exist as components of duplication is one that requires an untraversable distance from the object. Put another way, this distance between the mind of the recipient and the "real" that has captured that mind's attention is the basis behind Baudrillard's suggestion of "Integral Reality."

Linking this perspective from McLuhan—namely, that the mind is now interacting directly with the external world independent of the limits of the body—is where problems with locating CCTV might arise. Where, exactly, does CCTV originate? Where is the signal located? Where is the object that is the subject actually positioned? The realization that the human body is the locus of the process of governing—and this notion will be returned to later on in this text—is the point at which these alterations to the relationship between the body and physical space become central to an understanding of interaction and the way organization and systematic control are deeply personal as well as public events. This idea of "distance" is intrinsically tied to these points. The body's relationship with electronic media governs the way in which that media is used in the first instance. The point at which the body is located physically and the point it is moved to as a result of exposure to electronic media determines both the validity of an understanding of CCTV and the way in which it is used.

Put more specifically, CCTV is a position. Or, more accurately, CCTV is the creator and occupier of the position. The response to the televised image is one that, if McLuhan's thinking is followed to its logical end, would have an internal quality to it. McLuhan states that "the function of the body, as a group of sustaining and protective organs for the central nervous system, is to act as buffers against sudden variations of stimulus in the physical and social environment."[54] The signal, as an experience that is directly adjacent to the central nervous system, is a component of the initial comprehension system—it is something that happens within the mechanics of the mind. The mind recognizes the television signal, or the sound of another voice, or the sequence of letters in a piece of text that convey a message. The event of communication is the recognition of a signal. The event, the point of recognition that the signal exists occurs at once entirely within the mind of the observer and validates the preconception that there is an external reality that justified the attempt to view that external reality in the first place. The position of CCTV is that recognition—the justification of viewing lies in the recognition of the process of viewing and the validation of those preconceptions.

McLuhan postulated that "each form of transport not only carries, but translates and transforms, the sender, the receiver, and the message. The use of any kind of medium or extension of man alters the patterns of interdependence among people, as it alters the ratios among our senses."[55] This is the revelation of the primary discrepancy here, however; that CCTV is presented as though it is a reliable extension of the senses of all possible recipients of the signal. The element that makes this intrinsically problematic is this suggestion of homogeneity with respect to reception. The CCTV image fits into this dynamic in the sense that it presents itself at once as an acknowledgment of separation between viewer and viewed (I know that the image claims to be a reality outside of my personal reach, and I must trust it for the image to make sense) and a closure of that distance (the subject is next to the reality in that they are able to see it). The knowledge of that distance requires a closure of that distance.

In this sense, media—as a traceable social happening—establishes its existence in any conceivable pathway from its point of origin. To quote Bernard Stiegler in conversation with Jacques Derrida, "It is possible to read you and to understand that writing—any form of writing—is already a kind of teletechnology. The power to address a letter is a sending away from oneself which already breaks the circle of any proximity, of any immediacy."[56] While the focus is a form of communication that is independent of the interference of electricity—and can thus save McLuhan's argument about the extension of the body and the expansion of proximity—the creation of space with respect to the message is still consistent. If the focus is the event that is communication, it is inadequate to simply talk about the production of messages. The content of the message is, in a very real way, incidental to the idea of communication in the first place. In line with Stiegler and Derrida and their assessment of the effect of writing, the speed of electronic communication and the uncontrollable nature of the interpretation of that communication on the part of each individual recipient are unmanageable in the same way. Even with the most basic forms of communication, of course, there is no truly universal reality of communication; all signals require interpretation in order to be comprehended. With that in mind, the event that is communication—the act of producing an event that could only be described as recognition—is an event that can be verified almost entirely independently of knowledge of the qualities or the intent of the original signal.

Baudrillard weighed in with McLuhan when he stated that "there is no separation any longer; no emptiness; no absence: you enter the screen and the visual image unimpeded. You enter life as though walking on to a screen."[57] Further, "unlike photography, cinema and painting, where there is a scene and a gaze, the video image, like the computer screen, induces a kind of immersion, a sort of umbilical relation, of 'tactile' interaction, as McLuhan used to say. You enter the fluid substance of the image, possibly to modify it, in the same way as science infiltrates itself into the genome and into the genetic code to transform the body itself."[58] What should be looked at very carefully here is this reevaluation of position with respect to the idea of communication. This destruction of distance, of the way in which the body interacts with external input is crucial to ideas of surveillance and an understanding of the products of CCTV.

In terms of surveillance, of CCTV, this establishment of a destruction of distance is necessarily a point of recognition. Communication, as imperfect in any conceptualization, is at a basic level the introduction of new information into the thought processes of another person or thing. Let's try to apply that suggestion to the idea of CCTV. Looking into Baudrillard and McLuhan's suggestions that the result of electronic media is to extend the central nervous system (McLuhan) or to "enter the image itself" (Baudrillard), the result is the destruction of distance, of the barrier that would normally exist between text and audience. Baudrillard comes perilously close to hyperbole when he sates that "it is only with the strict separation of stage and auditorium that the spectator is an actor in his/her own right. Everything today conspires to abolish that separation: the immersion of the spectator in the spectacle, 'living theatre,' 'happenings.' . . . The spectacle becomes user-friendly, interactive. The apogee of spectacle or its end? When everyone is an actor, there is no action any longer, no scene. It's the death of the spectator as such."[59] There is a thread of validity to this statement, but the ability to move from one element of the equation (viewer) to another (subject) is one that presumes a definitive separation between the body and the event. McLuhan's suggestion that the body is extended via electronic media preserves the flow of information in this regard—you can see things happening elsewhere, but you are still only seeing. Being able to make this shift from the position of viewer to subject requires a dissolution of the position of the participants and this is impossible given the involvement of CCTV in the event. It determines the physical position of people as a by-product of its use. Someone has to be in front of the camera and someone has to be watching the monitor. Though the geographical distance is collapsed in the use of CCTV, the phenomenological positions of the participants wind up being more firmly entrenched. In this light, it is not that Baudrillard is *wrong*—he's writing about theatrical practices in 1960s France—so much as he's emphasizing the importance of the audience/performer relationship in the understanding of event. The collapse of distance, of proximity inherent in the televised image makes the presentation more immediate to the viewer, but further entrenches the separation between the two parties at the same time.

This totality of exposure or involvement is a direct consequence of McLuhan's argument regarding the extension of the body through electronic media. Though the person viewing the monitor is not within the confines of the source of that image, or the physical space of that is the locus for the production of the image, the necessity of that viewer, or even of the eventual viewer, for rationalizing the production of the image pulls the viewer into the text in the act of watching the monitor. The image is an extension of the eye and the body at the same time that it may be incorporated into images itself.

In this light, the idea of CCTV is curious insofar as it involves a massive readjustment of distance in order to provide a convenient exposure of a specific physical space. The curiosity is not necessarily a function of the qualities of the medium or the purpose to which that medium is put, but the importance of a geographical area that will inevitably be destroyed as a result of the use of that medium. In other words, surveillance inherently involves space. The use of a medium at best problematizes the integrity of that space and, at worst, annihilates it all together. In light of the theoretical insight covered so far in this text, the stability of the point of view is the only stable element in the equation:

> Psychically the printed book, an extension of the visual faculty, intensified perspective and the fixed point of view. Associated with the visual stress on point of view and the vanishing point that provides the illusion of perspective there comes another illusion that space is visual, uniform and continuous.[60]

This point of view is something experienced entirely by the viewer of the signal. It is important to remember that the primary element in a visual modality of communication is the visual and it is this extension of the visual that I would really like to pick up here.

The term "extension" implies both a dragging toward on the part of the central nervous system and an expansion, a distancing of the physical form, across space and, potentially, time. The result is the rupture of spatio-temporal stability in, admittedly, a minor form. The reason that this is worth mentioning, however, is that subsequent perception will be altered according to this rupture.

The ability to stretch, to move across the limits of the physical form is the primary reason to evaluate this event, that is, reception with a great deal of concern. At each interval, there is a little less of this relationship between the brain and the body left. McLuhan suggested that this "numbing" was a defense mechanism—that the act of extending the central nervous system outside of the corpus indicated a dangerous exposure and that the body would compensate by reducing the input delivered by that central nervous system.[61]

Reception must contend with the landscape. Under the most extreme of instances, language is dependant on the understanding of the recipient of the information. Virilio's writing about Einstein is instructive at this point. His basic contention was that Einstein's major revelation was the realization that things like "space" and "time" are elements of individual perception or intuition.[62] In light of this, the position of the camera, the understanding of the events taking place of that camera, and the position of the viewer's mind in the interpretation and subsequent positioning of these things is a matter of subjectivity and is deeply problematic. When general thinking on vision is applied to surveillance, it is problematic because the surveillance image is designed along a purpose of generalizability—the image or information captured must be presentable to other individuals after the initial capture and the integrity of the information generated should be stable when transferred from one person to the next.

It is then necessary to come to terms with the limits of notions of universality and the instinctive assumption that electronic media would bring the public closer toward true universality by homogenizing elements like perspective, distance, sound, and light. This argument amputates the viewer from the properties of the text and, as McLuhan and Baudrillard have noted, this is deeply problematic. If Virilio's point is integrated with McLuhan's arguments already discussed, the idea that media will influence the data presented is almost certain. What is less certain and, in fact, far less likely, is the contention that capture via electronic media will result in the flattening or homogenization of that information. The suggestion that the basic elements of the perception of the universe—space and time—are malleable from one sensory perception to another negates the possibility of an external actor rectifying this problem. The way in which information is interacted with cannot be flattened as the way in which that information is processed at the most basic levels can never be identical. Interpretation adjusts the characteristics of the information transmitted, but it also adjusts the relationship with the world around the subject. Writing about the state of human communication at the end of the twentieth century, Virilio argued that "we are not seeing an 'end of history,' but we are seeing an end of geography." Further:

> Whereas, until the transport revolution of the nineteenth century, the old time intervals produced an auspicious distancing between the various societies, in the age of the current transmission revolution, the ceaseless feedback of human activities is generating the invisible threat of an accident befalling this generalized interactivity.[63]

I don't necessarily think that calling the result of electronic media an "end of geography" is going too far. What I think is missing, however, from the statement is the clarification that "geography" here is linked inextricably to a now antiquated notion of distance. It would be absurd to suggest that humankind prior to the development of the steam engine understood distance in the same way that those who were able to take trains or steamers in order to travel from one place to another. Ultimately, Virilio is correct in his assertion that the expanse of media has resulted in a collapse of geography, but geography is not, as a result, dead. The antiquated notion of distance and space have been modified to such an extent that geography must be redefined according to the coordinates determined by electric media.

Reception, then, is a location. Or, rather, reception is recognizable according to the properties of that location. In other words, the recognition of the signal is something that takes place between the signal and the preestablished typical functions of the mind in question. There then are four separate schisms here working in tandem to construct the media experience: First, the production of the elemental properties of the signal—the person standing in front of the CCTV camera or the originator of the message broadcast on radio. This is the foundation of the "text" element of media transmission—that determined element of data that ostensibly becomes the content of the text. There are modifications to this, of course, but at a zero level this is the basis of the construction of all media products. It is the element of a determination, whether it be the decision to express a thought or argument across a vast distance or to position a media apparatus in a specific place and record the results, an expression of agency is required to produce the final text.

Second, the superposition of the signal—its total scope as a result of broadcast or direct transmission. There should be a qualification attached to this statement, however, which is that the intended limit of the medium and the individual text does not necessarily apply directly to each transmission event produced by that medium. There are many CCTV images that have escaped the intended confines of their existence and appeared in entertainment and news television broadcasts. *America's Dumbest Criminals* would be an example of the entertainment television instance. The best one I can think of with respect to news broadcasts would be the repeated display of images captured by CCTV cameras of the 9/11 hijackers before they boarded the planes or of the individual bombers on the bus and moving through the London Underground system on July 7, 2005. That said, the individual's understanding of the text presented does have to do with an understanding of, at the lowest possible level, an implied and recognizable geography. Though the signal may extend vastly from one area to the next, the locus of the source of that signal is fairly stable.

Third, the location of the recipient of the signal. This is arguably the most stable element of the entire relationship. Though I accept McLuhan's argument that electronic media has allowed the central nervous system to move beyond the brute physical limits of the body of the recipient, the nexus of the entire experience is still relatively stable—it is within the skull of the observer or audience. This root location of the observer, whether it be me on my couch watching television or a security guard in a booth in front of a number of monitors, will frame the experience of the text. The qualities of the message may be interpreted in different orders of importance depending on the circumstances in which they are being viewed.

The fourth principle is the mental impression of the location of the originator of the signal in the mind of the recipient of that signal. Guy Debord, in musing on French culture in the 1960s, argued, "This society eliminates geographical distance only to reap distance internally in the form of spectacular separation."[64] This spectacular separation generates a distance that conforms to the perceived gap between the producer of the spectacle and the receiver. The real physical distance is supplanted in favor of the distance implied by the content of the spectacle and the audience's relationship with it.

Briefly, the event itself is fundamentally outside of the immediate physical reality of the recipient. Media operates in multiple directions at the same time covering signal space and referential space. To borrow another line from McLuhan, "electric power, equally available in the farmhouse or the Executive Suite, permits any place to be a center, and does not require large aggregations."[65] The salient point to this statement, however, is that the center is always the point at which the signal is received. The pretense to the event of *reception* is something that takes place in the same way that air fills a vacuum; all available space is touched by the signal. The event itself, however, is contingent on the comprehension of the audience and that is where it is necessary to get into the distinction between the two spaces; signal space and referential space.

SIGNAL SPACE

Signal space would be the physical area covered by the traveling of the message—the recognition that the signal sent comes from somewhere past the printed page, the speaker on the radio, the screen of the television or computer. The signal space exists as a secondary characteristic relative to the content or presentation. There is an influence relative to all of this, however; it is muted and taken as a component of the transmission rather than a characteristic that is malleable and, ultimately, external to it. As signal space can only be comprehended at the point of reception and not dispersal/transmission, this is a universal characteristic of media—that media is formalized communication, communication is the formalized transfer of thought from one mind to another, and the efficacy of any transfer is judged on its reception rather than its transmission as a matter of validating the previous two points.

An illustrative, albeit antiquated illustration of this would be the relation via telegraph of the 1883 explosion of Krakatoa in what was then the Dutch East Indies and is now Java. Though the explosion was heard well beyond the visual elements of the event, the telegraph details sent to Europe and subsequently through to the New World gave shape and meaning to what had simply been a loud, unexplained "boom."[66] The signal space determined by the messages carried over the telegraph would have been the distance traveled across the wire. The content would have explained the events in Southeast

Asia and created some form of comprehension for an event that took place well outside the physical limits of the message recipients on the other side of the world.

It is this traversal of data, this movement of information from one physical space to the next that can be called signal space. The comprehension of distance is modified by media, but that modification must have a referent that allows for a rooting of an idea of the origin of the message. This occurs even in the case of science fiction, where there is invariably an overture to the audience at the start of the text—"A long time ago in a galaxy far, far away" in George Lucas's *Star Wars* or the endless announcement of a "star date" in opening moments of Gene Roddenberry's *Star Trek* television series. In the case of more mundane examples, such as CCTV, the signal space is the determinant of legitimacy—it is its claim to have come *from somewhere* that gives it its basic relevance.

REFERENTIAL SPACE

The second codification would be that of referential space. Simply put, the referential space is the response elicited within the mind of the recipient of the signal that corresponds to the characteristics of that signal—the personal, imaginary properties of the setting described on a radio show, the color content of a black-and-white photograph or the third dimension of a television signal. According to Baudrillard, simulation "corresponds to a short circuit of reality and to its duplication through signs."[67] Referential space exists as a self-defeating and, yet, indestructible presence. This negative state of being, however, is integral to the purpose behind the communication. It strives for universal reception where there is objectively no way that each individual is going to see the same image or imagine the same setting. Referential space is the optimistic side of the notion of media—the idea that there is something such as clean communication or the easy transferability of information and is also the way in which messages or transmissions speak to subjects through their own experiences.

Both signal space and referential space determine the understanding of place in relation to the object depicted in media. As CCTV is inevitably about the movement of an event via electronic means across distance, of the adjustment of space to see an event that is outside of the viewer's normal physical abilities, the problem of proximity is solved via the extension of the body with the new capabilities afforded by electronic media. The result of this extension is a reappraisal of space, distance, and the relationship with the idea of externality. From McLuhan's argument regarding the extension of the central nervous system to Baudrillard's allegation that the system of representation has expanded to the point of collapse (resulting in "integral reality") to Guy Debord's determination that the ubiquity of the spectacle has resulted in the collapse of geography, a person's relationship with the external is drastically modified with the introduction of new technologies of representation.

THE MECHANISM

First, it is useful to look at the function of the camera in Closed Circuit Television—the camera's role in the process of capturing surveillance—as a purely operative tool. How does the camera effect this process of capture? How does it relate to the idea of distance? How is "distance" constructed when an apparatus is the primary modifier in the equation?

Virilio was relatively direct in his assessment of the impact of the film camera on Western culture:

> With the apocalypse created by the deregulation of perception came a different kind of diaspora, the moment of panic when the mass of Americans and Europeans could no longer believe their eyes, when their *faith in perception* became slave to the faith in the technical *sightline* [line of faith]: in other words, the visual field was reduced to the line of a sighting device. [italics author's][68]

If Virilio is right, what the filmic image really changed was the faith people had in their own ability to view the world. The camera created a schism, a distrust between the observers and their faith in their ability to perceive. The addition of the prosthesis that was the camera drastically adjusted the relationship between the observers and their own bodies.

J. MacGregor Wise has argued that "the idea of telepresence essentially is the idea of being in two places at once—to be where you are, but to feel like you are someplace else. With the telegraph and telephone, and their sense of instantaneity and simultaneity, we began to move close to this idea."[69] The coup that was television when it was developed—it is important to remember that television was initially a purely live medium—was that the entire human was seemingly being teleported across space. With previous advances in electronic communication, the effects were more isolated; the voice (telephone), the thought process (books, newspapers), and so on. Media, at a very basic level, is really about the movement of the body beyond its normal physical limits.

This involved, at a basic level, two complementary ideas. The dependency on the mechanism of the camera in the delivery of authenticity is contingent on the viewer having a sense of connection with the image provided by the camera. Just as the observer understands the validity of something they perceive as being in front of them without constantly giving credit to the eye in the process of deciphering it, this faith in a "technical sightline," is an overture to their becoming dependent on this connection with the mechanism that delivers the image. A good example of this dependency is provided by the character of Ricky Fitts in Sam Mendes's film *American Beauty* (1999). In it, the protagonist's daughter is infatuated with a new neighbor and classmate who is hardly ever seen without a handheld video camera he uses to capture the world around him. At one point, the daughter, Jane—played by Thora Birch—attempts to arouse him from her bedroom window by removing her top. Upon his recognition of her, even before she has begun to disrobe, he begins filming her. The immediate impulse is to suggest that this is simply the dominant/male compulsion emerging. It is easy to think that he films her as a method of capturing or possessing her, in short so that he can play the tape over and over again as a cheap form of ownership of her image although it is possible that the situation is more complicated. As will be explained later in a more disturbing way when this analysis looks at Michael Powell's 1960 film *Peeping Tom*, the reason Ricky films Jane is because he is unable to feel a sense of profound connection with the external world unless it is presented through this filter of legitimacy, unless it is processed and displayed through the camera, through the lens. Virilio's assertion that the "technical sightline" has become the focus of faith in the visible external realm is well illustrated here. As an anecdote, I have also noticed in recent years a considerable increase in the number of people who attend concerts and spend the entire show filming the act on stage with the camera on their mobile phones. This need to capture, I think, has more to do with determining a legitimation of the experience than it does with what the ostensible purpose of the mechanism of the camera, which is to recall something that has already happened.

Marshall McLuhan has shown how electronic media functions as an extension of the central nervous system, while MacGregor Wise provides a more specific illustration of the connection between the image and the observer—he describes this as "telepresence." This idea began with the telephone and the telegraph that created a feeling of being transported while still remaining in the same place. With the modification of the processes of perception through the application of electronic media, a much greater sense of the authenticity of the image was created in the mind of the observer. To quote Guy Debord:

> The most abstract of the senses, and the most easily deceived, sight is naturally the most readily adaptable to present-day society's generalized abstraction.[70]

If culture today can be codified as a "generalized abstraction," the question becomes whether what MacGregor Wise calls "telepresence" is a result or a cause of this. On the one hand, it could be argued that the camera itself requires that viewers reach out from their bodies toward the image as a necessary precursor to comprehension. On the other, it seems reasonable to assume that the medium itself fragments the experience of its own content. In other words, the sending of a signal from the camera to a screen involves the construction of a text that will always be received in a different place from where it originated. Inextricably linked to this is how the viewers' understanding of their own physical position is willingly ruptured through the simple act of viewing the signal. In watching footage displayed during a news broadcast that is supposedly captured and presented without manipulation, the viewer is at once willing and encouraged to engage in this exercise of "telepresence" in order to understand the signal through their previous experience with the medium. The existence of television results in a willing fragmentation of the self as well as a social imperative to engage in doing so over and over again.

This sense of fragmentation, in addition to the feeling of being "where you are, but feel[ing] like you are someplace else" is the recognition that this "someplace else" is an incomplete reality compared to the one the subject knows themselves to be rooted in. In other words, the experience that is the televised image, two-dimensional and incomplete, is inevitably less clear than the unmediated visual world. When it comes to CCTV, therefore, it is inescapable that the presentation will be delivered with gaps in the visual input. What is outside of the camera's range must be determined—in an interpretive way—by the viewer. MacGregor Wise neglects the fact that this feeling of being somewhere else requires a degree of input from the viewer to be experienced at all. Not only does the video not provide full representation of the area photographed, there is also an inherent degradation in the visual quality of the image transmitted via live digital input. As the CCTV image is typically limited to a black-and-white rendering, it also requires an assumption of color, an incompleteness that requires the input of previous experience in order to make the impression delivered by the camera authentic or natural. To quote Aaron Doyle, "The footage is murky and inchoate and has a dreamlike or liminal property that makes it resonant with suggestions of the unconscious."[71] This incompleteness leads into a hyper-personalization of the image.

The camera, then, requires the viewer's input in order to complete the image as it cannot provide a verbatim depiction of what is happening. It requires participation in order to complete its function. This is what McLuhan meant when he made his distinction between cool and hot media: "A cool medium, whether the spoken word or the manuscript or TV, leaves much more for the listener or user to do than a hot medium. If the medium is of high definition, participation is low. If the medium is of low intensity, the participation is high."[72] The sort of television McLuhan would have been writing about is likely to have been closer to current CCTV images than today's high definition TV. In light of this, these overtures to television as a "cool" medium and the assertion that the image produced requires direct participation in order for the text to be comprehended complements the suggestion that the product of the CCTV camera requires input from the viewer to be comprehended. In other words, the low resolution image produced by the CCTV camera is an overture to a personal experience of media because the viewer must fill in the gaps in the transmission.

The camera, as a mechanism, reaches the viewer as a system of stimuli that is intrinsically incomplete. The image requires an immersion on the part of the viewer and a largely subconscious degree of involvement for the product of the camera to appear natural or believable. Debord, in outlining the properties of the "society of the spectacle," argued that, "The spectacle is not a collection of images; rather, it is a social relationship between people that is mediated by images."[73]

This notion that a physical reality can be moved across time is something that is more complex in CCTV than it is in simple photography. The photograph is static; the lack of movement and the stable perspective is comforting when viewing an unfamiliar object. Baudrillard pointed out that "most photographs (but media images too, in general, and all that makes up the 'visual') are not true images. They are merely reportage, realist cliché or aesthetic performance, enslaved to all the ideological systems."[74] While this may be true, Baudrillard ignores the importance of movement in the cognitive process or understanding media. The activity inherent in any televisual signal prevents the viewer from ever completely coming to grips with the information presented. The viewer must reevaluate the signal sent to them when the image moves. It is worth noting, however, that in a very real way the stable nature of the CCTV image may be more unsettling than that of a televised image designed to be broadcast as entertainment. The stable camera presents itself as though it were a photograph—uninterrupted and static until the image is invaded by something happening. Even in the case of CCTV cameras that are capable of some limited movement—pivoting or swiveling—the constant position from which the image is taken, the stable physical position, promotes a sense of stability to the image displayed. The mobile television camera, in contrast, prevents the viewer from relaxing with respect to the background—in a normal television broadcast, the focus moves from one angle to the next in order to give the presentation a sense of depth. In CCTV, on the other hand, the viewer is challenged to reorient the physical geography in which the characters are situated constantly and, therefore, can never fully feel at ease with the image that is broadcast. The CCTV camera is positioned entirely to capture the kind of disruption that broadcast television is designed to avoid.

The CCTV image is different in the sense that any injection into the stable image is a disruption. This disruption, at a basic level, is transmitted by the camera and necessarily involves two parties—the viewer and the subject. The camera operating as mechanism in this case operates as a delivery system and creates the viewer in its production of the image. The watching that the viewer does is enacted by the camera in its production of an image; the viewer is the person who is witnessing the image delivered by the camera. As much as a subject is required in order to justify the creation of the image, the viewer is the point of validation—the point at which the impulse is supposedly satisfied—and is created due to the operation of the camera. This is because the viewer has a responsibility to interpret and, in some cases, act on the image that is produced. The most noticeable and, arguably, the most significant way in which the CCTV image is acted upon is in court proceedings.

NOTES

1. J. Habermas, *Legitimation Crisis* (Boston: Beacon Press, 2005), 97.
2. Ibid., 99.
3. M. Foucault, *Discipline and Punish: The Birth of the Prison* (Harmondsworth: Penguin, 1979), 44.
4. H. Lefebvre, *Rhythmanalysis: Space, Time & Everyday Life* (London: Athlone, 2004), 28.
5. Ibid., 30.
6. Sunshine Press, "Collateral Murder—Wikileaks—Iraq." YouTube. April 3, 2010. July 24, 2014.
7. T. Edwards, "Police Watchdog Admits Ian Tomlinson CCTV Error." *The Week Online*. April 14, 2009. Web. July 26, 2014.
8. J. Finn, *Capturing the Criminal Image* (Minneapolis: University of Minnesota Press, 2009), 33.
9. J. Finn, *Capturing the Criminal Image* (Minneapolis: University of Minnesota Press, 2009), 36–37.
10. Ibid., 37–38.
11. P. Virilio, *The Vision Machine* (Bloomington: Indiana University Press, 1994), 42.
12. D. Harris, *Failed Evidence* (New York: New York University Press, 2012), 3.
13. Ibid., 4.
14. D. Harris, *Failed Evidence* (New York: New York University Press, 2012), 26.
15. Ibid., 29.
16. D. Harris, *Failed Evidence* (New York: New York University Press, 2012), 40–47.
17. P. Virilio, *The Vision Machine* (Bloomington: Indiana University Press, 1994), 42.

18. P. Manning, *The Technology of Policing* (New York: New York University Press, 2008), 7.
19. Ibid., 48.
20. Ibid., 55.
21. *The Guardian* newspaper reported in March of 2015 ("Police killed more than twice as many people as reported by US government," *Guardian Online*, March 4, 2015) that the police in the United States average about 928 killings per year. An annual average of 545 of those killings go unreported. It can only be hoped that Manning is ignorant of these statistics when he claims that there is very little use of force by police in the United States.
22. D. Burghart, "What I've Learned from Two Years Collecting Data On Police Killings." *Gawker*. August 22, 2014. Web. April 29, 2015.
23. P. Manning, *The Technology of Policing* (New York: New York University Press, 2008), 63.
24. D. Harris, *Failed Evidence* (New York: New York University Press, 2012), 57–58.
25. P. Manning, *The Technology of Policing* (New York: New York University Press, 2008), 79.
26. There are few long-form texts better than David Simon's *The Wire* (2002) at exhibiting this. An HBO series, the show followed the drug trade in Baltimore, Maryland, and over five seasons demonstrated how both the trade of dealing and importing drugs and the practice of policing the drug culture are both incapable of reform. I would encourage anyone who hasn't seen it to do so as soon as possible.
27. K. Gates, *Our Biometric Future: Facial Recognition Technology and the Culture of Surveillance*. (New York: New York University Press, 2011), 182–183.
28. Canadian Press, " 'How Old Do I Look' Website Raises Privacy Concerns." *CTV News Windsor*. May 5, 2015. Web. May 7, 2015.
29. A. Griffin, "Uploading Pictures to Find Out How Old You Are Gives Microsoft the Right to Post Them Wherever They Want." *Independent Online*. May 7, 2015. Web. May 7, 2015.
30. K. Gates, *Our Biometric Future: Facial Recognition Technology and the Culture of Surveillance* (New York: New York University Press, 2011), 10.
31. C. Zimmer, *Surveillance Cinema* (New York: New York University Press, 2015), 2.
32. Ibid., 4.
33. C. Zimmer, *Surveillance Cinema* (New York: New York University Press, 2015), 5.
34. Ibid., 23.
35. N. Parness, "Toronto Police Want to Keep Most G20 Security Cameras." *CTV News*. Bell Media. November 15, 2010. Web. February 20, 2014.
36. M. McLuhan, *Understanding Media: The Extensions of Man* (London: Routledge, 2001), 47.
37. Ibid., 39.
38. Ibid., 59.

39. "Artificial" or "manufactured" are loaded terms, but they are appropriate here within the context of the argument. The point being made is that traditional modalities of human contact such as speech or touch or physical gesture are absent in electronic media. Indeed, it is developed in order to replace these devices. The connection that is electronic media is a connection that is developed as a recognition of loss or inaccessibility.

40. There may be a point to make regarding the evolution of television presentations with respect to the experience of electronic media on the body. The awkwardness associated with the application of the televised image to dramatic and documentary styles is tangible when we look at the historical progression of the presentations. From the stable, single camera view where actors or newscasters would simply break narrative to perform an advertisement for the audience to the current explosion of "reality" television, the need for the pretence of format or plot dwindles in the face of the overwhelming need to experience the image and the presentation of something *immediate*. Television, specifically in the broadcast/infotainment-oriented context here, has had to reevaluate itself, to become more *human* in order to make sense to the viewer.

41. J. Baudrillard, *Simulations* (New York: Semiotext[e], 1983), 5.

42. S. Hall, "Encoding/Decoding," in *Media and Cultural Studies: Key Works* (London: Blackwell, 2002), 166–176.

43. J. Baudrillard, *The Intelligence of Evil or the Lucidity Pact* (Oxford: Berg, 2005), 17.

44. J. Baudrillard, *Simulations* (New York: Semiotext[e], 1983), 2.

45. Ibid., 21–22.

46. I. Fang, *A History of Mass Communication: Six Information Revolutions* (Boston: Focal Press, 1997), 80.

47. M. McLuhan, *Understanding Media: The Extensions of Man* (New York: Routledge, 2003), 47.

48. J. Baudrillard, *The Intelligence of Evil or the Lucidity Pact* (Oxford: Berg, 2005), 18.

49. Ibid.

50. Ibid., 18–19.

51. J. Baudrillard, *The Intelligence of Evil or the Lucidity Pact* (Oxford: Berg, 2005), 27.

52. M. McLuhan, *Understanding Media: The Extensions of Man* (New York: Routledge, 2003), 47.

53. Ibid., 67.

54. Ibid., 47

55. M. McLuhan, *Understanding Media: The Extensions of Man* (New York: Routledge, 2003), 97–98.

56. J. Derrida & B. Stiegler, *Echographies of Television* (Cambridge: Polity, 2002), 36.

57. J. Baudrillard, *The Intelligence of Evil or the Lucidity Pact* (Oxford: Berg, 2005), 75.

58. Ibid., 76.

59. Ibid., 76.

60. M. McLuhan, *Understanding Media: The Extensions of Man* (New York: Routledge, 2003), 187.

61. Ibid., 51–52.

62. Ibid., 22.

63. P. Virilio, *The Information Bomb* (London: Verso, 2005), 9.

64. G. Debord, *The Society of the Spectacle* (New York: Zone, 2004), 120.

65. M. McLuhan, *Understanding Media: The Extensions of Man* (New York: Routledge, 2003), 39.

66. S. Winchester, *Krakatoa: The Day the World Exploded, August 27, 1883* (New York: Harper Collins, 2003), 182.

67. J. Baudrillard, *Simulacra and Simulation* (Ann Arbor: University of Michigan Press, 1994), 27.

68. P. Virilio, *The Vision Machine* (Bloomington: Indiana University Press, 1994), 13.

69. J. M. Wise, "An Immense and Unexpected Field of Action: Webcams, Surveillance and Everyday Life." *Cultural Studies* 18, no. 2/3 (2004), 428.

70. G. Debord, *The Society of the Spectacle* (New York: Zone, 2004), 17.

71. A. Doyle, "An Alternative Current in Surveillance and Control: Broadcasting Surveillance Footage of Crimes." *The New Politics of Surveillance and Visibility* (Toronto: University of Toronto Press, 2006), 210.

72. M. McLuhan, *Understanding Media: The Extensions of Man* (New York: Routledge, 2003), 348.

73. G. Debord, *The Society of the Spectacle* (New York: Zone, 2004), 12.

74. J. Baudrillard, *The Intelligence of Evil or the Lucidity Pact* (Oxford: Berg, 2005), 93.

Chapter 3

CCTV and the Court System

THE CANADIAN COURTS

Invariably, the justification for the surveillance of people in public places is that, should a crime occur, a record will exist that proves the specifics of the crime, thereby eliminating the ambiguity that normally goes along with human reporting of crimes.

Law is a matter of process, however, and the mechanisms that are allowed into it are vetted extensively before they are granted access, particularly when it comes to new technologies. Fingerprinting, audio recordings, video surveillance, and emerging technologies of dataveillance all must be evaluated by multiple levels of judicial inquiry before they are considered legitimate evidence. In some cases, the complexities and nuances of the practice result in constant debate and reevaluation, as has been the case with fingerprint evidence and DNA testing.[1] In the case of CCTV, its use as a mechanism to allow witnesses to testify from a distance is a significant source of debate, but this typically has to do with the accused's right to confront their accusers and whether the mechanism of video conferencing (which is normally what it is—courtroom CCTV is a live feed run between the courtroom and the off-site location) might prejudice the jury or the presiding judge's interpretation of testimony given. Questions regarding the surveillance of public areas, as well as the reliability of the footage produced, are an element of Canadian criminal proceedings that continues to evolve.

Perhaps the most important court decision with respect to CCTV footage in the history of the Canadian court system was the 1996 Supreme Court hearing of *R. v. Nikolovski*. The case involved the robbery of a convenience store. The accused—Alexander Nikolovski—was captured on CCTV camera waving and thrusting a knife at the store clerk. The footage was introduced at trial and supplemented the additional eyewitness testimony scheduled for the prosecution's case.

During the initial police investigation, however, the store clerk failed to definitively identify Mr. Nikolovski from the photographs that were shown to him by police. Nikolovski's was one of three photographs selected by the clerk, but the clerk admitted at trial that he could be no more than "25 to 30 percent sure that any of them was the robber."[2] The clerk also failed to identify Mr. Nikolovski in court during the initial trial. The passage of time between the robbery and the trial may have played a role in the clerk's difficulties. A police officer who claimed to know the accused indicated that Mr. Nikolovski's appearance was different in court than it was at the time of arrest.

The trial judge, while acknowledging the flimsiness of the eyewitness identifications during the police investigation and during the trial, expressly privileged the CCTV footage in her own deliberations. The ambiguities resulting from the police investigation and the performance of the witnesses in court was, in the end, unimportant. The clarity of the footage and the amount of time the robber spent in frame on the footage left her with no doubt that the person on trial was the same person displayed on the CCTV recording. Mr. Nikolovski was convicted.[3]

The Ontario Court of Appeal reversed the decision, finding that a judge could not rely solely on her own interpretation of the appearance of the accused in court and her interpretation of the CCTV footage in order to make a decision. The conviction was overturned on the basis that she had overstepped her prescribed role in the process and enlisted herself as an uncalled witness. As there was no basis for the decision in other evidence presented at trial, the Appeals Court effectively decided that the trial judge had exceeded her prescribed agency in the matter and entered an acquittal.[4] In response, the Crown appealed to the Supreme Court of Canada.

Seven of the nine justices held that the Crown's appeal should be allowed and that the guilty verdict should be reentered in the case. The reasoning given in the decision was rooted in an unwavering faith in the reliability of the image delivered by the CCTV camera. The following quote from the opening of the decision sets the tone nicely:

> A video camera records accurately all that it perceives and it is precisely because video evidence can present such very clear and convincing evidence of identification that triers of fact[5] can use it as the sole basis for the identification of the accused before them as the perpetrator of the crime [. . .]. Once it has been established that a videotape has not been altered or changed, and that it depicts the scene of a crime, it becomes admissible and relevant evidence. Not only is the tape real evidence, but it is also, to a certain extent, testimonial evidence

> as well. It should be used by a trier of fact in determining whether a crime has been committed and whether the accused before the court committed the crime.[6]

The justices caution other jurists about the prospect of making identifications solely on the basis of videotaped evidence, but at the same time they endorse the practice. As far as they're concerned, the efficacy of machines trumps the frailty of human perception and the possible impact of emotion on cognitive ability. They even point to the obvious mental trauma inflicted on the store clerk as to why that person's use in the process of identification was effectively doomed from the outset.

Justice Peter deCarteret Cory wrote the decision for the majority and, in paragraph one, he set out the fundamental concern of the case: "Can a videotape alone provide the necessary evidence to enable the trier of fact to identify the accused as the perpetrator of the crime?"[7] In the words of the original trial judge (and, as cited by Justice Cory in his decision):

> I have directed my mind, but what about that video tape? I mean, the video tape does away with a lot of the frailty of identification by a witness who said to me he was frightened, he was nervous, he couldn't recall some of it. And look at the tape. The tape doesn't lie.[8]

And this is typically the issue when it comes to the introduction of new—or, in this case, not all that new—technologies in the identification of persons. Justice Cory points out that,

> The admission of new types of evidence is often resisted at first and yet, later accepted as commonplace and essential to the task of truth finding. Fingerprint evidence may be the first example of scientific evidence leading to identification. Similarly, blood typing with its ever increasing [*sic*] refinements can be extremely helpful in identification. DNA testing is yet another example. It must never be forgotten that evidence of this type can serve to establish innocence just as surely and effectively as it may establish as it may establish guilt. The case of Guy-Paul Morin[9] serves as a constant reminder of this.[10]

Cory referred to the case of *R. v. Pleich* in 1980 which resulted in the decision that it was the audiotapes presented during the case rather than a human interpretation of those tapes that constituted real evidence and that they had "many of the characteristics of testimonial evidence." The tapes in and of themselves were the most important evidence that needed to be considered by the jury.[11] The logic of the decision in *R. v. Pleich* implies that "the admission of videotapes as evidence seems to be a natural progression from audiotapes." *R. v. Leaney* rounds-off Cory's argument as, in that case, the identification of the offender hinged on videotape evidence of the crime in progress as well as the testimony of five police officers. Even though the appellate judge determined that the police testimony from the original trial should have been excluded, it was decided that the conviction should be upheld based on the videotape evidence alone.[12]

Cory points out that the frailty of human eyewitnesses is well documented and is, in fact, the basis behind the recognized need for cross-examination during trial.[13] He emphasizes the traumatic nature of crime and the inevitable effect that will have on the sensory perceptions of the witness during the event and the clarity of memories connected to it after the fact. As an alternative, Cory has nothing but enthusiasm for video evidence:

> The video camera on the other hand is never subject to stress. Through tumultuous events it continues to record accurately and dispassionately all that comes before it. Although silent, it remains a constant, unbiased witness with instant and total recall of all that is observed. The trier of fact may review the evidence of this silent witness as often as desired. The tape may be stopped and studied at a critical juncture [. . .]. So long as the videotape is of good quality and gives a clear picture of events and the perpetrator, it may provide the best evidence of the identity of the perpetrator.[14]

Bringing the analysis back to the specifics of the case before him, Cory is entirely willing to rely on videotaped evidence as the only method of identification:

> It is relevant and admissible evidence that can by itself be cogent and convincing evidence on the issue of identity. Indeed, it may be the only evidence available [. . .]. Should a trier of fact be denied the use of the videotape because there is no intermediary in the form of a human witness to make some identification of the accused? Such a conclusion would be contrary to common sense and a totally unacceptable result.[15]

The merits of the evidence as relatable to the determination of guilt, then, outweigh the traditional approach of allowing the accused to challenge the evidence given by his accusers. The pervasiveness of CCTV recordings—as well as other devices such as camcorders and mobile phones—was far lower in 1996, of course, and the foreseeable source of this kind of evidence for the judges making their decision would be either private businesses who'd installed CCTV security systems specifically because of their risk of robbery or vandalism or specific public spaces that would have installed systems for the same reasons. In other words, in Canada, before the dawn of the twenty-first century, the likely source of the footage would have come from either government channels or from the victims of the crimes being prosecuted.

As to whether there is anything of note in the moving image versus the still, Cory is clear: "There cannot be any distinction between a still photograph and a videotape. Indeed, a videotape may well provide stronger evidence than a still photograph."[16] As long as it has been established that the videotape has not been interfered with or modified and that it depicts the area that is of concern according to the specifics of the case, it qualifies as "real evidence" and is, for all intents and purposes, "testimonial evidence" also.[17]

A more recent example of the application of CCTV evidence in Canadian courts and the difficulty it presents for security forces who were initially very enthusiastic about the admissibility of the footage in court, is that of Tyrone Jackson, who was arrested in Ontario, Canada, in 2011.[18] He was charged with "resisting arrest, assaulting a police officer and possession of marijuana."[19] His legal representatives filed an application to stay the proceedings—in other words, to dismiss the charges—due to the excessive force used by the police in the process of arresting Mr. Jackson. The basis of Mr. Jackson's lawyers' argument was CCTV footage from the scene provided by two stationary cameras.

Mr. Jackson was stopped by police after a traffic officer ran the plate number of a borrowed car he was driving. The officer discovered that the tags had expired and that the owner of the vehicle was wanted on outstanding warrants for firearms charges. Mr. Jackson was followed into an underground car park and the constable confronted him there. Additional police eventually joined the fray and Mr. Jackson suffered a broken jaw as well as other injuries and faced the charges indicated above. A significant amount of the confrontation took place in front of a CCTV camera.[20]

The camera that provided the footage used in the trial was positioned opposite the stairwell entrance where the confrontation took place. The camera is activated by motion and there are some blind spots due to its positioning in relation to the location of the confrontation.[21] The result was that there were concerns at trial as to whether the footage constituted a complete enough record of the event and, if it didn't, what that might mean in trying to interpret the footage.

Judge O'Donnell noted that "The camera's recoding function is triggered by motion, which the camera cannot always detect due to the light source facing into it"; "The motion that is of interest to this case occurs at the very back of the camera's view, meaning that any motion is less likely to be detected than it would if it happened at the front of the car, where the officers and Mr. Jackson would be more obvious to the camera"; "[The camera] is only one of multiple cameras feeding its data to a central recorder. If that recorder's ability to record is less than the sum of the multiple video feeds coming to it at any given time, then data will be lost and there will be choppiness or even gaps in what is recorded. Both choppiness and gaps are evident in this recording."[22]

The judge's concerns with the continuity of the image and the ability for the camera to capture every available detail stand out as the primary problem with interpreting the footage. He didn't spend an enormous amount of time worrying about whatever limitations there might be associated with the intrinsic properties of a video signal. Whether the incident took place in a location that is optimal for the camera or not is a concern, and that what is captured definitively by the camera trumped whatever explanations were given of the event by the police. The camera is granted the final authority in locating where a person is in space and time and, in some cases, what the condition of that person is in that space and time. In the text of the decision, Judge O'Donnell notes that "Mr. Jackson's evidence that he was unconscious when he was removed from the alcove is much more consistent with the video than the police evidence."[23] The result is that the case was stayed in light of evident violations of rights guaranteed by the *Canadian Charter of Rights and Freedoms* by police.[24]

For the most part, though, CCTV footage is used in Canadian courts to legitimize human identification of the person on trial. In the case of *R. v. Zunic*, a restaurant was robbed by a two-person team. The police arrested one of the assailants on the street after the robbery and the on-site CCTV footage was used to verify the assumption that the person arrested outside the restaurant was the same person who'd carried out the robbery inside.[25] In *R. v. Mikolajczyk*, the identity of the accused as the person who'd committed three counts of breaking and entering was determined entirely on the basis of "expert"[26] review of closed circuit television footage and a review of the clothing he'd been wearing when he was arrested. The trial of *R. v. McLetchie* involved charges of "robbery, pointing a firearm, possession of an illegal handgun, possession of cocaine, aggravated assault, assault with a weapon and being masked with intent."[27] The CCTV footage at a nearby bank machine allowed the Crown to match eyewitness testimony of the description of the clothing the culprit was wearing with footage of a person fitting that description in the immediate vicinity.[28] This is just a very brief sample, but it does point to the increased acceptance of CCTV as a viable form of identification in trial proceedings in Canadian courts.

THE BRITISH COURTS

The difficulty in making comparisons between the application of CCTV in Canada and the United Kingdom is that, at least as far as British law is concerned, there is no enshrined right to privacy for its citizens.[29] Since the establishment of the European Commission on Human Rights in 1998, the assumption is that British subjects could petition Strasbourg for concerns regarding privacy, but the degree to which the domestic courts would provide protection for British subjects in anticipation of the continental reaction has been negligible. From Marianne L. Gras's article on the state of CCTV regulation in Europe:

> With reports of over 4 million cameras in use in Britain, European lawyers seem uneasy [. . .]. The Home Office, however, pronounces itself "confident" that British CCTV practice is in line with the Human Rights Act. The [...] hearing of Peck v. United Kingdom in Strasbourg, in spite of the complaint for treatment which can only be described as an ultimate breach of privacy (at least in continental European terms) being upheld seems to confirm this view. The court did not appear overly keen to criticise the prolific use of CCTV in Britain. Indeed there is reason to believe that the mere use of CCTV surveillance will not suffice to invoke article 8 [the specific provision in the European Convention on Human Rights that should grant British citizens the right to privacy].[30]

The barrier to carrying out significant surveillance via cameras in Britain, then, appears to be very, very low. As long as the domestic perspective is that the positives outweigh the negatives, there is little reason to believe that an inflicted right to privacy will modify the British use or implementation of CCTV cameras (or any other form of electronic surveillance for that matter).

An appropriate example of this is the case of *Henry v. HMA*.[31] Nicholas Russell Henry was convicted of a brutal assault in October 2011. The case concerned an attack using a machete and a pole on a man named Allan Scott by two masked assailants. Both of the attackers wore masks and hooded sweatshirts and the CCTV footage that captured the incident was (arguably) of poor quality. The appellant contended that no identification could reasonably have been made by the police who viewed the footage given these two factors.

The real reason to mention this case is that the definitive identification of Mr. Henry as one of the assailants did not come from the victim; it did not come from nearby witnesses; nor did it come from a second-hand tip—a story from someone who knew someone who'd heard something from someone else on the street. The final identification was made by a small group of police officers who viewed the CCTV footage after being made aware that Henry was the primary suspect in the case.[32] The basis of the appeal, then, was that the CCTV footage the police used to make the identification was of such poor quality that it never should have been admitted as evidence at trial in the first place and that, independent of police endorsement no reasonable jury could have convicted Mr. Henry using such poor quality CCTV footage for identification.

There is an interesting note in paragraph 7 of the Appellate court's decision that is linked to this question of identification and it is worth repeating here: "It is understood that the police witnesses aforesaid have no expert qualifications in facial recognition technique." The suggestion that there might be some sort of "facial recognition technique" is an intriguing one and, at least for the moment, appears to turn the basic justification for the reliability of CCTV on its head. The British population's seemingly universal familiarity with the photographed image as well as the supposed impartiality of the camera in its recording of events would seem to make the need for an expert approach irrelevant. In point of fact, this is supposed to be the entire purpose behind the use of the cameras—the unproblematic transferability of the image to the courtroom as a form of evidence.

Lord Brodie writes that he is,

> not persuaded that there exists any rule of law rendering inadmissible evidence from a witness of his or her understanding of what CCTV footage shows. As Lord Sorn observed in a characteristically illuminating judgment in *Hopes and Lavery v HMA* 1960 JC 104 that there is no rigid rule that only witnesses possessing some technical qualification can be allowed to expound their understanding of any particular item of evidence.[33]

The prose is a bit obtuse, but the point is clear after a few readings: The analysis of CCTV footage does not, as far as the court is concerned, require technical skills that are beyond the layman.

Naturally, this brings the police directly back into the frame. Their interpretation is as valid as the next observer and yet they possess a sort of intrinsic credibility that is linked to the social perception of their job. If there is no barrier to interpreting the image delivered by the CCTV camera—and it is normally sold in exactly that context—the investigative experience and the training of the police force augment an identification made by police officers via CCTV footage. In other words, Lord Sorn's assertion that there is no rule demanding that a witness possess technical expertise about the item of evidence in order to offer an opinion about it preempts a critical evaluation of how the viewer interprets CCTV images while leaving the professional aura of policing intact. The issues raised by theorists from McLuhan, Baudrillard, and Debord regarding the moving image, the interpretation of the image and the reliability of image-making technologies, evaporate and the only question left is whether the witnesses responding to council's questions is being truthful in their answers.

Of course there is a rational element in Lord Sorn's dismissal of a need for expert interpretation. Demanding expert interpretation on every use of CCTV in the court system would presumably slow down the trial process but, more importantly, hand over "legitimacy" in terms of interpretation to a select group of individuals. While this is necessary when it comes to something intrinsically abstract and technical like DNA evidence, it seems to fly in the face of the common social understanding of the photograph or the video image. Its simplicity is often a fundamental component of the endorsement of the technology and it is clearly what the courts are enthusiastic about in the context of this case.

At the original trial, the defense presented a former detective inspector and officer in charge of the scientific support department of the Grampian Police Department named Andrew Rolf and a psychologist and lecturer at Glasgow Caledonian University named Dr. Allan McNeill.[34] Rolf argued that the CCTV footage was of such low quality that there was "insufficient detail" in the CCTV footage in order to make a positive identification. Dr. McNeill indicated that Rolf's assessment fit with the current scientific literature on the subject.[35] Given the result of the first trial, the rational assumption would be that the jury ignored the expert testimony and relied entirely on the opinions of the three officers who concluded that Mr. Henry was the person captured on video.[36] In the end, they must have believed the police simply because they were police.

Dr. McNeill had just completed a project entitled "False Identification of Faces." To wit,

> Dr McNeill explained that while people are exceptionally good at recognizing faces if those faces are well-known, the opposite is true if the face is not well-known, even in optimal conditions. Even with a test designed to make the task as easy as possible, people still make errors in the region of about 20 per cent. While perhaps not entirely clear from the transcript of his evidence, Dr McNeill's report indicates that he had the opportunity to view the CCTV footage spoken to by the three police officers led by the Crown. In examination-in-chief Mr Jackson asked Dr McNeill whether he would consider using a CCTV image of this quality as a safe way to identify a person whom the police already thought might be the perpetrator of the assault on the complainer. Dr McNeill responded by explaining that what the research shows is that even if a CCTV image is of very good quality it is still a very difficult task to match it to another image of a person or even to a live person. If the CCTV image is occluded in some way or the image is degraded in some way, it becomes even more difficult.[37]

Regarding Mr. Rolph's testimony, the appellate ruling provides a selection of his time on the stand:

Q—"Now, let us say . . . that you were examining the CCTV footage, which you have done, and not examining it against photographs but against a

person. . . . Would you think that there is sufficient detail . . . on the CCTV imaging to use that as a base for positive identification of someone?"
A—"No."
Q—"Why do you say that?"
A—"Because there is insufficient information there for anyone, in my view, to positively identify someone."
Q—"We have had police officers in this case . . . who come in and say 'We have looked at the CCTV image. We then looked at a person, and we can say that that image allows us to identify that person' . . . do you have any comments on the quality of it, CCTV imaging, that would allow that identification to be made?"
A—"In my view no. In my police career, obviously this is one of the things I had to deal with on a regular basis, because I was in charge of identification, and I would not be happy with someone giving a finding like that, because I do not think, in my view, in my experience that there is enough information there, in that image, no matter what you are looking at, whether it is a photograph or a person or whatever, there is not enough information in that image to make a judgment like that, because you cannot see the eye, you cannot see the mouth, you cannot see the ear, all you are looking at is basically part of the nose."
[. . .]
Q—"Now let us say that you are back in the police . . . (and someone said) 'Using that quality, that level of CCTV, we can use that to identify someone we had never known before' would you be happy with that?"
A—"No, not at all, no."
Q—"Even if it was somebody you knew well you would not be happy with this level of imaging?"
A—"That is correct."[38]

The appellate court made a meal of the arguments put forward by the defense. Regarding the quality of the CCTV footage:

> Most of the points made by Mr. Jackson [council for the defence] as indicating the weakness of the identification of the appellant, would appear to be uncontroversial: eyewitness identification is a difficult task in which mistakes can be made; this is particularly so where the person supposedly identified is a stranger to the witness; while it may be thought to offer some advantages over direct eyewitness identification, identification on the basis of a still or moving photographic image, such as the CCTV footage here, introduces its own difficulties due to the imperfect quality of the image; identification will be the more difficult where the face is partially obscured, as by a hat or a scarf; any identification may be regarded as suspect in the absence of safeguards provided by a procedure

> equivalent to an identification parade; and an identification will be particularly suspect when the person identified is first introduced to the witness in circumstances suggestive of the person's guilt. *However, against these points, all of which we would see having been fully ventilated before the jury, there was the detail of the evidence given by the police officers and the explanations which they gave as to why it was that they were able to identify the person wielding a knife in the CCTV footage as the appellant, explanations which members of the jury had been able to consider as they viewed the relevant images during the course of the officers' evidence.*[39] [italics added]

In both instances—that of the initial trial and the appeal against the original verdict—the judges put greater weight on the assessment of the police officers in their instructions to the jury than they did the testimony of the expert witnesses. As Lord Brodie pointed out at the start of the decision, there is no designated rule that only witnesses who have some sort of advanced or specialized knowledge of how an item of evidence works or is produced are permitted to speak on the validity of that evidence. Anyone who has formed an impression of something may express their impressions on that thing as long as the court agrees that their perspective is relevant might assist the jury in reaching a verdict.

The temptation here is to think that the courts are more than happy to admit evidence that makes the normal mechanisms of a trial run more smoothly; police are logical witnesses in criminal proceedings and there is a rational assumption that their professional experience would make them better at making identifications under stressful circumstances or noticing elements that would make an identification more accurate or more complete. The problem with this line of thinking is that it reinforces the primacy of the human element of security and seemingly erodes the value of the technology that is supposed to fill in the gaps in human perception and the likelihood of human error.

What was really problematic for the courts in this case was the fact that both of the expert witnesses asserted that CCTV *as a technology* is unreliable as a means of identification. Dr. McNeill goes so far as to suggest that the idea of facial recognition is fallacious on its own and Mr. Rolph indicates that his personal experience as a member of law enforcement prevents him from believing that there is any special efficacy to CCTV at all. The salve is that the police were the ones who made the ID during the initial investigation and it is their immediate connection to the case that appears to trump the experts' concerns with the reliability of the image in the abstract. Whatever the problems might be with the technological aspects of the evidence, the instincts of the police officers will be able to cut through that haze and get to the facts of the case.

In light of the fact that the principal witness could not identify Mr. Henry at tria,l[40] all of this makes a sad kind of sense. Technologies that are used in the identification or the prosecution of offenders must augment rather than modify the existing process of investigation and prosecution. The plan has never been to throw the baby out with the bathwater. CCTV should add a layer of infallibility to identifications made by police rather than complicate the entire process. Like the McLuhanite contention that the content of any medium is the medium that came before it (the content of film is the book, the content of radio is speech, etc.), the introduction of new forms of evidence into the legal process is supposed to simplify or buttress the existing procedures without calling them into question. Allan McNeill's research on facial recognition flies directly in the face of this. The assertion that facial recognition *as a practice* is fundamentally flawed and the expansion of that practice to technological means does not eliminate the fundamental concerns complicates rather than simplifies or validates the existing practices.

More worrying, really, is the testimony of Andrew Rolph. As a former detective inspector and someone who is well versed in the "scientific" aspects of investigation, his declaration that the CCTV camera often does not assist or simplify the process of identification is problematic for its continued use. In essence, Mr. Rolph argued that the normal fallacies of identification apply regardless of the technical means included in the identification and this undercuts one of the primary justifications for the use of cameras in public space. If they are no better than human eyewitnesses, if the capture of the image does not make the process of identification simpler or more reliable under difficult circumstances, all you are left with is a suspension of privacy justified by the probable absence of a witness. The invasion of privacy is only justified by the expediency of having a witness always in place in specific locations and this expediency fits conveniently within the boundaries of the United Kingdom's ambiguous stance on privacy itself.

Since, conversely, Canada has had a national Privacy Commissioner since 1977, the assumption that Canadian citizens have a presumptive right to privacy permeates many of the cases involving surveillance evidence. In Britain, however, as the majority of the mechanisms that are used to keep watch on a population were implemented long before the establishment of the EU, the techniques and technologies are effectively normalized. The issue lies in the problematizing of something that the courts and the police have come to depend on as unproblematic and, frankly, convenient. A December 1, 2014, judgment from the Court of Appeal[41] illustrates the reliability British courts apply to CCTV footage.

On April 4, 2010, two men were detained under suspicion of drug abuse and possession in the Kentish Town Road area of London. One was well-known comedian Noel Fielding and the other was his friend James Browne. The officers would later claim that Mr. Browne had ignored police orders and, as a result, one of the officers, PC O'Leary, had needed to force Mr. Browne to the ground and carry him outside an Everbest convenience store. A significant amount of the confrontation was captured on CCTV footage both inside the shop as well as outside from a camera positioned on the opposite side of the street. The footage from the shop was lost due to a damaged DVD, but the footage from the camera on the opposite side of the street was intact.

The interaction inside the shop between PC O'Leary and Mr. Browne was physical. Mr. Browne suffered extensive injuries as a result of the confrontation and sued the police in court. The judge evaluating the civil action brought by Mr. Browne relied almost entirely on CCTV footage from outside the shop to make her assessment.

In paragraph 31 of the judgment, she makes extensive use of the available CCTV footage in rejecting the officer's version of events:

> The CCTV evidence shows Mr. Browne as he enters the convenience store. I find that he is walking perfectly normally. He is dressed perfectly normally, in fact quite smartly. He is not displaying any signs of being "high." I reject Officer O'Leary's evidence that the Claimant was stumbling. It is apparent that Mr. Browne could not be described as "incredibly dishevelled and looking unshaven and tired." He may very well have been tired having been up all night. He had been drinking over the course of the night and was not "razor sharp." I accept his evidence that he was not drunk. When he gave his evidence to me PC O'Leary was asked about the appearance of the Claimant on the CCTV and he said the he believed that he had sobered up quite well and had had to "switch off" when approached by the police [. . .]. PC O'Leary therefore gave his opinion that Mr. Browne was displaying signs of drug use immediately before he is seen on the CCTV, sobered up whilst on the CCTV and then began displaying those signs of drug use again whilst in the store. I consider this to be simply incredible.

Three paragraphs later, she laments the absence of more CCTV footage to cover incidents in dispute:

> In the absence of CCTV evidence I have to make findings as to what happened in the store on the basis of the evidence I have heard from the two protagonists, PC O'Leary and the Claimant [James Browne].

She is, however, content to evaluate the validity of testimony on the basis of what is depicted on the footage in paragraph 37:

> The CCTV shows the point at which PC O'Leary goes into the store and the point at which he emerges carrying Mr. Browne. The time-lapse is 17 seconds. I reject PC O'Leary's account of what happened inside the store on the basis that I find he simply did not have time to do all that he says he did.

She is also content to determine the likelihood of the cause of injuries in paragraph 41 from the images available on CCTV footage:

> The CCTV footage does not show any sort of twisting or forceful movement that would have caused this fracture. Under the circumstances I have reached the conclusion that the fracture did not occur outside the store and must therefore have occurred inside.

Given the circumstances of the case, it would have been irresponsible for Judge Coe not to take the CCTV footage into account. It was effectively a matter of one person's version of events versus another. The CCTV functions in this instance as the perfect impartial observer.

A more distressing example from the British use of CCTV is the case of *Peck v. The United Kingdom*.[42]

Brentwood Borough Council began implementing its own CCTV system in 1994. A little more than a year later the council decided to "authorise the release of regular press features on the CCTV system" and to "cooperate with third parties in the preparation of factual programmes concerning the CCTV system" in order to fund the operations of the system and to demonstrate its viability and justify the cost to local inhabitants.[43] The archives that were kept on hand for ninety days[44] were subsequently searched for what one can only assume would be sensational or titillating material to share with the media.

One of the items released was footage of Mr. Peck (the applicant in the case) at a central junction in Brentwood. He was carrying a kitchen knife he'd taken from home. He'd been suffering severe depression brought on by personal and family circumstances. He later stated that his intent was to commit suicide by slashing his wrists. The camera caught him as he was leaning over a railing at the junction, facing traffic with the knife visibly in his hand. The CCTV operator was alerted to the image of a man carrying a knife and in turn alerted the police who raced to the location, approached Mr. Peck and diffused the situation without anyone being injured.[45]

Images of Mr. Peck were released to the council's press feature, *CCTV News*. His face was clearly visible. The *Brentwood Weekly News* also ran the images. Mr. Peck's face was still clearly visible. The unmodified images then appeared in the *Yellow Advertiser* under the headline, "Gotcha." Finally,

Anglia Television obtained video footage of the incident and ran it with Mr. Peck's face obscured (although the quality of masking was later determined to be inadequate by the Independent Television Commission). The *Yellow Advertiser* reprinted the original photograph in February 1996 under the headline, "Eyes in the sky triumph." Finally expanding the embarrassment to a national level, the council agreed to furnish CCTV footage that would necessarily contain that of Mr. Peck, to the producers of *Crime Beat*, a BBC series with an average of 9.2 million viewers.[46]

Those who knew Mr. Peck were easily able to identify him from the images and the footage. In fact, he was only aware that the images existed and had been released because his neighbor told his partner that they'd seen him on television.[47] None of the exposure had put the incident in context and, for all intents and purposes, the viewer might believe that Mr. Peck had intended to either threaten or harm other people with the knife. Having to explain over and over again that he'd intended to end his own life would have been humiliating and only have added to his depression.

With regard to the High Court's review of Mr. Peck's original application for judicial review, however, the release of the footage to the media appears to be unproblematic:

> By publicising information about the successful operation of the CCTV, the Council was providing information about its effectiveness and thereby reinforcing the deterrent effect of its operation. The making available to the media of footage from the CCTV film to show the effectiveness of the system can properly be said . . . to be incidental to and to facilitate the discharge of the Council's function under section 163 [of the 1994 Act] because it thereby increased, or tended to increase, the preventative effect of the equipment which [the Council was] providing for the purposes of the prevention of crime.[48] (*Brackets in original*)

The presumption being, apparently, that if Mr. Peck had wanted to kill himself privately, he should have done so at home. The judge lamented the circumstances, but pointed out that the lack of specific privacy protection under the law at that time—before the United Kingdom incorporated the European Commission on Human Rights—permitted the release of footage captured by the government or third parties.[49] As long as he ventured into public space, any captured image of him was open to reuse and, indeed, recontextualization by whatever opportunist was able to get access to the footage.

The European Court of Human Rights appears to have agreed with the High Court in its review. As the British government "maintained that the applicant waived his rights [to privacy] by choosing to do what he did, where he did"[50] and the applicant "was not complaining about being filmed by

CCTV (as this saved his life),"[51] the issue became whether or not the council had the right to release the footage to the media.[52]

Indeed,

> The applicant submitted that there was no sufficiently important countervailing public interest. He was not a public figure and he had no public role. The disclosure was made not to catch a criminal or find a missing person but to satisfy the general aim of publicising the effectiveness of the CCTV system, with which aim properly masked images or other less intrusive footage would have been consistent.[53]

The contention regarding the non-criminality of the event was reinforced by the European Court of Human Rights.[54] It also argued that the British standard for violation of privacy under the law, particularly since there was no legally established *de facto* right to privacy in the country, was so high that it precluded a rational challenge to abuse of privacy by private citizens.[55]

Peck won the challenge, and it does raise a concern regarding the application of video footage in policing. As much as it is possible for the court to gather information from what is captured on camera and, arguably, to make determinations that would otherwise have been tainted by personal interest as was the case in the Browne trail mentioned above, the footage does not have a shelf-life and is not captured by the court. It comes from somewhere else. Someone else owns it and can do what they like with it. Whether it is a council that is attempting to justify its own surveillance system or a private company that might see a financial benefit in passing the footage on to entertainment or news producers, the context that is intrinsic to the events captured on tape evaporates once it is repackaged for broadcast or print. At that point, the data is reinterpreted according to the social practices of looking and the differences in how the information is understood between the two perspectives can be found in the socio-political properties of the gaze.

NOTES

1. J. Finn, *Capturing the Criminal Image* (Minneapolis: University of Minnesota Press, 2009), xviii–ix, 57, 65.
2. *R. v. Nikolovski*. 1996. 3 S.C.R. 1197, S.C.J. No. 122, 1996 CanLII 158, File No. 24360. Supreme Court of Canada. para. 1. Web.
3. Ibid., paras. 1–2.
4. *R. v. Nikolovski*. 1996. 3 S.C.R. 1197, S.C.J. No. 122, 1996 CanLII 158, File No. 24360. Supreme Court of Canada. para. 3. Web.
5. "Trier of fact" is Canadian legal jargon. It really is just a pseudonym for the trial judge.

6. *R. v. Nikolovski*. 1996. 3 S.C.R. 1197, S.C.J. No. 122, 1996 CanLII 158, File No. 24360. Supreme Court of Canada. para. 3. Web.
7. *R. v. Nikolovski*. 1996. 3 S.C.R. 1197, S.C.J. No. 122, 1996 CanLII 158, File No. 24360. Supreme Court of Canada. para. 1. Web.
8. Ibid., para. 6.
9. Guy Paul Morin was accused of the murder of a nine-year-old girl in Ontario in 1984. He was acquitted at his original trial but the prosecution appealed the result. At a second trial ordered by the Ontario Court of Appeal, he was convicted and sentenced to life in prison. Morin languished until 1995 when he was cleared by recently developed DNA testing technology. A full breakdown of the Ministry of the Attorney General of Ontario's website: http://www.attorneygeneral.jus.gov.on.ca/english/about/pubs/morin/.
10. *R. v. Nikolovski*. 1996. 3 S.C.R. 1197, S.C.J. No. 122, 1996 CanLII 158, File No. 24360. Supreme Court of Canada. Para. 14. Web.
11. Ibid., para. 15.
12. Ibid., para. 17.
13. Ibid., para. 19.
14. Ibid., paras. 21–22.
15. Ibid., para. 22.
16. Ibid., para. 25.
17. Ibid., para. 28.
18. *R. v. Jackson*, 2011. ONCJ 228. O'Donnell J. Web.
19. Ibid.
20. Ibid., para. 1.
21. Ibid., paras. 32–33.
22. Ibid., para. 33.
23. Ibid., para. 41.
24. Ibid., para. 73.
25. Ibid., para. 29.
26. There are no specifics offered in the case file as to what specifically qualifies one person as an "expert" on CCTV footage.
27. *R. v. McLetchie*, 2011. O.J. No. 1244. ONSC 1440. March 23, 2011. Web.
28. Ibid., paras. 18–21.
29. M. Gras, "The Legal Regulation of CCTV in Europe." *Surveillance & Society* 2, no. 2/3 (2004), 216.
30. M. Gras, "The Legal Regulation of CCTV in Europe." *Surveillance & Society* 2, no. 2/3 (2004), 217.
31. Lord Brodie, *Opinion of the Court delivered by Lord Brodie in Appeal Against Conviction by Nicholas Russell Henry, Appellant, against Her Majesty's Advocate, respondent*. HJAC 128. Appeal No: XC724/11. October 17, 2012. BAILII. Web.
32. Ibid., paras. 7, 10.
33. Ibid., para. 10(6).
34. Ibid., para. 9.
35. Ibid., para. 12.
36. Ibid., para. 13.

37. Ibid., para. 27.
38. Ibid., para. 28.
39. Ibid., para. 20.
40. Ibid., para. 11.
41. *James Browne v. The Commissioner of Police of the Metropolis*, High Court of Justice Queen's Bench Division. Case No. HQ11X01233 (2014).
42. *Peck v. The United Kingdom. European Court of Human Rights*. 4th Section. Application no. 44647/98. Judgment. Strasbourg. 28 January 2003.
43. Ibid., para. 12.
44. Ibid., para. 9.
45. Ibid., paras. 10–11.
46. Ibid., paras. 13–16.
47. Ibid., para. 18.
48. Ibid., para. 29.
49. Ibid., para. 32.
50. Ibid., para. 53.
51. Ibid., para. 54.
52. Ibid., para. 60.
53. Ibid., para. 74.
54. Ibid., para. 79.
55. Ibid., para. 106.

Chapter 4

Theoretical Elements of CCTV as a Media Format

THE GAZE

The person who is looking at CCTV footage will be doing so from a specific perspective. The use of the camera is one element, but another is what is motivating the person who is looking at what the camera produces. I have experience of being in this position because while completing my master's degree I worked as a building security guard at a "sports entertainment complex" in London, Ontario, Canada. The arena was brand new and outfitted with an integrated camera surveillance system that linked motion sensitive video cameras to a monitor and recording system in the security booth at the back of the building. During my many overnight shifts, I would be trying to write my thesis and only looked at the security monitor when a movement set one of the cameras off (usually it was mice, but sometimes it was the hockey team's trainer who lived in the locker room unbeknownst to the owners of the building).

The monitor, linked with the motion sensitive cameras, altered the feeling of the building. During events, there was an enormous amount of activity and the monitor would simply cycle through the cameras at regular intervals, displaying visitors at all of the surveilled corners of the building. At night, however, there was an eeriness to a static image suddenly popping up on screen; movement was suspicious particularly since I was the only person who should have been in the building. The cameras were supposed to draw my attention to something displayed in front of them but, all too often, whatever had set the sensor off was gone by the time I looked up to check what it was. The effect was a little unnerving as I was supposed to be using this equipment to assess anything in the building that shouldn't have been there and yet I found myself staring at static images of the concourse or the hallways behind the private boxes hoping that whatever had left the frame before I'd reacted would wander back into it. I discovered that the surveillance image is not something casual. I became conscious that the way I was looking was not the same as simply looking out the window of a car while riding along the road or casually glancing around a public square while you sit and sip a cup of coffee. It is an image that is delivered for a purpose and one that the viewer is compelled to interpret by an institutional demand.

I was not allowed to use my own initiative in reacting to something on the screen. The instructions for the job I was being paid to do were that I would use the monitor and, by extension, the cameras as a tool to keep an eye on a building that was far too big for one person to oversee. The false alerts that I witnessed repeatedly coming from the security system, however, made the job frustrating and more than a little unnerving. Like a phone ringing or a knock at the door, the expectation that there will be someone on the other end of the line or in the doorway once I've responded to the ringing or the knocking is natural—it fits the normal expectations of what those prompts mean. Oddly, the absence of what is expected at the other end of the line, on the other side of the door, or even on the transmitted image from the CCTV camera only leaves questions as to the origin of the signal and no definitive answers. Yet I was required to analyze the fact that the camera had begun sending me a live feed without any obvious reason for it and would feel compelled to watch the static image for long enough that I could justify turning away again. I felt responsible for the image, for understanding why it was there because I understood that to be my job. If there was no apparent reason for its being on the monitor in the first place, I would still have somehow to connect my futile watching with the reason for my being employed. I became certain each time the monitor switched on that it would tell me nothing I needed to know and yet I was certain that I was supposed to evaluate it anyway. The CCTV system seemed to exert more power over me by sending blank images to the security booth; there was no point in paying attention and yet I was absolutely required to pay attention. The camera seemed to have all of the agency. It somehow created a dynamic whereby it defined s significant part of my job without providing any significant assistance in doing my job. This realization, however, did not grant me any independence—I was still entirely dependent on what the cameras sent through to the monitor.

There is an analogous connection between the use of the camera in CCTV and the use of it by the main character in Michael Powell's 1960 film *Peeping Tom*, an important film about the pathology of looking. He is a "focus puller" on a film crew, a part-time soft-porn photographer, child abuse survivor, and serial killer named Mark Lewis (played by Karlheinz Böhm aka Carl Boehm) who has managed to hide a knife blade inside the tripod leg attached to one of his cameras and has attached a large mirror around the outside of the lens.

This makes it possible for him to film his victims watching their own terrified faces as he stabs them to death. The camera allows him to capture what he wants from whatever perspective he wants. It is an idealized form of looking that allows the experience to be captured and repeated over and over again. The camera allows Lewis to immortalize his victims' last mortal moments. It allows him to turn what would normally be a passing moment into something that he can control and reexperience an unlimited number of times. The camera in this instance, and all others, is an object that must be directed by someone.

In *Peeping Tom*, Mark is both the director and the person who watches what is filmed. He does so to make his world real, since his father's abuse has created in him a pathological sense of distance from the real world: he can only relate to it by creating representations of it. Unlike Mark, the person who watches the CCTV image on the monitor is rarely the same person who directed its installation in the first place. More often than not, these cameras are erected by institutions rather than individuals even though individuals like myself end up having to watch what the cameras record. The reason to look at the CCTV image is administrative. It is looking that is directed by an institution—whether it be the owners of the building where the CCTV camera is located or whether it be the police officer who is watching feed delivered by a camera in a public place. In *Peeping Tom*, Mark is like the subject of the gaze in CCTV, having been under the constant surveillance of his father's camera from his birth. As a result, he is only able to experience the world through his camera in a way that might be comparable to (although obviously in a much more extreme way) the way I was starting to feel as a CCTV operator. This sense of being detached from direct experience of the world seems to be comparable to what Michel Foucault called "the medical gaze":

> The medical gaze was [. . .] organized in a new way. First, it was no longer the gaze of any observer, but that of a doctor supported and justified by an institution, that of a doctor endowed with the power of decision and intervention. Moreover, it was a gaze that was not bound by the narrow grid of structure (form, arrangement, number, size), but that could and should grasp colours, variations, tiny anomalies, always receptive to the deviant.[1]

This will be what is meant when I use the term "the institutional gaze" in this argument. For Mark, the need to reclaim power as the viewer rather than the subject—as he was in his own father's filmed experiments of him—pairs with the overall power of objectifying something through surveillance. For Mark's father, the impetus came directly from the institution itself in that his research was no doubt funded in the interest of furthering research into the psychological effects of fear experienced by young children, which he did by using the camera to experiment on his son. The footage provided by the camera was used to either validate Mark's father's hypotheses or further his work and would be presented to the wider world for what he probably thought was the greater good, oblivious to the damage being done to his son. Mark's father was therefore working as an agent of the institutional gaze in much the same way as those councilors who authorize the use of CCTV. The power relationship that Foucault outlines works in both directions here. The use of the camera has effects on the viewers as well as the subjects. The institutional gaze provides an alibi for the creation of the image in the first instance and provides the subject with an instant value—that of being worthy of being watched. It is tempting to draw a link between the cultural acceptance of being viewed and the popularity of "selfies" among younger citizens as well as the enthusiastic use of social surveillance applications like Instagram, Facebook, and FourSquare. The normalcy of the condition of being watched coupled with the presumption of legitimate authority that goes along with security surveillance practices offers a sense of codependency in the relationship of being watched. That normalcy, however, only involves a limited interaction that is shaped and even permitted by the user. Social networking is something that is intrusive, but ultimately voluntary. The institutional approach, and this is the key element of Mark's father's surveillance, is carried out for the benefit of the institution or the person who enacts the surveillance rather than the subject of that surveillance. Regardless of who is finally watching the footage captured, be it Mark's father, Mark, the building owner or me, the footage was captured without the subject's explicit consent and yet has direct consequences for that subject. The looking that is done with CCTV footage is the result of an identified need to watch and this need comes from an administrative, distanced perspective rather than a participatory one.

The product of surveillance, of CCTV, is much more than simply the result of applying logic to fluid happenings in Cartesian space. The modalities of interpretation are not determined as much by the individual observer as they are by the observer's understanding of what is of interest according to the predictable events taking place within the limits of the image. These understandings are as much a result of directed interpretations offered by the organization that owns the cameras and which has trained the person watching the image on the monitor as they are the result of the viewer's personal experiences. The image determines the spatial limits of the information that can be gathered, but the value of the information captured in the image proper is determined by the predictions, limitations, and advanced understandings of the clinical gaze. There is no tangible difference between this and the way CCTV images are meant to be interpreted. This is what is meant when the idea of the gaze is discussed with respect to surveillance. The authority that Foucault allocated to the medical profession, the ability to determine its own reflexive accuracy ahead of the event—thereby preemptively validating its own conclusions—is in principle the same reason to erect a CCTV camera or, indeed, to the establishment of any surveillance system.

It is possible to speak of the institutional gaze when authority is attached to the idea of looking. It involves looking with a kind of certainty that the endorsement of a larger authoritative structure imbues it with. This is what Foucault meant, in the above quote, when he distinguished the doctor's observations from those of the ordinary observer. This same institutional direction and authority extends to the practice of viewing CCTV footage. Whatever is captured by the camera becomes available to the observer in a way that is premeasured according to the social dynamics of surveillance. The CCTV image pre-interprets its findings in a similar way to how Foucault argued that the eighteenth century assessed disease as a system of significations:[2] the position of the camera, what can happen; the image as captured, what has happened; the reaction of the observer, what will happen. Although it would be too deterministic to suggest that all events that become CCTV images are anticipated, the general qualities of movement in front of the camera are assessed before the camera is erected. The process of observation validates the erection of the camera and the resulting actions that take place when deviance is detected are the justification for the observation made. In short, the gaze comprises the predictable outcomes of the act of observing, as Foucault noted:

> The formation of the clinical method was bound up with the emergence of the doctor's gaze into the field of signs and symptoms. The recognition of its constituent rights involved the effacement of their absolute distinction and the postulate that henceforth the signifier (sign and symptom) would be entirely transparent for the signified, which would appear, without concealment or residue, in its most pristine reality, and that the essence of the signified—the heart of the disease—would be entirely exhausted in the intelligible syntax of the signifier.[3]

Is this not the exact same dynamic that is applied in surveillance? If so and if, as McLuhan has argued, the body is extended upon exposure to electronic media, then there is a need for elements in the social world that are foreign to the population, that are perceived as a threat, to be diagnosed in the same way that the subject would interpret a threat to their own bodies. This necessitates a vocabulary of seeing, a particular way of organizing the event of seeing, and the reactions to what takes place in it. The codification of that experience event is best described as "the institutional gaze."

There is an interesting relationship here between the use of Closed Circuit Television cameras which are, by definition, cameras that produce images specifically for an identified source and the increase in access to image recording and distribution technology for the public. In CCTV, the circuit that connects the camera and the monitor is not shared by any other entity and, as such, the delivery of the image is controlled. The ubiquity of camcorders and, more recently and far more importantly, camera phones has complicated the position of power in relation to the production of images. From the unanticipated recording and publication of the beating of motorist Rodney King by the Los Angeles Police Department in 1992[4] to the photographing and filming of the police assault on protestor Adam Nobody during the 2010 G20 summit in Toronto, Canada,[5] the ability for images to be created that put institutions or representatives of institutions in the spotlight is relatively new and certainly not fully appreciated by the institutional gaze. Those images that are produced outside of the loop of CCTV and the institution are much more freely interpreted by the public and the commercial media and are far more transportable and promotable on Facebook news feeds, Twitter accounts, and traditional information channels like network news and newspapers (both online and in print). The fluidity of the image and its morphability in the form of popular use and consumption makes the instant authority of the "institutional gaze" infinitely more important for practitioners and the users of the CCTV image in that there is supposedly a stable point of interpretation. The institutional gaze not only legitimizes the capturing of the image as it is happening but the legitimate interpretation of that image as it is being viewed. If it is released for use in court proceedings or even for an entertainment television program, it is as something that has been deemed worth looking at by the parameters of the institutional interpretation.

The authoritative background of the medical gaze, the foundation of what I am calling the "institutional gaze," sets limits to the possible interpretations of what it discovers and provides a procedure for dealing with that discovery. Continuing with Foucault's analysis of the emergence of scientific diagnosis in the nineteenth century,

> medicine discovered that uncertainty may be treated, analytically, as the sum of a certain number of isolatable degrees of certainty that were capable of rigorous calculation. Thus, this confused, negative concept, whose meaning derived from a traditional opposition to mathematical knowledge was to be capable of transforming itself into a positive concept and offered to the penetration of a technique proper to calculation.[6]

Here again there is a direct parallel with Mark's father's research in *Peeping Tom* here in which the father records his son in moments of abject terror in order to better understand the condition. Mark's father is a famous psychologist engaged in the study of the psychopathology of fear who used his son as a guinea pig, filming him constantly from the moment of his birth. To do so, he set up situations that would terrify him and recorded the boy's reactions over and over again. The hope was that the practice would refine itself in the process of collecting data and a technique of analyzing and controlling fear would be the result. What is described here is decidedly less horrific than Mark's father's approach, but the interpretation of the surveillance image is the result of an institutionally prescribed assumption of what constitutes acceptable action in front of the camera and what does not. It is important to keep in mind that the purpose of surveillance is the analysis of behaviors but it is also crucial to remember that the analysis can only come from within the interpretive framework defined by the institution carrying out that analysis.

To sum up, the sort of institutional authority that Foucault claims is afforded to the medical professional conducting a diagnosis is the same kind of authority that applies to the interpretations of surveillance images by security or government agencies. Inasmuch as the gaze in medicine is both the application of myriad smaller measurable variables to larger, more nebulous problems the institutional gaze in security is an application of blanket assertions of authority to unique and distinct social events.

It is this uncertainty in the visual that makes necessary the institutional system of determination Foucault has described in *The Birth of the Clinic*. The process in surveillance thus shares characteristics with that of the clinic—it is the naming of the unknown, the making solid of ghosts. In this specific context, the ghost is that which cannot be comprehended by the viewer without a structural interpretation. Elements that sit outside of the perceptual limits of the viewer remain intangible, nebulous. The solution to this follows the same intrinsic procedure Foucault described; the use of smaller measurable elements that can be identified in order to explain that which, for the moment at least, defies explanation.

This relationship between known and unknown on all levels is invariably in a state of perpetual flux. If the person initiating an action is viewed—becomes subject to the gaze—it can reasonably be assumed that whatever that person does initiates the application of standard interpretations by the viewer. As there is no dialogue with the person in front of the camera, no opportunity to determine the actual thought processes that have caused the person to be of interest, the solution is to attach preconceived notions to whatever happens. In the same sense that Foucault describes the solution to uncertainty as the application of "the sum of a certain number of isolatable degrees of certainty that were capable of rigorous calculation,"[7] so the gaze in surveillance is a technique for making sense of the actions of subjects. This process of the gaze integrates the actions of the subject into the matrix of "isolatable degrees of certainty." To put it simply, the gaze weaves the subject into this schematic of quantifiable and definable properties that makes the unknown knowable.

Once the institutional gaze is enacted, once the subject is identified by the viewer, the subject becomes a text in need of interpretation. While Debord claimed that "the spectacle is not a collection of images; rather, it is a social relationship between people that is mediated by images,"[8] in CCTV this mediation is enacted with the identification of the subject as an object of interest. Debord was worried about the infiltration of the spectacle into daily life, about the effect that it could have on human interaction and the population's collective grip on power relationships. In CCTV, this influence now bleeds into the way institutions function: gaze moves beyond direct, personal interaction and so becomes institutionalized.

This again follows on from Foucault's conclusion that the patient, under the regime of the institutional gaze, became an object of comparison against all subsequent patients. The person in front of the camera is in an equivalent position to Foucault's patient: she/he fits into a pattern by which behavior is judged first on the basis of how people were viewed on the monitor beforehand and then will become a point of comparison for those who come into the frame afterward.[9] What this does is institute a pattern, a system of predictable causes and outcomes that predetermines the way the viewer evaluates the surveillance image. Though the viewer may perceive the person viewed as acting in a spontaneous way, the interpretation that can be applied to those actions is commanded by the historical paradigm laid out by every pervious individual who has been similarly interpreted. In this sense, the actions of the person being viewed no longer belong to him or her; they are tainted by the institutional gaze and the history that informs it.

The result is that the person being viewed lacks a substantive agency. The person under surveillance or, specifically, in this discussion the person in front of the CCTV camera, necessarily becomes at once an object for investigation by the viewer and an opportunity for validation of the tenets of the gaze. The question becomes how this condition of being viewed situates the subject in light of the gaze.

BEING VIEWED

Insofar as Foucault described visibility as a trap,[10] the trap snares both the viewer and the person being viewed. Both are trapped by the institutional gaze. The watching of the image, the act of viewing and understanding the message transmitted by the image necessarily transfers responsibility for the "event" from what is actually happening to what the person watching thinks is significant about it. If the person watching is doing so because it is their job, they are acting as the instrument of the institutional gaze, and if they see something happen that would require the attention of the police, they have a professional imperative to report it. Failure to do so—should it be discovered—would mean they would lose their job, even if it should turn out not to have been anything of significance. Acting on behalf of an institution in the practice of surveillance means that the viewer must constantly bear in mind the institutional practices that demand the image be monitored in the first place. In a sense, it is impossible for the viewer to act as an individual as the reason they are involved in watching the feed from the camera is to apply the interpretive framework of the institution to whatever they happen to see. In my personal case, the monitoring of the CCTV feed during my security job involved assuring that the reason the camera had switched on was not an uninvited guest in the building, regardless of why they happened to be there in the first place—that is, if they were homeless and needed a warm place to sleep for the night or if it were someone trying to hide from an attacker. Neither of those things would have mattered according to the guidelines given to me by the people who owned the building and the cameras. In my case, as well as virtually any comparable one, the knowledge of an event via the use of surveillance creates a liability for the viewer. Once they've seen something, they can't un-see it and they can only legitimately act on it according to the defined acceptable responses given to them by the institution.

The regime of legitimate interpretations and actions that are integrated into the institutional gaze very often are naturalized for those who are part of the structure. No matter what happened while I was staring at the monitor in the security booth at the arena in London, Ontario, I was aware that I was expected to react if I had witnessed something that fit within a field of unacceptable events. The myriad times, however, that the cameras activated and I couldn't see any reason for it over time dulled my response to a sudden image. Before long, I found myself hoping that every camera that awakened was doing so only because of mice. The two alternative explanations were more frightening for differing reasons; either someone had in fact broken into the building but had slipped past the cameras before I could look up or the cameras didn't work and my employment was a matter of perpetuating an illusion of watchfulness. In the first instance, I might be in physical danger and that was bad enough. Somehow, the possibility that there might be no actual efficacy to the security system was worse since no one had told me in advance that that was the case. In that instance, then, I was part of a machine that didn't work rather than simply watching a machine that didn't work. The only rational response was to try to salvage my sense of self worth and simply treat the security system as a flawed but forced component of my job.

In any case, it began to feel like the job was more about a performance that announced security rather than an actual act of securing something. An interesting metaphor for the advanced stages of my job working in that security booth might be the beginning of the Wachowski brothers' first *Matrix* film, a film that leans heavily on Baudrillard's work and the question of simulacra and ambiguity of the idea of the "real" in a mediatized culture. In the film, the lead character Neo (played by Keanu Reeves) is contacted by a mysterious Internet figure he's been searching for named Morpheus. Morpheus, played by Laurence Fishburne, tells Neo that he is searching because, deep down, he can feel that "something is wrong with the world." Morpheus proceeds to offer Neo a choice. Either he can continue living in the world he knows even though he can't shake the impression that something is wrong with it, or he can shatter that illusion forever and learn the truth. Once he's through the looking glass, however, there will be no way to return.

The knowledge that "something is wrong with the world" is not so much the understanding that everything is a construction, but that the interactions taking place between individuals in the world Neo had inhabited were not real. The demonstrative desire on the part of Neo is that all events, all witnessings, are constructions to which the only actual witness is this elaborate illusory world the audience later learns is called "the Matrix." The immediate disruption on realizing a disconnection from the Matrix was a claustrophobic awakening in a fluid-filled tube, or, according to Slavoj Žižek, the sudden awareness of a total connection to disciplinary mechanisms.[11] These disciplinary mechanisms, however, are invariably inhuman or apathetic.

The ache that plagues Neo during the beginning of the film is one of being disconnected—of feeling a lack of authenticity in all life world interactions. The desire with which he seeks out Morpheus is indicative of a desire for an actual connection. The knowledge that the life lived is one that is not witnessed is traumatic, frustrating. The moment at which Neo joins others aboard a rebel ship called the *Nebuchadnezzar* and is able to verify being seen, is the moment at which he is able to verify his existence: he can see the reactions of others to his presence. The validation of his suspicions, of his seemingly irrational actions is the discovery that they have been witnessed. This knowing that there are others who would have witnessed his actions, who had followed him suppresses any lingering doubts.

This safety in being witnessed is present in CCTV. The knowledge that someone is watching offers reassurance that someone else knows what is happening. If something significant happens in front of the camera and the person monitoring a live feed sees it, they have a decision to make: they can either report it or ignore it. In this instance, the viewer is obligated by what happens on the screen and the person in front of the camera is no longer the only person who would definitely have knowledge of what happens. The transfer of power is the liberation of the subject as he/she/it no longer has full ownership of the actions carried out under the institutional gaze.

It would be too much to suggest that this is a conscious recognition on the part of the person being filmed. Living in surveilled environments, however, must produce at least a passing knowledge of being watched. There is a degree of personal security in the knowledge of constantly being seen. At the very least, it seems more likely that someone who assaults you in view of the camera will be identified and caught. The camera promises the possibility of a negative connotation to being viewed, however, it records anyone who passes in front of its lens regardless of the connotation. The effect on the citizen is the creation of a desire to be invisible and a recognition that the event of being visible is not necessarily within their personal control any longer—you don't have to intentionally draw attention to yourself to get people looking in your direction any longer. Whatever may happen, you always have someone looking in your direction.

Foucault's investigation of the clinic indicated that "description" was more a matter of giving a voice to that which everyone sees without realizing it. There is a limit to the translatability of this speech in that it works toward an already developed and specific vocabulary.[12] It is worth noting that CCTV works in similar fashion. Whatever is captured by the camera will be described in a context that fits the overall dialectic of surveillance. In this way, the actions that are captured, the activity that is taken and processed through this vocabulary, becomes part of that vocabulary. The data that is captured by the surveillance apparatus treats the subject of the surveillance according to already established criteria and works the data into the existing vocabulary. Whatever changes come about as a result of new information do so after passing through the preexisting filter of the institutional gaze and the scope of the gaze is expanding rapidly.

According to David Lyon, the pervasiveness of media systems that enact surveillance has become so ubiquitous that their acceptance is nearly a *fait accompli*.[13] People are profiled when they use debit or credit cards (the data is captured and recorded by the banking or lending institutions), they are monitored when they use mobile phones or the Internet (GPS systems in mobile technology regularly relate locations back to the parent company and Internet Service Providers record and share the browsing history of their customers) and they willingly participate in social networking systems that catalogue massive amounts of data that they willingly provide. This watching, then, is less an intrusion than it is a condition of the landscape. Lyon's argument that the public is currently living in a "viewer society" is correct. The problem is that the theoretical narrative applied to surveillance societies concentrates on the operational effect of the viewing rather than what is to be done with the footage or the data that is produced by it.

Taken literally, in a viewer society all things are to be viewed. The limit of what is visible disappears and the idea of invisibility becomes unthinkable.

The trauma of being visible, then, disappears. It is worth noting that this is most likely the reason for the popularity of Internet entities like Facebook, Twitter, YouTube, and the like. The goal now is to verify one's own existence by being witnessed. The expanse of the "viewer society" results in a need for constant validation in the realization that one is being witnessed.

It works on the same principle as confession or psychotherapy except the release takes place in tandem with the act. Lyon makes the point that "Those who permit themselves to be watched generally do so because of some perceived benefit to them."[14] This is undoubtedly true, though the idea of the benefit has changed. In the purest sense, and in light of the pervasiveness of Closed Circuit Television in the contemporary Western urban environment, the simple benefit is a promise of safety when simply going shopping or using the public transit system. The public is no longer consciously choosing to be viewed in the active sense. They are, however, so accustomed to the knowledge that they are being viewed on a regular basis that the possible absence of being surveilled might give an unsettling sense of insecurity.

This sense of vulnerability is immediately alleviated by being viewed. The relief is instant; unlike confession or psychotherapy where the subject must recall the actions that would be of interest to the viewer or audience and express them specifically in the knowledge of being watched happens in tandem with the actions themselves. In other words, if the desire is to be witnessed, the satisfaction is immediately achieved upon the realization that one is being witnessed.

Perhaps this relief is linked to the notion that personal responsibility for anything is inversely proportionate to the number of people who might know about it. The transfer of knowledge of events to the viewer by the person being viewed distances the person in front of the camera from ownership of the actions carried out—it is now someone else's problem. The knowledge that the actions captured on camera are known *or have the potential of being known* by another individual standing for a higher authority removes a degree of responsibility from the person subject to the image. If it were that important, if the actions I'd done something bad, someone would have reported it, right? The creation of the surveillance apparatus, and the conditioning of the public to the idea of being constantly viewed offers the public a permanent confessor who never needs to be addressed directly.

The act of viewing thus makes the viewer a participant, although the participation is rooted in knowledge only. The decision to disclose what has happened makes the viewer a party to the situation but only after the fact. The viewer can act on the information, pass it on to someone else to act on it, or they can keep it to themselves. Their only agency is in deciding what to do after whatever happened has taken place. They cannot stop it from happening and they did not participate in it. Their position is purely reactive.

Being viewed alleviates the sense of personal responsibility at the price of granting the viewer the ability to judge. This is where I break with Foucault's analysis of the gaze in the clinic. Whereas in the case of the clinical gaze the "observing gaze refrains from intervening,"[15] the CCTV gaze interferes as a matter of course. The condition of being viewed is relevant to people. The physiological properties that the clinical gaze observes probably won't change their behavior if they become sentient and realize they are being viewed. Cancer doesn't care if someone is watching. The act of observing, then, records events taking place without changing them. Whereas the clinical gaze is able to "leave things as they are," the positioning of a CCTV camera changes the landscape. Those who pass in front of the camera are aware that they have become a text. In the case of the clinic, the event that has caused the gaze to focus on the patient's body happened to that body before it was observed by doctors. By contrast, the process of surveillance is the establishment of the gaze *before* an event has taken place.

All of this is relevant when evaluating the effect of being viewed on the products of surveillance. As much as the clinical gaze relies on this already-there property of the disease or the injury affecting the patient, live surveillance links the viewer and the subject in its happening. Viewers will either watch the event taking place on a live feed or they will review the event as a recording. In this specific context, it can be assumed that the camera itself counts as a party to the event—the event of capture is enough to construct a kind of simultaneity in the image. Even if the footage is not watched immediately, the event of watching it is still within the confines of simultaneity. The possibility of judging the actions depicted in the image and taking the information from the point of viewing to the point of an action in the world outside this relationship is enough to involve the viewer in the content captured in a very immediate way.

By agreeing to witness, the viewer places him/herself in an entirely reactive position. This reaction comes at a price, of course. The knowledge that something has happened instantly becomes a responsibility. This responsibility necessarily involves a decision; if an action witnessed would normally require a subsequent action on the part of the viewer—whether or not to order officers to the scene, to turn the footage over to investigators, or to simply ignore the event. The ostensible reason for surveillance is the gathering of information and ignoring that purpose would be a blatant violation of the reasons for doing the viewing in the first place. As such, the autonomy that belongs to the viewer stretches only so far as they are willing to ignore the implicit purpose of their bearing witness in the first place. It is in this sense that this argument, once again, comes close to Foucault's interpretation of the clinic. According to Foucault, the act of description "does not mean placing the hidden or the visible within reach of those who have no direct access to them; what it means is to give speech to that which everyone sees without seeing—a speech that can be understood only by those initiated into the true speech."[16] The vocabulary of medicine is necessarily out of reach for those who have had no training. It does, however, entail a responsibility in light of that knowledge—the vocabulary, the speech, that Foucault writes about is in effect a condition of permanent responsibility. The knowledge that allows the physician to describe the disease, to explain the properties of the ailment, is the productive aspect of the medical or the clinical gaze—the ability to describe it in an authoritative way. The reception of the CCTV signal works in a similar way in that there is effectively no passive response to experiencing the image and there is no passive way to describe the events depicted in the image either. Either the viewer will act on the details of the image or will ignore it.

Despite these similarities, the communication that follows the viewing of the CCTV footage requires a different sort of speech to that of the physician. The implicit demand for judgment, the inherent relationship that emerges as a result of having watched the footage requires a communication on the part of the viewer. Like the close attention to detail that is necessary to fully evaluate the patient, the viewer of CCTV is linked to the event in that they have witnessed its happening. Their requirement is to remove themselves from the situation by making a decision. The ability to judge the acts of the subject is not so much a measure of the authority of the viewer over the one being viewed as much as it is the point at which viewers are able to remove themselves from the situation and evaluate it. There is an old joke that fits this situation in a way:

> Two mental patients decide that they've had enough of being confined to the asylum and develop a plan to escape. One night, they put their plan into action and sneak up onto the roof of the building. There is a short gap between the roof they're on and the one that they have to get to in order to get to freedom. The first patient runs at the gap and jumps over to the other building without any problem. The second patient, however is frightened. After trying to coax the second patient over for a few minutes, the first patient has an idea: He picks up the flashlight he stole from the orderly's cart and offers to shine the beam across the gap. The second patient, he suggests, can walk across the beam over to the other roof and they can both escape. The second patient screams at the first patient, "What, do you think I'm crazy? . . . You'd turn it off when I was halfway across."[17]

The first patient is the viewer who is already on the other side and essentially free. The second patient would be the viewed, aware of the tenuous connection between them and ever aware that if the connection is severed, it will be at the whim of the viewer. The decision to keep the flashlight on is equivalent to the viewer's ignoring something they would otherwise need to report. The fear that the flashlight might be turned off is the equivalent of switching the flashlight off. The relationship between the viewed and the viewer only exists for as long as the viewer allows it to exist. The judgment event is the equivalent of turning the flashlight off.

DELAY

Another fundamental issue is the delay, however slight, between the actual events occurring in front of the camera and their transmission back to whatever screen may be displaying them. Jacques Derrida, in conversation with Bernard Stiegler, suggested that,

> Now at this very instant, we are living in a very singular, unrepeatable moment, which took place only once, of something that was live, that is live, that we think is simply live, but that will be reproduced *as live*, with a reference to this present and this moment anywhere and anytime, weeks or years from now, reinscribed in other frames or 'contexts'.[18] [italics author's]

Derrida was speaking to the fact that the conversation he and Stiegler were having was being videotaped. Derrida's argument was focused on the presentation of the television image. The sense that television always appears live is one that has more currency than might appear at first glance: From television shows like *Cheers*, which proudly proclaimed that they were filmed "in front of a live studio audience," to the canned laughter used in other comedy programs, to this irritating new trend that moves news broadcasters out from behind the desk so they can stand in front of the camera rather than sitting behind a desk and, presumably, give the shot a sense of action, the medium seems to beg an overture toward "liveness." The concerns that Derrida is voicing are that the temporal reality of the conversation he is having can never be fully recognized because of the intrinsic properties of television as a medium.

This idea of delay, then, is fundamental to television. During their conversation, Derrida says to Stiegler, "no matter how soon after their recording we die, and even if we were able to die while recording, *voila*, this will be and will remain 'live,' a simulacrum of life."[19] The image retains this essence of being a present happening long after the actual event has transpired. I've touched on this point in the previous section, but after the effect of recording, of the production of a repeatable image that can be retrieved after the life world has taken place, preserves this sense of "liveness" for posterity.

Derrida argues that "we should never forget that this 'live' is not an absolute 'live' but only a live effect . . . an allegation of 'live.' Whatever the apparent immediacy of the transmission or broadcast, it negotiates with choices, with framing, with selectivity."[20] The CCTV image consequently trades on this essence of the televisual. The ascription of "live" that is woven into the reception of a televisual image is the very quality that gives televised surveillance its legitimacy.

The logical move is to bring this line of thinking back to Baudrillard's idea of "integral reality." This "live" that resonates out of the television screen is built on the disappearance of the idea of the copy. The suggestion that the television image carries with it a sense of "live" that cannot be removed from the overall presentation plays directly into the suggestion that the idea of duplication has no real meaning anymore. Derrida argued that presentations that are labeled "live" are in fact produced ahead of broadcast, and he did argue that what is produced is "not a faithful and integral reproduction of what it is thought to reproduce."[21] He was talking mainly about broadcast television, most of which would have been fictional stories constructed for broadcast or sporting events that worked off a number of different camera angles. That being said, the argument that Derrida is making—that the televised image is inextricably linked with a notion of "live" even though this property is demonstrably not an accurate reading of the presentation—is relevant to the subject of this book. The delay that is temporally linked to the image—either because the video being watched was called up a significant amount of time after it had been produced or simply by virtue of the recording apparatus that captured the events in the first place—is fundamental to the way someone will view the footage when they encounter it.

McLuhan's contention that electronic media functions as an extension of the central nervous system brings a sense of temporal consistency into the equation. It is unusual to assume that a sensation that is directly experienced is not on the same temporal plane as the body having the experience. This possible delay that is linked to CCTV and television in general, then, encourages the viewers to lie to themselves in order to fully relate to the image displayed. There will be a delay. However, the properties of television reception require that viewer ignores its delay and experiences it as though it were live. The image appears to the viewer as though it were immediate, *a la* Derrida's comments, and we receive it as immediate according to McLuhan's assertion that the central nervous system is entwined with the delivery apparatus. The way audiences interact with the televised image and the way the televised image is presented to them interact in such a way that the question of "liveness" becomes much more pliable and subjective. When I was working security, I always felt I was watching something as it was happening (even if, strictly speaking, nothing was really happening) even though there must have been a delay given that the camera had to activate in order to record and then send me the image on the screen.

In a mechanical context, CCTV is both immediate and subsequently delayed. Images must be captured by the camera, transmitted into electronic signals, sent to a receiver that then converts those signals into data and reconstructs the image on a screen for the viewer to witness. An image of a person waiting for a train at New Cross Gate station displays as though it were a disconnected window into that actual event. That the camera has captured the light bouncing off of the physical objects in front of it, organized the reflective properties of that light into a flattened, two-dimensional representation of that physical reality, and moved that image from the circuitry of the camera onto a screen for the viewer to see is typically overlooked when viewing the image—it has to be. In much the same way that someone is walking, if they were always conscious of the fact that this involves taking the body from a stable position, throwing it into space, stabilizing it, and repeating the action again and again they wouldn't move very fast. Likewise, the constant evaluation of video representations would slow the intake to intolerable levels. It would be less frustrating to view sequential photographs.

It is in this sense that I think I can make a convenient but defensible generalization: The current urban Western landscape is inundated with representations, moving images and endless significations in the form of television screens, advertisements, and auditory interpellation proclaiming late trains, crosswalks, the sale of newspapers, and so forth. This constant appeal for the attention of the individual attempting as she/he moves through this barrage of media and communication requires the development of a kind of shorthand. McLuhan pointed out that the development of electronic media extended the central nervous system outside of the body of the individual. Over repeated exposures, this results in an increased ability to trust the integrity of the information being delivered in the same way that a person learns to trust their own sense of touch or taste. Just as individuals don't evaluate the properties of their phone every time they answer it, it is unlikely that they would debate the veracity of what is shown to them in a televised image every time they encounter one.

Ordinarily, the experience of a reality outside of the individual's immediate physical location is limited by the speed and accuracy by which the brain processes information presented to it—reality is subjective and contingent. The body that learns to move in this environment learns to privilege the experiences of one sense that is being actively engaged over the others that aren't. McLuhan referred to this process as "numbing." In order to deal with the information being delivered, the individual will adjust sense ratios to manage the information and process it quickly enough to keep up with the transmission speed of that information. McLuhan argued that "To behold, use or perceive any extension of ourselves in technological form is necessarily to embrace it,"[22] and this act of embracing requires an acceptance of the presentation that simply accepts the incoming information without evaluating the involvement of the technology that delivers it. Delay, in this instance, is the element of the data transmission that is ignored in order to embrace the signal.

Previously, there had been tools that allowed the human body to witness events outside the normal limits of their senses. The telescope, for instance, allowed humans to view distances that were beyond the functional limits of the human eye. Where Virilio pointed out that this advance obliterated the human understanding of "near and far,"[23] the development of electronic media warped the idea of the linearity of space and the stability of time connected to observation. The CCTV camera requires an indulgence by the viewer not only with respect to the accuracy but also to the temporal accuracy of information presented. Even in the instance of watching a recorded CCTV event, the sense of immediacy is still present. This explains the sense of urgency that accompanies footage of police beatings, automobile accidents, and assaults that are easily found on YouTube.[24] The understanding that the footage could be relatively old in most cases does nothing to diminish the urgency of the image depicted. The presentation carries with it a sense of "now" that cannot be removed regardless of whatever the understanding might be of the temporal details of the event captured. At once, both the immediacy McLuhan outlined in the extension of the central nervous system and the "liveness" addressed by Derrida in his conversation with Stiegler come into sharp relief.

The television screen's dominant characteristic as opposed to that of the telescope is that it is electronic and, since it is powered by electricity rather than the manipulation of preexisting physical elements, it requires a departure from the world of spatial physicality. As much as Virilio outlined the type of adjustment humanity has had to make at the introduction of new media formats, the total rupture that accompanied electronic media changed the perception of the subject's body in relation to the world around it. Electricity powers the brain, enables the phenomenon of sight, and, when it comes to electronic media, draws the external world into the body. The new extension of the nervous system both implodes the sense of distance and, paradoxically, intensifies its presence in the happening of things. The audience is introduced to an intense sense of *thereness* that accompanies the signal.

It is tempting to assert that electric media—exemplified by CCTV—reduces the world to nothing more than a psychedelic experience. A literal reading of McLuhan certainly gives this impression. It is important to note that the adjustments that must be made when regularly interacting with electric media will result in a modification of the basic understanding of things like proximity and time. As a CCTV operative, I was able to view all different areas of the sports complex where I was working as though I was reacting to something in real time without moving my body. It did have the slightly unsettling effect of making me feel stretched across the building without having to stand up or turn my head. It also made me wait to have things that were worth looking at delivered to me rather than my having to investigate odd sounds or impressions on my own. When exposed to that style of watching, the initial exposure is confusing at best and traumatic at worst. As an amusing example of this I'd recount my grandmother's first exposure to "instant replay" during a live sporting event: An avid American football fan, she was watching a National Football League game with my uncle. The first touchdown displayed during the broadcast was shown live. The network then replayed the event, prompting my grandmother to scream, "They did it again!" This anecdote, while adorable, I think belies a deeper reality with respect to media in general and television in specific; even though it would have been impossible for a team to score again that quickly—something my grandmother would have known all too well—the immediacy that is present in the image was enough to temporarily suspend her critical faculties.

Media powered by electricity transports the external world onto the recipient. Regardless of any background knowledge of when the image was captured or where, the way in which the body of the person viewing it negotiates exposure to it is by granting it the "liveness" that Derrida described. This subject of *delay* is, subsequently, never a matter of negotiation. It is a matter of adaptation. It is something immediate. This immediacy paves over the awareness of delay and presents itself as "live" no matter how much technical delay the signal requires. Therefore, this treatment of the image *as live* is not a matter of comfort or preference but of relating to the impression delivered by the image according to its inherent properties. As Derrida pointed out,

> In principle, every event is experienced or lived, as one says and as one believes, in "real time." What we are living, "in real time," and what we find remarkable, is access precisely to what we are not living: we are "there" where we are not, in real time, through images or through technical relation. There happen to us, in real time, events that aren't happening to us, that is to say, that we aren't experiencing immediately around us.[25]

The idea of "delay" is obliterated in light of this. As much as all CCTV must involve some amount of delay between capture and display, no matter how small that delay might happen to be, it is still a property of the signal. This does not affect the way the signal is interpreted. Derrida has argued that the televised image in particular appears to the person viewing the image as though it were live. The CCTV image will be presented from one of two possible operational approaches—either it is used as a method of capturing reality for review after the fact or it is used as a way of viewing something that is happening presently but is out of immediate physical reach because of spatial limitations—but this sense of "liveness" is not limited to one of the uses and not the other. The image produced will be viewed as "live."

This tension between "live" and a delayed reception is the point at which it is possible to link the extension of the body and a greater distance between that body and the physical reality of the experiences that can be witnessed. The "delay" that is ignored outlines this moment where the body is confronted with the inherent contradictions of media and forced to alter its relationship with the world around it and even the body's relationship with itself. The viewer, in order to cope in a world that is saturated with media, is required to accept "liveness" even when the image is not actually live.[26]

AUTOAMPUTATION

The typical interpretation of exposure to electronic media involves the stretching of the human out of the natural breadth of experience while maintaining the tactile connection people have with objects close enough to brush their skin. In this sense, the viewer experiences the actions of the person viewed via electronic media as though they were mentally rather than spatially present. This would appear to make sense: Subjects are aware the signal is delivering information to them and they reconstruct the information delivered according to the information transmitted; the audience imagines the setting described in a radio broadcast or they fill in the third dimension of a television image in order to have this new information conform to their previous understanding of the world. The problem here is that even though these media don't entail conscious immersion, the level of unconscious concentration that is required when attempting to make sense of a continuing stream of representations requires that a considerable amount of the experiencer's cognitive faculties are invested in the act of interpretation.

This seems a relatively simple point, but it is one that is worth stressing: Media is, at a basic level, a method of communicating information from one person or a group of people to another person or group of people who are not within the immediate physical reach of each other. Recipients do, however, have to meet the author(s) of the message in a way; the information must make sense to them in order for the communication to have taken place. This is what McLuhan is talking about when he refers to autoamputation: "Any invention or technology is an extension or self-amputation of our physical bodies, and such an extension also demands new ratios or new equilibriums among the other organs and extensions of the body."[27] In this case of CCTV or security surveillance, the type of divorce being experienced is not comparable to the type of phantom limb syndrome that is often experienced by amputees.[28] The rupture that accompanies the experience of media in general and electronic media in specific is one that divorces the mind from the body while the body is *still an intact part of the life experience*. In this sense, autoamputation does not imply a fragmentation of the body so much as a realization that the body is no longer the immediate source of sensation. It is an introversion of a sort. To borrow a line from Baudrillard, "Unlike photography, cinema and painting, where there is a scene and a gaze, the video image, like the computer screen, induces a kind of immersion, a sort of umbilical relation, of 'tactile' interaction, as McLuhan used to say. You enter the fluid substance of the image possibly to modify it, in the same way as science infiltrates itself into the genome and into the genetic code to transform the body itself."[29] This entrance is one that takes place in the mind, of course, but it is still a movement on the part of the viewer. In actively monitoring or reviewing the CCTV image, the viewer effectively enters the screen in order to be certain of what she/he is seeing. There is a compulsion not only to recognize, but to believe the image displayed through direct experience. The relationship between the audience and the televisual image is one of immersion but an immersion that necessarily leaves the immediate properties of the body behind and engages the image as though it were physically present.

Later in the same text, Baudrillard argued that working on a computer negated the previous properties of text and shifted the practice to that of working "on it like a computer-generated image, which no longer bears any relation to the transcendence of the gaze or of writing."[30] I disagree. It is tempting, once we've decided that the medium has a profound effect on the perception, body or stability of the recipient, to assume that the medium-being-the-message necessarily trumps the content of the message in question. While it is likely that the properties of the medium bring certain elements forward and push others back, the message conveyed by the medium always remains static. To take a random example, it would be incredibly silly to suggest that the subject matter of the Champions League football final would disappear under the weight of the properties of the respective mediums when carried in a newspaper and in a television program. The essential point here is that the operations carried out in order to interact with different media are necessarily related to the properties of that specific medium but that this does not erase the data delivered by the medium itself. It may impoverish the delivery of some elements of the information, where print may highlight the abstract properties of an event—the names of the players on the pitch, for instance, and which of them scored—or televised images may highlight the physical movements—a dramatic cross or a moment of physical contact that lead to a disputed penalty—the basic properties of the event will still be woven into the retelling or the footage of what happened. The way in which subjects use their bodies to interact with the medium is different depending on the properties of the apparatus. McLuhan wasn't wrong in his suggestion that "the medium is the message" but there is a rider to the content that is media. The way in which the medium reveals itself to those who encounter it is as an active component of the reception of the message as the data conveyed in the message itself.

This is the point at which it is possible to start to look seriously at autoamputation. The arrival of the message is announced by the particular medium that is carrying it. The divorce that the subject must make with the physical properties of the typical life world area around them, however, is shaped by their initial desire to witness that signal in the first place. People are exposed to transmissions, they hail them in incredibly urgent ways, and they are forced to make these adjustments without thinking about it. This is, at a basic level, what McLuhan was talking about when he suggested that "Each new impact shifts the ratios among all the senses."[31] As such, there is an alteration with respect to the mind's relationship with the body. The reaction to the development of media that can negate the presence of space and time in the normal quantum-physical sense is that the world turns inward on the body rather than remaining the providence of the viewer or listener's physical extremities.

Virilio pointed out more than twenty years ago that

> With the industrial proliferation of visual and audio-visual prostheses and unrestrained use of instantaneous-transmission equipment from earliest childhood onwards, we now routinely see the encoding of increasingly elaborate mental images together with a steady decline in retention rates and recall. In other words, we are looking at the rapid collapse of mnemonic consolidation.[32]

This rupture, or autoamputation, then, might affect areas of the mind as well as the larger corpus. The kind of numbing that McLuhan was talking about, the type of shutting-off of the unnecessary elements of the body in order to fully engage the incoming signal with the parts that are able to comprehend it, would have to precede this. The focus on the fluidity of the CCTV image and the need to pay active attention of what comes next in the events unfolding on screen requires a willingness to take in information and dispense with it almost immediately—at least, for as long as it takes something of interest to happen. While attention is being paid to the stream of video imagery, then, the need to focus distances other immediate elements of the life world like the body itself, memory as linked to the senses that are not actively engaged, and situational awareness of the immediate physical surroundings.

The concern that Virilio was raising was necessarily that this estrangement in the relationship with media and the typical sensorial methods of experiencing the world through it collapses under the weight of constant exposure to media. Granted, regular exposure to electronic media necessarily entails that one gains a different perspective upon the external world than would have been possible for those who interacted mainly with print or the spoken word. With that in mind, the argument that the construction of the mental world and the understanding of the surrounding world through the primacy of the image degrades the ability to construct ways of remembering things takes on the full weight of the idea of autoamputation and leaves no room for nuance.

If, then, electronic media forces the amputation of the senses across space and time, does this mean that the stability of space and time have been split by removing physical integrity from the human form? Virilio quoted Einstein as claiming that "space and time are *forms of intuition* that are now as much a part of our consciousness as concepts like form, colour, size, and so on."[33] The point, then, is that the whole of human experience is a matter of negotiation between the mind's understanding of itself and the world external to it. The focus on some immediate input that demands direct attention, that demands that anyone in contact with it must bear witness to something beyond the reach of their physical bodies, makes the intrinsic connection people have with their own physical presences more pliable, more fluid. The privileging of one sense over another typically occurs in a situation where the mind is attempting to come to grips with new data and to readjust the existing impression. When the image appears on the monitor, CCTV demands that the person looking at that monitor make sense of what they are seeing. In this light, it is worth preserving this contention of autoamputation as it preserves the element of constant negotiation and the adjustments that are made in the process of it.

The allegations that were initially made regarding autoamputation in the face of electronic media came about long before the type of saturation coverage people typically experience in the contemporary urban environment. The type of divorce that McLuhan was talking about was simply the result of sitting down to watch a specific program on television or listen to an hour's worth of radio. The degree of difficulty in escaping electronic media in today's cities and towns would have been entirely beyond the scope of the initial assessments. Areas like Times Square in New York looked relatively banal in the mid-1960s, 1970s, and 1980s when McLuhan would have been thinking about these issues. The current incarnation involves massive television screens functioning in the place of traditional billboards as well as endless overtures to access more information through the Internet or via mobile phones. This process of amputation, this idea of having to split oneself in order to comprehend the signal, is something that no longer happens in very intense time frames—the notion of an end point is almost absurd. The split, the matter of negotiating among the senses in order to comprehend the signal interpellating the recipient, is no longer a momentary issue to cope with but a constant state of experience.

To quote Louis Althusser, "*all ideology hails or interpellates concrete individuals as concrete subjects*" [italics in original].[34] The focus of the signal is indeed a concrete person, and the image encourages the viewer to experience him or herself as hailed or interpellated as a whole being. The experience of what concrete feels like or freshly mowed grass smells like are part of what a viewer would put into a CCTV image to fully comprehend it. These details are not necessary to gathering the relevant information, but they are a natural component of fully viewing the image. The interpellation delivered by the monitor—the way the audience is hailed by that image—demands that they become concrete subjects, full subjects, entirely present subjects as they experience the image.

It is therefore tempting to come back to Baudrillard's assertion that writing on a computer is a matter of working with and altering images rather than writing in the traditional sense. What should be read into this idea is the recognition of the event of autoamputation—the realization that the body is now interacting with some aspect of the world outside of it. The problem is that the interpretation often goes in the wrong direction. People are perpetually trying to determine how the outside world appears to them as it changes and how the interaction taking place is different from previous interactions. As with the computer, Baudrillard suggests that users simply alter their relationship with the element of phonetic writing in order to accommodate the introduction of a new medium. Yet it is useful to remember Einstein's dictum that the larger elements of life world experience are always a matter of perception rather than defining external constants. Therefore, in response to the suggestion that the medium alters the way in which the subject interacts with previous media, I would argue that the basic tenets of the data and the tools being are used by the subject to interact with their own thoughts do not change. Nevertheless, how people have traditionally processed and used data is strengthened when they are threatened by a new mode of receiving information people hang onto those things that do not change in light of those things that have. The degraded quality of a pixelated image gives enough information to cue up data from personal experience that will fill in the gaps in the immediate transmission. Using memory to negotiate new input has the added benefit of making any new input appear manageable for the viewer. Organizing new information according to how it has been processed before allows for this reorientation of the sensory apparatus that McLuhan postulated to seem natural.

This element of autoamputation, then, is conditional on the level of exposure and its frequency. This is a more mediated world than McLuhan would have envisioned when he argued about the split between the body and the central nervous system. The fact that the body is a component of the physical world is crucial to the way an individual interprets the world. This is relevant because the signal inherent to CCTV involves awareness of something that has happened outside of the normal perceptive limits of the body. CCTV wants viewers to believe that they are witnessing reality, but the conception of reality has been torn between the act of direct experience and the ability of electronic media to marry perception with events that are not taking place within the subject's immediate physical field of engagement. From a procedural perspective, Baudrillard's formulation of Integral Reality is the social application of autoamputation. The split experienced as a result of being stretched across space and time in order to experience the televised image as real is the same one that necessitates a move from a traditional understanding of duplication to one that erases the idea of the original and replaces it with a contention that everything is now real and the idea of an "original" in the precession of simulacra is obsolete.

What viewers are witnessing on the monitor can only be interpreted as reality due to the cultural conception of this use of the television medium. Viewers are, however, aware that the image displayed on the television screen is an electronic representation of a confined view of a happening in another place at a marginally different time. As was the case in *R. v. Nikolovski*, the judge was willing to accept her interpretation of the video image overtop of the store clerk who'd actually been at the scene during the robbery. The judge "saw" the robbery as captured by the CCTV camera, but what is not announced in her reasoning is that "seeing" in this sense means accepting a representation as an accurate depiction of a reality she can only access through the video image. She only sees it as related by the camera. This split is the element it must be remembered is present in all electric media communications and is the main reason interpreters should be very careful when talking freely about witnessing "realities" that are communicated via the circuitry of contemporary communications.

INVERSION

The ability to perceive the surrounding world has been reworked according to the effects of electronic media. A person's ability to act on media—or, indeed for media to act on that person—has modified the general sense of distance to such an extent that the external world has become an internal entity in terms of self-perception. This is not to say that people are now at one with the world, of course. Far from it: the inversion of the senses creates a reflective isolation on the part of the viewer. The input transmitted by electronic media invariably comes from outside the body. The crucial point is that, due to the nature of electronic media—the *deus ex machina* nature of the reception of it—the brain does not experience the input as a transmitted source. The immediacy is enough to make it appear as though it has arrived inside the head spontaneously. The world turns inward. The processing of signals that would normally come from outside of the body is now immediate. It is present in the mind of the subject and impossible to ignore.

By this, of course, I do not mean to suggest that the experience of the outside world is no longer based on truly outside stimuli. Paul Virilio moved in the direction of this idea in *The Vision Machine*:

> If all that appears in light, *appears in its speed*, which is a universal constant, if speed is no longer particularly useful, as we once thought, in displacement or transportation, if speed serves primarily *to see*, to conceive the reality of the facts, then duration, like extent, must absolutely be "brought to light." All durations, from the most minute to the most astronomical, will then help to expose the intimacy of the image and its object, of space and representations of time. Physics currently proposes to do this by tripling the once-binary concept of the *interval*: on top of the familiar intervals of the "space" type (negative sign) and the "tome" type (positive sign), we have the new *interval of the "light" type* (zero sign). The interface of the live television screen or the computer monitor are perfect examples of this third type of interval." [italic's authors][35]

It is this "zero" signifier that leaps out at me immediately. In the previous section, the question of how a person's physical relationship with the external world is altered through exposure to electronic media was framed around interaction with the physical world. This introduction of a time property, this problematization of the idea of "interval," appears to follow the same initial force albeit on a slightly different trajectory. The delivery of the live televised image is normally most notable because of a recognition of the distance between the point of origin and the place where it is viewed, of its erasure of traditional space. It is a common element of North American culture that people will refer to distances as though they were stretches of time—something is 2 hours away rather than 170 kilometers. Much of this comes out of the contemporary relationship with the car and its integral linkage to people getting around, but the understanding of space as a unit of time, as something that is traversed over seconds, minutes or hours rather than physically measured between two determined points is so much taken for granted that it is no longer noticed. This assertion that "light" or "light speed" creates a new determination in the understanding of interval has profound implications with respect to how subjects interact with media.

To exemplify this, let's take Mel Brooks's 1987 spoof classic *Spaceballs*. In it, an exchange between the primary villain, Dark Helmet, and one of his underlings, Colonel Sandurz, is strangely illustrative here. In this scene, the two characters are watching a VHS copy of the very film they are currently characters in with the hopes of finding a group who have escaped their surveillance. Colonel Sandurz, played by George Wyner, is attempting to walk Dark Helmet, played by Rick Moranis, through the act of fast-forwarding so they go beyond the point in time they currently occupy in the film in order to find the other characters:

Helmet: What the hell am I looking at? When does this *happen in the movie?*
Sandurz: "Now." You're looking at "now," sir. Everything that happens now is happening "now."
Helmet: What happened to "then"?
Sandurz: We passed "then."
Helmet: When?
Sandurz: Just now. We're at "now," now.
Helmet: Go back to "then"!
Sandurz: When?
Helmet: Now!
Sandurz: "Now"?
Helmet: Now!
Sandurz: I can't.
Helmet: Why?
Sandurz: We missed it.
Helmet: When?
Sandurz: Just now.
Helmet: When will "then" be "now"?
Sandurz: Soon.

Is this not precisely the way in which viewers interact with the immediacy of the image? Is there not some sort of collapse in the basic continuity of time inherent in an interaction with the data captured by the camera and transmitted via electricity? The basic determinate factor in all perception is the realization of the self in relation to the objects under investigation. Subjects know the world around them in relation to themselves.[36] The degree to which this is problematized by electronic media is ultimately determined by the way in which physical bodies interact with that media.

What therefore does this modification of the understandings of time and distance do to the subject's relationship with their bodies? Ultimately, the domination of the interpretive and processing networks of the brain means that a conscious response to external data is no longer possible. Even though memory is used in constructing the finer details of the CCTV image, that input is added as a matter of reflex—not a considered plan of adjustment. The immediacy of the presentation therefore prevents the normal tactile filters from analyzing the incoming data. Information is taken in as quickly as it is available and the viewer adds their own contextualization. What is the adjustment necessary, then, if a new technology causes information to make contact with the audience more quickly than it might previously have done, or independently of the traditional filters already established to navigate the surrounding world (fingers, feet, ears, etc.)? Is the viewer, the reader or the audience able to arrest the flow of information with a view to interpreting it? Is the speed at which information arrives at the audience now an antidote to the danger of the body functioning as a kind of processing hub for that information?

To borrow another point from McLuhan, "To behold, use or perceive any extension of ourselves in technological form is necessarily to embrace it. To listen to radio or to read the printed page is to accept these extensions of ourselves into our personal system and to undergo the 'closure' or displacement of perception that follows automatically. . . . By continuously embracing technologies, we relate ourselves to them as servo-mechanisms."[37] The utilization of new technology, then, results in an increased dependence on it. Perceptions become wedded to the items that function as the body in lieu of the body. As in the case of *R. v. Nikolovski*, where a judge was content to take the image provided by a CCTV camera over the testimony of an eyewitness of the crime, familiarity with a technology can have the effect of overshadowing traditional methods of gathering information and evaluating that information. As in the alarming number of people who confess to having the television on when they're home alone—even though they are not watching it—the removal of the stimulus is akin to the removal of a part of the body. Not only are people accustomed to being able to sense the world outside of their normal physical limits; the dependence upon that new item or prosthesis has dulled the presence of the physical frame from their instinctive matrix. Subjects are now accustomed to touching the world through their electronic prosthesis.

The fallout from exposure to new media was of interest to McLuhan: "The selection of a single sense of intense stimulus, or of a single extended, isolated, or 'amputated' sense in technology, is in part the reason of the numbing effect that technology as such has on its makers and users."[38] Television, utilizing primarily sight, though often supplementing the focus with sound, further turns the sense of the body inward on its own physical frame via a dilution and concentration of the input dispersed to both of these senses. The sense of touch is relegated to the visual information regarding the texture of the objects represented—the look of wet pavement, the appearance of rain beating down in the light cast by a street lamp, the image of water beading on the collar of an overcoat can provide data regarding the feeling of damp or the smell of the air depending on the quality of the transmission. The brain is commanded to another temporal and physical sphere and has its normal extremities substituted via the movement and the transmission itself. A viewer's notions of friction, distance, the very tangibility of the world around them may melt when interacting with television. The psychological result of immersion in a reality removed from the physical frame that actively fights against interpretation is a removal from the direct, tangible physical world experienced by the body and total submersion into a world that cannot be fully experienced.

Virilio, in continuing his analysis of the speed of light as an element of the act of perception, suggested that,

> We accept the paradox of a veritable "observation energy" made possible by the Theory of Relativity. The latter sets up the speed of light as a new *absolute* and thereby introduces a new type of interval—light—alongside the classic intervals of space and time. If the path of light is absolute, as its zero sign indicates, this is because the principle of instantaneous emission and reception *change-over* has already superseded the principle of *communication* which still required a certain delay.[39] [italics author's]

Virilio has here located the kind of immediacy that McLuhan was reacting to when he began to talk about the fracturing or the amputative properties of electronic media. While Virilio goes on to suggest that the introduction of the property of light into the typical physical understanding of the surrounding world would drive the process of evaluation toward determinations of "paths" rather than objects, the immediacy characterized by light-as-delivery-mechanism plugs the analysis back into McLuhan's suggestion of autoamputation. This collapse of distance, this amendment of the properties of time as relative to distance that is connected to the idea of reality as transmitted via light, elevates the mind's relationship with media to "servo-mechanism." The speed with which the signal is received coupled with the lack of traditional sensorial input that would illustrate the signal and to make that illustration immediate for the viewer[40] is the kind of truncation that McLuhan was thinking of.

NOTES

1. M. Foucault, *The Birth of the Clinic: An Archaeology of Medical Perception* (New York: Vintage Books, 1994), 89.
2. Ibid., 90.
3. Ibid., 91.
4. J. Medina, "Rodney King Dies at 47; Police Beating Victim Who Asked, 'Can We All Get Along?' " *New York Times Online*. June 17, 2012. Web. June 29, 2015.
5. A. Hasham, "No Jail for Toronto Police Officer Convicted of G20 Assault." *Toronto Star Online*. January 29, 2015. Web. June 29, 2015.

6. M. Foucault, *The Birth of the Clinic: An Archaeology of Medical Perception* (New York: Vintage Books, 1994), 97.

7. Ibid., 97.

8. G. Debord, *The Society of the Spectacle* (New York: Zone, 2004), 12.

9. M. Foucault, *The Birth of the Clinic: An Archaeology of Medical Perception* (New York: Vintage Books, 1994), 97.

10. M. Foucault, *Discipline and Punish: The Birth of the Prison* (London: Penguin, 1991), 200.

11. S. Žižek, *Welcome to the Desert of the Real* (London: Verso, 2002), 96.

12. M. Foucault, *The Birth of the Clinic: An Archaeology of Medical Perception* (New York: Vintage Books, 1994), 115.

13. D. Lyon, "9/11, Synopticon, and Scopophilia: Watching and Being Watched," *The New Politics of Surveillance and Visibility* (Toronto: University of Toronto Press, 2006), 36.

14. Ibid., 41.

15. M. Foucault, *The Birth of the Clinic: An Archaeology of Medical Perception* (New York: Vintage Books, 1994), 107.

16. Ibid., 115.

17. A. Moore, *The Killing* Joke (New York: DC Comics, 1988), 46.

18. J. Derrida & B. Stiegler, *Ecographies of Television* (Malden, MA: Polity, 2002), 38.

19. Ibid., 39.

20. Ibid., 40.

21. Ibid., 40.

22. M. McLuhan, *Understanding Media: The Extensions of Man* (New York: Routledge, 2003), 50–51.

23. P. Virlio, *The Vision Machine* (Bloomington: University of Indiana Press, 1994), 4.

24. A search on YouTube on June 7, 2015, using the terms "CCTV" and "assault" delivered, "About 26,100" results almost instantly. Viewing any of the videos on the first page will verify this argument.

25. J. Derrida & B. Stiegler, *Ecographies of Television* (Malden, MA: Polity, 2002), 128–129.

26. M. McLuhan, *Understanding Media: The Extensions of Man* (New York: Routledge, 2003), 51–52.

27. Ibid., 49.

28. It is sometimes claimed by veterans or those who have lost body parts in traumatic circumstances that they are still able to experience physical sensations from the body part that was lost. Those who have lost arms have sometimes claimed that they still feel an itch or an ache where the wrist might have previously been located. The subconscious element of this would be where amputees will often experience their whole bodies when dreaming and, upon waking, have to come to terms once again with the loss of the body part.

29. J. Baudrillard, *The Intelligence of Evil or the Lucidity Pact* (Oxford: Berg, 2005), 76.

30. Ibid., 76.

31. M. McLuhan, *Understanding Media: The Extensions of Man* (New York: Routledge, 2003), 71.

32. P. Virlio, *The Vision Machine* (Bloomington: University of Indiana Press, 1994), 6–7.

33. Ibid., 22.

34. L. Althusser, "Ideology and Ideological State Apparatuses." *The Visual Culture Reader*, 2nd edition (London: Routledge, 2002), 139.

35. P. Virilio, *The Vision Machine* (Indianapolis: Indiana University Press, 1994), 72.

36. A useful, though admittedly problematic, touchstone for this point might be Descartes's *Cogito*. The suggestion that there must be a mind that exists in order to question and subsequently verify its own existence is the original point in this argument that location determines perception. We have to begin from the source of the data in order to explain its trajectory.

37. M. McLuhan, *Understanding Media: The Extensions of Man* (New York: Routledge, 2003), 51.

38. Ibid., 48.

39. P. Virilio, *The Vision Machine* (Indianapolis: Indiana University Press, 1994), 74.

40. The Internet really has become the epitome of interrupted experience in many ways. The ability to open windows and tabs and scroll over connected sources of information the moment one comes into contact with information that requires explanation from another source has made this experience of panic linked to not-knowing-something relatively rare for most Westerners. The true privilege of contemporary Western existence is the luxury of never having to be uncertain for a significant length of time. Google, in a very real way, has turned the condition of ignorance into something more akin to Virilio's light-based "zero intervals" rather than something that must be alleviated over time.

Chapter 5

Speed Cameras, the Courts, and the Recorded Image as Positive Identification

Tri-M is a company that produces power supplies for industrial equipment—the kind of equipment that is normally used in difficult and remote environments. From their website, it appears that they do a lot of business with the mining industry. The company works in industrial power supply systems, mining, transportation, aerospace, and so on. The movement of physical material over large areas is part of the business model and, as in any area of production where filling orders is a matter of maintaining a fleet of delivery personnel, making sure those personnel are where they need to be quickly is key in getting and/or keeping contracts. This might be why one of their company vehicles was photographed exceeding the speed limit in British Columbia, Canada, in 1998.

The specifics of the case are not particularly relevant to the study of surveillance until the case gets to the level of the B.C. Supreme Court. The Crown appealed a decision issued by a lower court that declared driving to be a protected right. The lower court had taken issue with the presumption of guilt in the act of driving (as evidenced by the taking of the driver's photo) and decided it was a violation of the citizen/company's constitutional rights.[1] The British Columbia Supreme Court stated at the outset that "the issue on this appeal is whether the radar scheme in British Columbia [. . .] contravenes s. 7 [the right to 'life, liberty and security of the person'] or s. 11(d) [the presumption of innocence] of the Canadian Charter of Rights and Freedoms."[2]

Photo radar systems have a rocky history in Canada. They were almost universally unpopular when they were first implemented. The automated systems—as evidenced by this trial and a number of others—did not complete their tasks quickly and many people were notified of fines they'd supposedly incurred months after the event had taken place. The system appeared to be broken from the outset and no one ever claimed to have solved the problems.

The primary issue, though, was the overall lack of acceptance of camera surveillance as a viable tool for security. Whereas this technology has flourished in Great Britain, police services in the Great White North have had a tough time selling the exchange of anonymity for security. What they tend to rely on is the notion that these technological invasions of private life are justified because of an intrinsic objectivity rooted in scientific principles.

In general, courts are very comfortable with the notion of scientific fact when it comes to evidence:

> It is not uncommon nor is it unconstitutional to use evidence gathered by scientific means to prove elements of the criminal charge against an accused. This may be done by various means including photographic evidence, audio and video evidence, DNA evidence or radar gun evidence. The Supreme Court of Canada has held that such scientific evidence may constitute cogent and convincing evidence not subject to the frailties of eye witness testimony and that such evidence alone can be a sufficient basis to establish guilt.[3]

Whether something is common or not is not really the real issue in situations like this. Something might be very common, but it also might be deeply problematic. The fallacies that are connected to eyewitness testimony are a clear indication of this. The area of interest in the above quote is the assertion that it is not "unconstitutional" for evidence gathered from "scientific means" to be used in proving a charge. The parameters of what qualifies as "scientific" are not enumerated here and, thanks to Jonathan Finn's work among others, it is easy to argue that what is accepted as scientific data can change drastically over time.[4] The fact that a camera is involved, at least when it comes to speeding, is enough to pre-validate the accusation that a person was speeding. This is, of course, the element of the case that caused the trial judge to take issue with the protected right of presumed innocence overtop of the debate over an intrinsic "right to drive."

When it comes to the presumption of accuracy that is linked to photo radar, the courts have a surprisingly nuanced interpretation. Judge Hayes of the British Columbia Provincial Court states that,

> We can gather that the radar component monitors speeds of vehicles and if a photograph is taken of a vehicle, its speed is *simultaneously and accurately* recorded. This speed reading, along with other encoded data, is embedded in a black strip along the bottom of the vehicle photograph, referred to as the "data line." The combination of these two components forms the "captured image." Strictly speaking, the presumption of accuracy found in the definition applies only to the speed reading.[5] [italics added]

It is interesting here that the more abstract data, the information that cannot be verified from personal interpretation in the same way that the photographed image can be, is the information the court is willing to accept without question. The lack of ability to interrogate presumes that the data is somehow beyond ambiguity and the only reasonable approach is to accept the information as presented. The purpose of the image, then, appears to provide a recognizable physical object on which to apply the abstract data. Whether the car and, subsequently, the driver of the car are the objects depicted in the image is the only thing the court will need to address. The validity of the suggestion that the car in the image is moving above the posted speed limit is validated by the fact that the photograph was taken in the first place. It is, really, a very pure sort of circular reasoning.

> The same cannot be said for photo radar prosecutions. The captured image is "a frozen moment in time." A vehicle image is recorded photographically, while simultaneously and accurately the speed reading is imbedded in a data line. Also simultaneously, other data is embedded on the data line such as, film roll number, frame number, date and time, location code, and qualified operator number. Aside from the speed reading in the data line, there is nothing in the photographic component of the captured image that would provide a "visual estimate of speed" to corroborate the speed reading.[6]

In other words, the output of photo radar works across two distinct lines of data. The first is the speed reading which indicates that the law was broken; an object moving at the speed indicated caused the machine to spring into action. The second is the photograph that attempts to specify the object that caused the machine to spring into action. One is an indication of an event and the other is an attempt to tie the abstract validation of the event to a concrete physical entity. The speed is the indication that something must be guilty, the photo is an attempt at specifying what that something might be.

Great Britain, as I've already noted, has no enshrined right to privacy, so the debate around the use of surveillance cameras for traffic purposes is a bit more muted. The main similarity would be the declaration that an offense has taken place and the presumption of guilt on the part of the registered owner of the vehicle in the photograph. In *O'Halloran* and *Francis v. The United Kingdom*, the European Court of Human Rights reviewed the case of Gerard O'Halloran, whose car was photographed traveling at more than 20mph over the posted limit on the M11 on April 7, 2000. Ten days later, Mr. O'Halloran received a letter from Essex Constabulary[7] with a declaration that the vehicle had been speeding and that he was identified as the registered owner of the vehicle. The letter included a demand that he affirm that he was the driver or he would face an additional fine and the loss of points on his driving license.

Mr. O'Halloran confirmed that he had been driving at the time, but later thought better of it. Mr. O'Halloran argued to the European Court of Human Rights that the letter containing the command violated his right against self-incrimination.[8]

Mr. Francis's case was very similar. His car had been photographed by a speed camera, the Surrey police sent a letter to his home containing virtually identical demands and a reassurance that the allegations are "supported by means of photographic/recorded video evidence."[9] Unlike Mr. O'Halloran, however, Mr. Francis wrote to the police service and "invoked his right to remain silent and privilege against self recrimination."[10] He was ordered to identify who had been driving the car when the photo was taken but continued to refuse. He appealed to the European Court of Human Rights after an inflated fine had been levied against him for not settling the matter quickly or quietly.[11]

Unfortunately for both of the appellants, a majority of the justices presiding over the European Court of Human Rights sided with the authorities and rejected the appellants' arguments that they'd been compelled to incriminate themselves.[12] There were dissenting opinions offered at the end of the case, but none of them make mention of the use of the camera as a component in the case. The existence of the photograph of the car tied to the speed reading is a regular point of departure in the decision transcripts, but the arguments are put forward in a way that indicates the photograph is equivalent to, though more nuanced than, sending a printout of the license plate number along with the alleged date and time of the offense. The car is identified by the photograph and that is where the consideration of the image seems to end. Beyond that, the concern is with the way in which the photograph can be used to intimidate the owner of the car into disclosing who was driving the car at the time of the offense.

Probably the most famous example of the ambiguity between the photo and the identity of the driver in the United Kingdom was the case of Chris Huhne and Vicky Pryce. Huhne was a member of the British Parliament, first elected to office in 2005 and he quickly ascended to the position of energy secretary in the Conservative/Liberal Democrat coalition government formed after the 2010 election.[13] Vicky Pryce is a prominent economist and author who has held visiting professorships at City University's Cass Business School, Imperial College Business School, and Nuffield College, Oxford.[14]

On March 12, 2003, Huhne's car was photographed speeding down the motorway between Stanstead airport and Huhne's home in South London. Huhne apparently has a heavy foot—he'd already accumulated enough points on his license that another citation would have meant a driving ban. Huhne and Pryce were married at the time and Ms. Pryce agreed to accept responsibility. The points were applied to her license rather than his.[15]

In June 2010, Huhne left Pryce ahead of the publication of a newspaper article detailing a long running affair with a PR consultant. Livid, Pryce began talking to newspaper editors about the plan to shift the points from Huhne's license to hers.[16] The information became public, the two were charged and eventually convicted of perverting the course of justice.[17]

The majority of the hard information in this story has to do with partisan politics, a messy divorce and a lot of "he said, she said" banter in the press that measures up to one of the most sordid political scandals in tabloid history. Very little of it has to do with the practice of using speed cameras or the idea of the image as evidence. The key reason to mention it here is that the identity of the driver in this instance—as in the cases of Mr. Francis and Mr. O'Halloran—was unknown to authorities even though there was photographic evidence that someone had been speeding. The image supposedly exists to tie a specific physical entity to the output of the speed camera, but all it really does is to verify the license plate. In other words, it can indicate which specific object was moving too quickly down the road, but cannot directly implicate the person who was causing it to do so.

The use of photo radar attempts to put a specific person in a location and time where the abstract data indicates that an offense has been committed. It cannot specify the person in most instances, however, and the result is the kind of intimidation mentioned in the Francis and O'Halloran cases and the kind of maneuvering exhibited by the Huhne/Pryce case. In both instances, however, the image works as a kind of leverage. It is presented as representative of an obvious fact and one that implicates whoever owns the vehicle. The only option once the shutter has closed, then, is to either accept the charge or implicate someone else.

It seems like photo radar or, if you prefer, speed cameras occupy the same conceptual ground as CCTV cameras. They are justified intrusions on public space that only the guilty would object to. If you have done nothing wrong, you have nothing to fear. The use of cameras to establish a seemingly indexical proof of the visual properties of an event is justification enough for the threat of photographing anyone who might come within view.

Privacy as regards the use of cameras—still or video—has been mentioned earlier in this text, but the idea of privacy stretches across a couple of different areas. In the first instance, there is the question of whether public space should be monitored at all. In the second instance, there is the question of who should have access to this information and who gets to interpret it. In the third, which this book hasn't really touched on yet, the question becomes how long this information is to be kept on hand for. In the case of *R. v. Sharma*, the disposal of CCTV footage was suspicious, inconvenient, and sometimes deleterious.

In January 2013, Vijay Kumar Sharma was arrested in Calgary under suspicion of impaired driving. The police officer alleged that Sharma had been unable to walk from the police cruiser into the station under his own power. Sharma disputed that version of events and requested a copy of the surveillance footage from the front of the station. The police claimed that they destroyed the surveillance footage after thirty days, but the request was made within the timeline. Mr. Sharma was still not provided with the footage and the Alberta Provincial Court granted a stay of proceedings on the basis that his rights were violated.[18]

In Judge Fradsham's decision, he outlines a number of cases related to several Canadian police departments and the conspicuously inconvenient destruction of videotaped evidence. Citing the case of *R. v. Leung* (2008), he includes the following paragraph from the decision:

> I join my colleagues who have expressed their frustration over many years that the destruction of videotaped evidence because of the police retention policy remains a problem that has not been corrected. Valuable time and resources of the court, the police, the Crown, defence counsel and the defendant continue to be spent on *voir dires* related to this issue, when, as has been suggested before, the solution is simple: the police must retain the tapes until all the related trial and appeal proceedings are completed.[19]

This quote works as an example of a sizable number of decisions that contain the same sentiments. When it comes to Mr. Sharma's situation, Judge Fradsham has trouble with the suggestion that the thirty-day retention policy is not indicative of the footage's potential use in a future investigation. The retention policy indicates a plan to use the footage if it is helpful in prosecuting a suspect and a rationale for conveniently destroying it if it isn't:

> The facts in the case at bar are that the video was intentionally destroyed 30 days after it was created. The evidence before me was that the video was destroyed because it was considered to be part of the security system of the district office, and that it was not considered to have any investigative function. *However, it is interesting to note that the video recording was kept 30 days, and one might reasonably conclude that any need to review it within that 30 days would be related to some type of investigative function.*[20] [italics added]

This process of self-governance when it comes to retention of CCTV footage seems to be an intrinsic conflict of interest. The decision to destroy the footage resides in the hands of one of the two parties included in the content of the images. From the perspective of those arrested, however, the desire to demonstrate mistreatment to the court or to demand restitution from the authorities in a civil suit would be overwhelming (and perhaps justified). Whatever the case, the policy of destroying videotaped evidence only benefits one party in the binary universe of policing.

Simply declaring that the camera was unable to capture the footage requested is another possible outcome as evidenced by the case of *Order MO-2758*. An appellant petitioned the Hamilton Police Services Board for information relating to an assault they'd suffered at the hands of a police officer in April 2011. The police provided access to documents relating to the incident but claimed that CCTV footage demanded did not exist.[21] The specific camera in the area was fixed and not pointed squarely at the location of the event and, as such, there was no footage to provide. The language from the report is a bit troubling, however:

> As a result, the evidence of the police is that the information recorded on the camera on the date and time in question was unrelated to the incident. Accordingly, the FOIC [Freedom of Information Coordinator] states that the Acting Sergeant did not retain a copy of the footage and erased it after 72 hours had elapsed in accordance with the police's retention schedule.[22]

Here, the impression left at the end of the report is that the adjudicator is either willing or simply resigned to taking the Hamilton Police Service's word for it. There might have been a record, but it certainly doesn't exist any longer, so the visual contours of the incident can only be constructed by weighing each party's version of events against each other in court.

It becomes a bit more complicated when this question opens up to spaces where the occupants have no choice about their exposure. In *Order F2015-02*, Adjudicator Teresa Cunningham evaluated a request for CCTV footage of an incident inside the Edmonton Remand Centre. The inmate alleged that officers in the prison had used excessive force in restraining him and demanded the footage relevant to the time and date of the event using the *Freedom of Information and Protection of Privacy Act*.[23] The authorities challenged the request arguing that the privacy rights of those who were within the frame in the footage would automatically have their own privacy violated if the footage were released. The tribunal decided that the inmate initiating the complaint had a right to the footage and that the faces of the bystanders in the footage should be blurred out or otherwise obscured,[24] but this case raises an interesting point; namely that it is possible for people to find themselves in areas where they are unable to prevent their image from being captured and that that image does not belong to them. The image may be of interest to others for reasons that have nothing to do with them and to what extent do subjects have control over an image they were unwilling or unable to consent to in the first place?

In May 2003, the Edmonton Police Service (EPS) issued a "privacy impact statement"[25] requesting reactions to a proposed CCTV system set up in the central area of the city during the forthcoming Canada Day weekend. In support of it, the police cited historical statistical data demonstrating that there had been an increased number of incidents and calls for police service in the area during the festivities. The situation had deteriorated year after year until a riot erupted in 2001.[26] In assessing the case, the privacy commissioner provided a useful definition of what "privacy" means:

> "Personal information" is defined in section 1(n) of the FOIP Act [Freedom of Information and Protection of Privacy Act] to mean recorded information about an identifiable individual. A "record" is defined in section 1(q) to mean "a record of information in any form and includes . . . images . . . and any other information that is . . . photographed . . ." I concluded that an individual's image that is photographed using a video camera is recorded information about an identifiable individual and therefore personal information.[27]

The commissioner decided that the collection of that information is acceptable even though it is a wholesale collection of information regarding specific individuals. This collection is excusable because the monitoring is happening in "public places"[28] and the information is collected under the "law enforcement provision of the FOIP Act."[29] The Edmonton Police Service's sensitivity to the issue is demonstrated by the fact that they issued a "privacy impact assessment" even though they were not required to do so by law.[30] The commissioner echoes the EPS's concerns regarding the use of CCTV in public spaces and states that "Surveillance cameras and general public surveillance must not be seen as the common solution to every crime or security problem."[31] It is, however, permissible since the increased monitoring of the area might improve police response times and assist in future prosecutions.

And this is the normal reaction to the use of CCTV cameras where individuals might not openly volunteer to be monitored. Even in private workplaces, as in the case of R.J. Hoffman Holdings Ltd. where CCTV cameras were installed in two of their oilfield maintenance locations in Alberta and Saskatchewan,[32] the assertion that the information is only accessible to those in positions of directly related authority (the police in public, the employer in private) is enough to justify the data collection. Even though the commissioners in the Hoffman case admitted that other arbitrators had found the monitoring of employees for the purpose of performance evaluation to be unacceptable,[33] they were willing to accept the use of the surveillance system for "loss prevention, safety and security"[34] purposes as legitimate.

The use of cameras to monitor people in public areas raises a number of concerns but none seemingly more urgent than what the ultimate purpose of the surveillance is. In the case of photo radar, it appears to provide additional leverage for bullying speeders into paying their fines without a fuss. In the case of police-controlled CCTV footage, it appears to be either a welcome addition to a prosecution if it shows the accused in a negative light or a liability that must be destroyed if it contradicts the police version of events (or displays outright misconduct). In its most benign form, it might allow police to manage difficult and historically dangerous events in public areas by improving their ability to coordinate efforts among their ranks. In the private sector, it could either be used to Taylorize the work force or to prevent theft of the company's property. In all of these instances, the camera's presence is a tactical method of managing or improving a situation. It is deliberate.

TESTIFYING VIA CCTV

The hardest cases to read are usually the ones that deal with allowing witnesses to testify in court via CCTV. In these instances, the argument revolves around whether the trauma inflicted on the victim of the crime by giving testimony in person in court outweighs the person on trial's right to confront their accusers. In researching this text, all of the cases that examined this procedural use of closed-circuit television dealt with sex crimes and the majority also involved children.

In the case of *R. v. Rockey*,[35] where the defendant was accused of raping his friend's two-and-a-half-year-old son, an early concern for the court was adding to the child's potential trauma by bringing him into a courtroom to face the man who had assaulted him. The question of whether the use of the camera might affect the truthfulness of the child's testimony shows up in the cross-examination of a number of expert witnesses. In the end, however, the court agrees that the use of CCTV was a way to get around traumatizing a child (again) and represented an acceptable adjustment. The questions would remain the same—it is just the setting where the child will speak that changes. As the camera is believed to provide an unimpeachable representation of what is happening in front of it, there is no argument about some perversion of the basic information delivered by the testimony. The only concern is the foundational right of the accused to confront those who would offer testimony against him/her versus the likelihood that exposure to the accused would deepen the child's existing trauma.

According to the Canadian Criminal Code,

> 486.2 (1) [. . .] in any proceedings against an accused, the judge or justice shall, on application of the prosecutor, of a witness who is under the age of eighteen years or of a witness who is able to communicate evidence but may have difficulty doing so by reason of a mental or physical disability, order that the witness testify outside the court room or behind a screen or other device that would allow the witness not to see the accused, unless the judge or justice is of the opinion that the order would interfere with the proper administration of justice.[36]

Under the heading "Conditions of Exclusion," the procedure for using CCTV at trial is detailed:

> (7) A witness shall not testify outside the court room under subsection (1), (2), (4) or (6) unless arrangements are made for the accused, the judge or justice and the jury to watch the testimony of the witness by means of closed-circuit television or otherwise and the accused is permitted to communicate with counsel while watching the testimony.[37]

There is no fear here that the use of the camera will modify the result of the testimony, only that this apparent way out of a terrible situation does not modify the process of the trial as it is taking place. What is paramount is that nothing should occur that would prevent the accused from communicating with his counsel as the testimony is being delivered. If the introduction of a technology allows the court to function in essentially the same way it would without that technology, while being sensitive to the emotional gravity of the case before it, there is apparently no reason not to allow its use. McLuhan or Baudrillard might have had something to say about the consequences of introducing the video image into an active court case, or about the suggestion that distance from the courtroom and the intrinsic immediacy of the trial as it takes place does not affect the course of the proceedings, the only issue for the Supreme Court of Canada is whether the normal procedure of a trial can continue without a major modification. The concern, in a word, is about maintaining some sense of stability between the use of the technology and the traditional practice of the trial. The CCTV camera provides a disembodied version of the witness rather than a physically present one, but the testimony is still delivered and that is all that matters.

NOTES

1. *R. v. Tri-M Systems Inc.*, 1998. B.C.J. No. 2702. New Westminster Registry No. X051688. British Columbia Supreme Court. Brenner J. Abstract. Web.
2. Ibid., para. 1.

3. Ibid., para. 37.
4. J. Finn, *Capturing the Criminal Image: From Mug Shots to Surveillance Society* (Minneapolis: University of Minnesota Press, 2009), 126–129.
5. *R. v. Ng*, 1998. B.C.J. No. 1716. Burnaby Registry No. SA01982380. British Columbia Provincial Court (Traffic Division). Hayes, J. P. Para. 4.
6. Ibid., para. 16.
7. *O'Halloran and Francis v. The United Kingdom*, 2007. Application Nos. 15809/02 and 25624/02, Grand Chamber. European Court of Human Rights. 29 June, 2007. Web. May 24, 2015. Paras. 9–10.
8. Ibid., para. 14.
9. Ibid., paras. 17–18.
10. Ibid., para. 19.
11. Ibid., para. 24.
12. Ibid., para. 63.
13. P. Walker, "Chris Huhne and Vicky Pryce Each Jailed for Eight Months." *Guardian Online*. March 11, 2013. Web. May 26, 2015.
14. "Profile: Who Is Vicky Pryce?" ITV Report. *ITV News Online*. March 7, 2013. Web. May 26, 2015.
15. P. Walker, "Chris Huhne and Vicky Pryce Each Jailed for Eight Months." *Guardian Online*. March 11, 2013. Web. May 26, 2015.
16. Ibid.
17. C. Davies, "Chris Huhne Ordered to Pay £78,000 Costs for Speeding Case." *Guardian Online*. May 9, 2014. Web. May 26, 2015.
18. *R. v. Sharma* (2014). A.J. No. 640. Docket 130113343P1. Alberta Provincial Court. A.A. Fradsham Prov. Ct. J.
19. Ibid., paras. 58–62.
20. Ibid., paras. 142.
21. Order MO-2758; Hamilton Police Services Board. 2012. O.I.P.C. No. 138. Appeal No. MA11-392. *Ontario Information and Privacy Commissioner*. Panel: Bernard Morrow, Adjudicator. Tribunal Summary.
22. Ibid., para. 27.
23. Order F2015-02; Alberta (Justice and Solicitor General). Re: Alberta Justice and Solicitor General. 2015. A.I.P.C.D. No.2. Case File Number F7276. *Alberta Information and Privacy Commissioner*. Panel: Teresa Cunningham, Adjudicator. January 29, 2015. Tribunal Summary.
24. Ibid., para. 67.
25. Report on the Investigation into Complaint Regarding Collection of Personal Information Re: Edmonton Police Service. 2003. Report F2003-IR-005. A.I.P.C.D. No. 31. Investigation No. 2777. *Alberta Information and Privacy Commissioner*. F. Work, Commissioner. August 7, 2003.
26. Ibid., para. 4.
27. Ibid., para. 11.
28. Ibid., para. 15.
29. Ibid., para. 22.
30. Ibid., postscript.

31. Ibid.
32. Ibid.
33. Ibid., para. 49–50.
34. Ibid., para. 58.
35. *R. v. Rockey*, 1996. S.C.J. No. 114. File No. 24784. Supreme Court of Canada. Lamer, C.J. and La Forest, L'Heureaux-Dubé, Sopinka, Gonthier, Cory, McLachlin, Iacobucci, Major J.J.
36. "Testimony Outside of Courtroom—Witness Under 18 or Who Have a Disability." Criminal Code (R.S.C., 1985, c. C-46). *Justice Laws Website*. Government of Canada. May 22, 2015. Web. May 24, 2015.
37. Ibid.

Chapter 6

The Certainty in Images

People operate in life according to prejudged, previously experienced outcomes. Be it through the use of specific data that relates to abstract signifiers or through the use of previous experience to illustrate the gaps in a presentation, the process of interpretation is one that is always personal. This is what is normally missing from an endorsement of camera surveillance; the acknowledgment that although the image may exist independent of personal nuance, the interpretation of that image cannot. The reality that is experienced is invariably different from the reality that is conveyed due to the gap in density that is inherent to all information. The CCTV signal, being typically pixelated and typically silent requires the interpretation and the active involvement of the viewer to decode it. McLuhan hit on this point specifically when he argued that,

> Although the medium is the *message*, the controls go beyond programming. The restraints are always directed to the "content," which is always another medium. The content of the press is the literary statement, as the content of the book is speech, and the content of the movie is the novel. So the effects of radio are quite independent of its programming. Those who have never studied the media, this fact is quite as baffling as literacy is to natives, who say, "Why do you write? Can't you remember?"[1]

McLuhan had a gift for hyperbole, of course, but there is some validity here. When the "content" of things is discussed, it is the reasons that they are noticed, or the reasons they feel familiar that is being analyzed. With that in mind, McLuhan would have been straddling the divide between origin and reception. The suggestion that the content of media signals is rooted in the prior comparable media format is as much based on the understanding of how media are used as much as it is in the understanding of how media are approached in the interest of saying something. The use of any medium will be the secondary mechanism associated with the thought pattern that created the message. If I am interested in writing a paragraph, I will formulate the words as a whole pattern, almost as though it is a conversation with myself, slightly before I commit them to print. I will think the spoken words, then I will record those thoughts in written language. The concern with respect to these divisions, these recognized steps between the original event that generates the content and its delivery, is the ability of the delivery mechanism to reproduce the information accurately.

The content of CCTV is the belief in the accuracy of a conveyed reality, or the accuracy of the information conveyed as though it were a reality. This is the key point, really—that the image appearing on the screen is something that can simply be accepted as factually true. The rift here, or at least the augmentation should be made with respect to McLuhan's argument is the general understanding of the density of the content, or the participation in the creation of content that is the act of the viewer. As there are different reactions to subtle nuances conveyed in written language from one reader to another, there are different reactions to different images from one viewer to another. The relationship the viewer has with the visual world operates on the same interpretive relationship as that of the linguistic in that she/he must call upon previous experience in order to flush out the raw data presented.

This question of "reality," then, is something that must straddle the gap between an acknowledged subjectivity and a supposed uniformity of reception that validates the images produced by the camera. It is important to remember that when CCTV is the subject of discussion, the focus is on something that is intended to function as an unproblematic record of something that has happened. The point in erecting the camera is to state unequivocally that the person who has been arrested, or publicly denounced, or decided to sue in court is demonstrably the person who was captured on video. This was undeniably the case in *R. v. Nikolovski* as it was in the case of James Bulger's abduction, *R. v. Jackson*, *R. v. Mikolajczyk*, and particularly in the case of *Henry v. HMA*. Culturally, the camera is understood to be a machine and can therefore operate free of bias, that it is a technology and is therefore immune to prejudice. The result is that the camera conveys an irrefutable reality.

What is typically happening, here, then is that the apparatus is used as a type of technological purification of the witness' interaction with the world. These gaps that the viewer is compelled to fill in with their own experiences are the substance they use to create a "reality" out of an arguably vague visual representation. Surprisingly, however, this content that must be included in the presentation is antithetical to the expressed purpose of the presentation itself: The use of personal experience to fill out the lack of density or specificity in the product of the CCTV camera negates the supposed sterility of its process of capture. If there is still some element of subjectivity to the viewing of the image, to the understanding of the image, there is no stability to the claim that the image is inherently unbiased. There are a number of instances[2] where people have been erroneously identified on CCTV footage and convicted almost solely on that evidence. The belief, then, that the image is a utility that might be usable as a sterile tool in the operating room of the control society is deeply problematic. Where it must be acknowledged that current technology that delivering information must still be processed by individuals who have their own biases and prejudices, it must also be realized that the delivery mechanisms require the input of those biases and prejudices in order to be fully comprehended.

FLIR is an acronym for Forward Looking Infra-Red. It is a technology that police have used to detect significant amounts of heat emanating from buildings. Some illegal drug manufacture practices involve producing a significant amount of heat. In the case of cannabis, indoor growing operations usually require a great deal of artificial light which produces a noticeable amount of heat (and, depending on the bulbs used, electricity consumption). FLIR readings measure the presence and intensity of heat in structures or, more tellingly, in individual sections of structures—a room or a basement, for instance. The inference being that, should there be an indication that cannabis is being grown in a building, FLIR imagery will be able to confirm or deny the possibility.

FLIR as a form of image generation is an image representation of nonvisual phenomena. Much like an MRI, FLIR images function as a sort of virtopsy carried out on a building—the structure itself is not violated and information is still gathered about the contents. It allows for the collection of information without physically "seeing through walls." This, in a nutshell, is the point of conflict for the courts. It is a technology that police have used to determine if there might be drug growing or manufacturing operations without physically having to walk onto the premises. In some cases, the information gathered was used as a major component of the justification for a search warrant. The pertinent question is whether it is reasonable to suggest that someone has been "searched" in the traditional sense if the mechanism used to gather information does not physically touch the subject nor does it form or evaluate photorealistic images.

In 2004, the Canadian Supreme Court heard a case concerning the use of FLIR imagery in investigating information given to police regarding a cannabis growing operation (cannabis, at this point, still being a controlled substance in Canada). Walter Tessling was tried and convicted for running a grow op but won his appeal. The Supreme Court of Canada ultimately reversed the Appellate Court's decision, declaring that the process of gathering information via FLIR technology did not meet the threshold of being invasive. According to the judgment:

> Whereas the Court of Appeal treated the FLIR imaging as equivalent to a search of the home, and thus "worthy of the state's highest respect," it is more accurately characterized as an external surveillance of the home to obtain information that may or may not be capable of giving rise to an inference about what was actually going on inside depending on what other information is available to the police. *FLIR is not equivalent to entry.*[3] [italics added].

What, in the context of this book, is significant is the realization that the Supreme Court appears to require the production of an image that is photo-realistic in order for that photo to qualify as invasive. The American courts make the distinction between "off-the-wall" technology and "through-the-wall" technology.[4] The difference between the two being the information that is gathered in order to produce a picture. In the case of "off-the-wall" technology, readings are gathered from heat signatures, noise impressions, or some other form of nonvisual data. From that, speculations are refined about what is happening inside. In the case of "through-the-wall" technology, an image is generated by generating photo-quality images of the inside of a structure either by physically inserting a camera or by using technology that will allow for the reproduction of a physical scene. In the first case, the image generated is abstract. In the second, it presents a positive identification of individuals, objects, and, arguably, circumstances.

The deciding opinion points out that the majority of the law regarding surveillance of any kind finds its roots in the "law of trespass."[5] The limits of how a person or a dwelling could be observed were limited by the ability of the observer to physically gain access to the area or the people in question. As tools were developed to assist in accessing things from greater distances, "the protection offered by property rights diminished. Wiretaps, for example, require no physical intrusion, but can be implemented at a distance. FLIR images can be taken from an airplane. The courts were reluctant to accept the idea that, as technology developed, the sphere of protection for private life must shrink." The convenient adjustment—that Section 8 of the *Charter of Rights and Freedoms* "protects people, not places"—was established in *Hunter v. Southam*[6] and provided the foundation for a permissive attitude toward the use of technology to investigate real estate rather than human beings. The usual friction is still present in the minds of the jurists, but the rule established by the Canadian Supreme Court is that "Expectation of privacy is a normative rather than a descriptive standard."[7]

This is the crux of the problem. The subtext to this distinction between the abstract and the indexical is that there is an assumed certainty about what is witnessed in images. The presumption that the camera never lies, that the image is self-explanatory is enough to elevate it to a higher standard of evidence. The fact that images can be misleading, that misidentifications from photo imagery have happened in the past does not appear to matter. FLIR imagery only provides abstract representations of a nonvisual characteristic. Temperature is something that must be connected to other factors in order to be of significance. It needs additional verification or validation that would connect it to the subject of an investigation. The photographic image, at least at a cultural level, stands on its own.

At a basic level, this is the significance of CCTV. The technology is not exotic. In fact, it has been in common use for more than half a century. The image is, as far as a causal observer is concerned, self-explanatory. This "reality," then, this sterility that is inherent in the image is all the more problematic when it becomes a component of the management of a population. The image as a sterile representation of reality is embraced because there is a utility to it: The ability to capture information and move it, supposedly unmolested, from the point of capture to the point of delivery is the purpose of the use of the technology. That old adage that "the camera never lies" is not just something that justifies the use of the camera in the first place but it also how the viewer approaches the image produced by that camera. Where Baudrillard argued that "we prefer the exile of the virtual to the catastrophe of the real," McLuhan's assessment of the content of that virtual drags the focus back into the difficulty of the real all over again. The image as a tool of understanding allows for a belief in that comfortable distance that Baudrillard argued viewers were after, however, the unpacking or the understanding of that virtual requires that they inhabit it entirely.

NOTES

1. M. McLuhan, *Understanding Media: The Extensions of Man* (London: Routledge, 2001), 333.
2. One, but by far not the only, example would be the case of William Mills: Rowley, S. "Wrongful Conviction Throws Spotlight on Unreliability of Eyewitness Evidence," *The Guardian*. August 18, 2009. Web. May 5, 2012.
3. *R. v. Tessling*. 2004. 3 S.C.R. 432, 2004 S.C.C. 67, para. 3.
4. Ibid., para. 5.
5. Ibid., para. 16.
6. Ibid.
7. *R. v. Tessling*. 2004. 3 S.C.R. 432, 2004 S.C.C. 67, para. 42.

Part II

THE IMAGE AS A COMPONENT OF GOVERNING

Chapter 7

Governmentality and the CCTV Image

RECEPTION LEADING TO GOVERNMENT AND TRANSMISSION

In the previous sections, I've looked at how CCTV functions as a media format in relation to the viewer and to the subject. Principally, I was looking at the effect of the medium in a localized sense—what the use of the televised image does to the perspective of other people, the landscape, what the condition of viewing a televised image does to the perceptions of familiar and unfamiliar spaces, and how a system of duplication might shift or problematize the relationship with the ideas of reality or the temporal. The logical progression of this line of thinking is to evaluate how CCTV would then impact on the larger aspects of a person's relationship with the world around them and upon systems of organization, or power relationships. In short, what does CCTV as a component of the overall surveillance structure do to the process of government and the experience of being governed?

Embedded in this question is the issue of whether something as seemingly innocuous as a camera can have a noticeable impact on the practice of governing. Considering the ideas discussed earlier in this text, it seems reasonable to conclude that it will have some effect on how the subject and the viewer relate to the world around them and will also affect how larger and more fluid organizations that comprise multiple individuals will suffer such alterations as much as individuals. It seems likely therefore that the improvements and modifications of systems of surveillance will have considerable effect on the practice of governing. The process of governing naturally assumes an attempt to maintain control of a population.[1] According to Mitchell Dean, "to govern [. . .] is to structure the field of possible action, to act on our own or other's capacities for action."[2] This imperative toward the limiting of possibilities, toward control of a population, is at the very heart of both the impulse to govern and the process of governing. Elements that exist in a given culture will bring about approaches to the process of governing; the current structure of the power system, the technology available to it, the general familiarity of that technology to both the government and the subjects on whom all of these variables will converge are elements that shape the functioning of a system of power and limit and define the possible outcomes.

A natural theoretical tool in analyzing this is Foucault's concept of "governmentality." Foucault defines the term as "the ensemble formed by the institutions, procedures, analyses and reflections, the calculations and tactics that allow the exercise of this very specific albeit complex form of power, which has as its target population, as its principal form of knowledge political economy, and as its essential technical means apparatuses of security."[3] He is speaking about a collected format of tactics that has been developed in the past two centuries and is designed to replace the structure of power that was prevalent from the Renaissance to the Industrial Revolution. During this period, authority structures had relied on a demonstration of power based on a familial approach with the government occupying the position of the head of the household[4] and the citizenry managed like children or servants. This familial approach to the management of a population was practical so long as the primary seat of power was rooted in a symbolic entity—for instance, a monarch appointed by God. With the expansion of capital systems and the development of more complex forms of social arrangement, the stability of a distant-yet-ever-present form of power began to waver. The movement by which governmentality was transferred from a process of pure performativity to being inscribed in state institutions that claimed to enact the law in a disinterested way is intrinsic to the development of contemporary policing tactics. To quote Foucault again, "The pastoral, the new diplomatic-military techniques and, lastly, police: these are the three elements that I believe made possible the production of this fundamental phenomenon in Western history, the governmentalization of the State."[5] This overture toward the militarization of the domestic space is something that will be dealt with in greater detail later, but the intrinsic linkage of "policing" and the "governmentalization of the state" in the establishment of security is crucial to framing why I am investigating CCTV and the use of the image as a component of the security system.

Mitchell Dean introduces "governmentality" as, "the emergence of a distinctly new form of thinking about and exercising power [. . .] that is bound up with the discovery of a new reality, the economy, and concerned with a new object, the population."[6] A massive component of this evolution in practices of governing is that it "seeks to enframe the population with what might be called *apparatuses of security*" [italics author's].[7] CCTV is one of the most recent components of this apparatus and it operates within the context of these new realities. The way the population is envisaged by the control system determines how the available tools will be used on that population. As the population and the economy develop, new demands for security arise that entail increased monitoring of the population. Technology is also developed, partly to respond to such demands and to maintain the potency of the administrative system.

Toby Miller, in *The Well-Tempered Self*, built off of Foucault's formulations, looked at the ways in which citizens were increasingly incited to recognize "their moral obligations" to the state. These obligations are produced, transmitted, and maintained via what Miller called "technologies of governance." These technologies act on individuals, determining them as "subjects"—as people who are identified and monitored according to administrative processes. The two technologies Miller was most concerned with and, coincidentally, that matter most for the purposes of this narrative are " 'Technologies of power,' which form subjects as a means of dominating individuals and bringing them to define themselves in particular ways; and 'technologies of the self,' which are applied by individuals as a means of transforming their conditions into those of a more autonomous sense of happiness."[8]

The link between the concerns of this book—CCTV, media theory, the politics of control, and so forth—and Miller's line of thinking here is entirely pragmatic. In the interest of developing a theory of surveillance that incorporates a solid understanding of the properties of electronic media, it is necessary to examine how those who operate the cameras and those who are subject to it are affected by it. Whether the specific focus is the recorded image and its interpretation or about the subjects caught on camera and their relationship with the space under surveillance, the inevitable source of information will be the result of a personal interpretation. The persons viewing the recording will draw upon their own understanding of self and space and citizenship and participation in that act of interpreting and those who are aware that they are being watched will relate to their own condition of being in that space at that time according to their sense of self. The text created by the image reflects a power dynamic that is acted out in the watching of the video by the viewer. It is also enacted in the knowledge or acceptance of being part of the image by the subject. When Miller, following Foucault, refers to "technologies of power" and "technologies of the self," he is speaking about internalized and practice-oriented conditions of citizenship that enact governmentality. The CCTV image is at once a producer and a reflection of these conditions.

What does this mean, exactly? The use of these "technologies" creates a landscape that manages a population in specific ways. The movement from systems of discipline to the condition of governmentality naturally entails some format of recognizable social signs. Miller, in determining the shape of a political system, emphasizes discourse:

> A discourse is a set of statements that determine actions and thoughts. So a given discourse is a particular vocabulary and grammar that permits the making of choices only within its own rules. It decides what can and cannot be said, done, or represented.[9]

Contained within this schematic is the question of interpretation. The CCTV image is inextricably bound up with an anticipated reaction and an actual reaction. Discourse imposes limits, which also implies limits to interpretation. The properties of discourse fundamentally affect the way something is understood because the doctrinal system imposes acceptable parameters onto the conversation that invariably restricts the field of understanding. These limitations will evolve over time in a history that always produces barriers or borders to demarcate where acceptable behavior reaches its limit and beyond which, should the citizenry try to cross it, the security apparatus will enact an excessive exercise of power.

A fundamental concern in considering "governmentality" through media analysis is the way in which the process of communication that occurs through media systems like CCTV enables other elements in the process of control. How does the CCTV system modify the operations of the courts, for instance? Does its operation reduce the need for the physical presence of police? Is there some residual understanding of the presence of the control structure that is the result of the presence of the camera (whether it is operational or not)? For Miller, "Television is seen to be a medium and form that can reveal the traces of domination and the cultural politics of the prevailing mode of production."[10] He is talking specifically about broadcast television rather than CCTV, but this assumption that the television medium is able to produce, perpetuate, and legitimize systems of domination and control is also important for the latter. Discourse develops and establishes limited vocabularies that complement and perpetuate governmental systems. Broadcast television fits more comfortably as a propaganda-transmission tool but the ubiquity of television is extended by the prominence of CCTV and its authority as a transmission system is exemplified by the state's willingness to trust the credibility of the images it captures.

Of course the model that lies behind both Foucault and Miller's understanding of this process is Bentham's "Panopticon," originally a design for a prison characterized by a circular design and a central guard tower that would allow for constant surveillance of all inmates.[11] The body of the building included openly visible cells stacked six stories high. In the center of the structure stood a single guard tower. The cells were constructed in such a way that the prisoners—housed one to a cell—would be unable to see each other but were always able to see the guard tower. The guard tower was constructed so as to permit the guard to see into any cell or number of cells at once but hid the occupant from the view of the prisoners. As such, the inmates would be unable to determine when they were being watched but would understand that it was possible they were being watched at any time. Theoretically, the prison might operate without a guard in the tower at all; as it was impossible for a prisoner to see into the tower but it is understood that the guard is possibly watching at any given point.

Bentham's prison was never built, but the link with CCTV is obvious. To quote Foucault, the desired effect of the Panopticon was "to induce in the inmate a state of consciousness and permanent visibility that assures the automatic functioning of power."[12] The dream of total visibility is now fully realized by the conversion of the urban setting into the panoptic dream itself. Each setting becomes a cell. Each camera becomes a guard tower. The discourse of control is suddenly expandable outside of brute architecture and can potentially encompass any designated area.

Foucault, in reviewing panopticism decided that:

> This enclosed, segmented space, observed at every point, in which the individuals are inserted in a fixed place, in which the slightest movements are supervised, in which all events are recorded [. . .] in which power is exercised without division, according to a continuous hierarchical figure, in which each individual is constantly located, examined and distributed among the living beings, the sick and the dead—all this constitutes a compact model of the disciplinary system.[13]

This idea of a "compact model" is particularly attributable to CCTV. The subdivision of a population—the compartmentalization of different social spheres and spheres of activity—is a direct consequence of the structure of the CCTV apparatus. Physical areas come to be seen as a series of images displayed on a monitor. The superficial division of space created by the frame of the monitor, by the limits of the peripheral scope of the lens, present areas under surveillance as though they were isolated spaces. The determination of what is worth surveilling also has an impact—the creation of the image makes the area depicted a focus of attention, giving it a sense of importance as a place where things happen or are likely to happen. The CCTV image therefore makes an area phenomenologically different from those areas that are not monitored by cameras.

It is likely that the realization of that spatial exposure would cause those passing in front of the camera to recognize a risk, resulting in a strategic evasion of the surrounding area. Though there is a validation in being photographed there is also the uncomfortable impression of being identified and tracked. It could simply be a reflection of a person's mood at the moment, but as much as there is a sense of validation in the knowledge that one is being watched, there is a corresponding risk as well. This would no doubt frustrate those advocating the introduction of CCTV. The goal of surveillance is to capture all possible deviations rather than create a window that will only capture a percentage of what is going on. In the abstract, the degree to which "governmentality" can be effective in a political system is directly linked with the ideological system's apparent ubiquity. This ubiquity naturally results in a sort of passivity on the part of the people who live in and move through the area under surveillance of course—the camera and any other element of the surveillance structure simply fades into the background with repeated assurances that these tools and processes exist to maintain order or protect the public. In a way that communicates both menace and consolation, the use of CCTV over a given area functions as a concrete reminder and agent of the system of control. In so doing it speaks to the scope of the state's technologies of power—both literally and figuratively. Yet the realization that the view of the camera is limited might also have a mitigating effect on the efficacy of state surveillance.

Foucault was using Bentham's formulation of the Panopticon to illustrate the method by which a larger population may be managed by a smaller entity. The text of *Discipline and Punish* begins to address this idea of governmentality around the same time as it works through panopticism. Foucault described the panopticon as "a kind of laboratory of power."[14] This immediately places the emphasis on defining some sort of enclosure, or limited space. However, the enclosure that Foucault was describing transcended the bricks-and-mortar interpretation that is typically made of Bentham's design. He cautioned the reader against understanding the design as a building:

> it is the diagram of a mechanism of power reduced to its ideal form; its functioning, abstracted from any obstacle, resistance or friction, must be represented as a pure architectural and optical system: it is in fact a figure of political technology that may and must be detached from any specific use.[15]

It is this warning against "specific use" that is noteworthy for the purposes of this argument. At a basic level, the panoptic has political implications. The structure developed by Bentham is probably the most compelling articulation of the desire to monitor all things at all times or, at least, to convince the population that all things are being monitored at all times. It is, however, a metaphor rather than a schematic. The prison model describes the impulse more than it explains the political ideas and maneuvers that would be involved in creating something like it.

One of the things CCTV does is to make possible the control of fluidity. The shifting and flow that is a normal component of human movement in an urban environment places architecture in a contingent rather than a deterministic position. Surveillance by governmental and commercial forces must learn how to use the landscape as it is rather than seek to shape it. In other words, if the practice of monitoring a population necessarily extends beyond controlled environments like prisons, schools and clinics, the technology employed must adapt to the landscape. The question then becomes how to establish a form of control.

CONTROL

In looking at the applicability of television to the practice of governing, it is necessary to consider whether treating a visual medium like television in terms of the purposes of control places too much specific credit on its compatibility with the dynamic of governing. In the development of techniques of control, Foucault did not see it as a hindrance to shirk nuance: "It's a case of 'it's easy once you've thought of it' in the political sphere. It can in fact be integrated into any function (education, medical treatment, production, punishment)"[16] The system of control loves the discovery of an effective tool or process. If it works in one context the tendency is to immediately test its efficacy in other processes. There is an instant repositioning of that application to other spheres of the process of government.

Stephen Graham, in *Cities Under Siege*, wondered, "Are cities, then, becoming little more than a series of interconnected 'camps' organized through militarized and surveilled passage-points, where all presences and circulations are pre-screened and pre-approved through continuous electronic calculations?"[17] Living or working in a city like central London necessitates participating in this dynamic. The saturation of CCTV cameras increases annually, and the degree to which citizens become units of data, or elements of analysis for security systems, depends on its fluidity and the number of uses it is being put to. With that in mind, the entry points of data on these systems are usually mundane no matter where they are found. In London, the use of CCTV throughout the public transportation system, the administration of the congestion charge through CCTV observation to ensure that all drivers pay it, and the almost mandatory use of the smart cards or contactless cards means that people become units of surveillance in the course of getting from home to work and back again. In Ontario, in order to use the 407 "express" toll highway, motorists are required either to preregister their details with the government and mount a tracking device on the windscreen of their cars or have their license plates photographed upon entry onto the highway and agree to be billed later. In the United States, and presumably elsewhere, motorists are being encouraged to have surveillance devices installed in their cars that will record their driving habits supposedly in exchange for reduced premiums.[18] The devices record the average speed cross-referenced with the GPS locations the vehicle travels through. They record the speed with which the vehicle brakes and decelerates. Every aspect of the use of the car in traffic is recorded and those numbers are used to determine whether the driver qualifies for a rate related to a "safe" driver or not. The fact that these devices have been adopted by drivers voluntarily indicates a level of comfort with exposure to organizations that have power over them as well as a willingness to forgo privacy for a perceived reward. In this light, it is important to emphasize that "governmentality" is something that is not continually inflicted. In order to work properly, it must be participatory. It might even appear voluntary at times as it does in the case of these monitoring devices offered by toll highway or insurance companies. The acceptance of the promise of surveillance is intrinsically linked to the internal normalization of the idea of surveillance that is reinforced by a perceived system of reward. Cameras and monitoring devices offer something (supposedly) tangible; safety or financial benefit. The incentive behind all of these "improvements" to the simple process of moving through urban areas is reward or convenience. At first, there was a certain amount of resistance to the monitoring practices at the opening of the 407 highway in Ontario, but as there were free-of-charge alternatives regarding the route of the road, indignation quickly devolved into a division between those willing to be charged and monitored versus those who didn't mind having to deal with congestion. The implementation of the Oyster card system in London also generated a significant amount of blowback due to privacy concerns, but the possibility of swiping a magnetized card for entry to the Underground rather than dealing with notoriously flimsy and—for this user, at least—easily lost printed tickets drew a number of skeptics in over time. The way in which these practices, this condition of forced participation in a surveillance structure, is sold to the public is always under the guise of personal benefit. The Oyster card is easier to use and there is less paper waste, which is good for the environment. The 407 typically has fewer cars on it which means fewer accidents and, consequently, a lower probability of traffic jams. The little box installed in your car simply tells your insurance company what a good driver you are and so, the they insist, it allows them to justify offering you below average rates for your coverage. The installation of CCTV cameras on every platform in the Network Rail system in Britain supposedly scares away "chavs," "yobs," and the other undesirables the public has been conditioned to fear, and it results in greater safety overall. The selling point is always personal. It tends to play into feelings of bigotry or unsubstantiated fear that are easily exploited by security companies or the government and, by extension, the police.

A crucial element of Foucault's governmentality principle is that the citizen should carry out the practices that it defined as acceptable without having to be constantly reminded to do so. In this sense, governmentality fits comfortably within the traditional determinations of citizenship. Traditionally, one of the more effective ways to engender this consent and endorsement is to establish a system of personal desire linked to reverence for the culture. Absurd exercises like singing the national anthem before sporting contests is a classic case in point. The link between the celebration of a national history and spectacular competition for its own sake is never actually mapped out. That being the case, the practice continues and questioning the validity of it is usually met with sour indignation on the part of the participants. Inclusive exercises that are expected to be accepted without question dampen critical interpretation by seeking to impose a feeling of camaraderie. Those who participate are true citizens, those who do not are instantly suspect.

This division within the domestic population requires a process of identification. The codification of acceptable behavior carries with a need to identify, to mark those who conform to the parameters set out and those who still share the same space yet are not fully integrated into the political fabric. The ubiquity of these depictions serves to normalize the subjects' condition of non-citizenship and normalize whatever punitive state actions might be carried out against them. What emerges, then, when new technologies of surveillance and new methods of identification and determination available to the power structure are considered, is how these determinations are modified and whether they retain the same operative characteristics. The opportunity it offers to visually identify subjugated groups such as those mentioned above makes the visual surveillance of these groups with technology like CCTV appear obvious if not rational.

There must be a process or structure that would determine which individuals in a culture are essentially phantom and those who are allowed to exercise agency. According to Miller, the citizen, in the abstract, is "an open technology"—it is one that "the elements of the state use to make [citizenship] a cohesive technology."[19] These elements, the procedures and the tools that fit the procedures, have characteristics of their own, and they are able to influence the perception of data or information gathered. The presentation of footage captured by a camera frames the details of that footage before it is even seen. The knowledge that footage is being watched for a specific reason also influences the way details are interpreted. The individual captured on screen is assumed to have certain characteristics even before they have "acted" in front of the camera. This is the oldest tragedy of the social narrative. Bigotry can be either momentary or something that frames an entire lifetime of impressions. These technologies intertwine with one another and between the citizen and the mechanism that determines the citizen. What can be said with some certainty is that the closeness of media coupled with the temporal flexibility of exposure that is intrinsic to the media allows for a greater flexibility in determining a person's "phantomness" or agency.

The lived world now allows for representations, in fact requires representations, that are directly linked to each citizen. The necessity for passports, birth certificates, social insurance numbers, and so on results in a connection between the physical person and a spectral person who lives in databases and travels along fiber optic cables. The two entities are entirely symbiotic in that the violence done to one will invariably affect the other in some way. While the death of a person naturally results in a sudden inertia regarding their data—the closing of bank accounts, the cancelling of driving licenses—the violation of the data of a living person can directly impact on the life of the person connected to it—identity theft being an obvious case in point. The desire for control in the act of governing allows for greater inroads in the proximity of the citizen to the political system, but also creates greater complications of what a citizen is understood to be. Representation always involves a split between the real and the copy, between the authentic and the duplicate, but, as Baudrillard has pointed out, this division begins to blur and implode the greater the depth of field becomes.

The establishment of the idea of citizenry is predicated on the necessity for control. A substantial part of this control is the determination of who is a citizen and who is not and it is the unspecified element of that designation that becomes its active component; the other is therefore defined through its exclusion. The mechanisms that make possible this process of control usually arise accidentally in the process of their development and their longevity depends on the extent to which they are able to maintain and perpetuate the power relations that put them in place. Foucault says as much in *Discipline and Punish*: "The panoptic mechanism is not simply a hinge, a point of exchange between a mechanism of power and a function; it is a way of making power relations function in a function and of making a function function through these power relations."[20] The element of process, or of a series of connecting technologies that operate in a way that benefits the system is the point at which it is possible to point to the direct connection between systems of surveillance generally, but specifically that of CCTV and the system of power relations that culminates in governmentality. Whereas the primary purpose of the construct is control, its establishment is dependent upon the mechanism that allows the system to continue functioning. While this interdependence is somewhat counterintuitive when under close scrutiny of the nuts and bolts of the relationship that is being described, the proof of it is in the cyclical justifications that perpetuate the use of the mechanism. The

CCTV camera provides a video record of crimes. The crimes provide the justification for the use of the CCTV. The presence of the CCTV camera supposedly curtails or discourages the commission of acts of deviance on the part of the citizenry. The ignorance of the CCTV camera and the subsequent commission of acts of deviance justify the presence of the camera—it is possible to know who the criminals are and it is also possible to catch them thanks to the presence of the camera.

Toby Miller outlines what is called the "Repressive State Apparatus." In brief, this "involves the use of force and the threat of it as a means of eliciting obedience to authority."[21] The application of a mechanism like CCTV to this practice allows an amplification of the second part of that schematic and is, arguably, the more important element in the process of controlling a population. It is the promise of violence rather than its delivery that prevents deviance.[22] As such, the system of control must present itself via a state of constant awareness and preparedness to act.

If this analysis is accepted it follows that control involves an interdependent system of action and nonaction. The action should be routine—it is simply the collecting of data, the monitoring of a situation. The nonaction should appear for all the world to demarcate a procedural resolution that immediately follows an event requiring the involvement of the security system—the trial rather than the summary punishment, the incarceration rather than the execution. As in Miller's formulation, the key element is not so much the use of violence, or the threat of it, but lies in the collection of reasons that will be used to justify the use of violence that is inherent in the threat. The review of CCTV camera footage operates in exactly this fashion. The very presence of the camera and the fact that footage exists acts as a promise to complete the procedure mentioned above. The collection of data provided by the camera and the promise it offers of evidence that may be used at trial round out this procedure. The active element of the system of control lies in the assumption that the violence used must be justified, that the system must always be prepared to justify its use, and that being able to justify the use of violence is an intrinsic component of any potential use. There must always be an excuse handy. The feed from the CCTV camera, the tapes from a well-placed wire tap, the "voluntary" confession obtained after fourteen uninterrupted hours of interrogation. The document that provides the reason for the use of force is the locus of control. The prevention of indignation, the establishment of an excuse for uncivilized behavior in the interest of preserving civilization, is the point at which the ideological need is satisfied.

The permanent branding of the individual is no longer necessary. Credit cards, mobile phones, loyalty cards, as much as the CCTV camera, allow for the monitoring of the individual. Citizens become performers in a never-ending system of justification and need to demonstrate proper citizenship.

This is the key element in the panoptic dream; this push toward performance requires the endless demonstration of the subject's innocence through mechanisms required by the security system. The wearing of a hooded sweatshirt to avoid exposure to CCTV cameras is an indication of probable criminality or deviance. Rather than proclaiming the accused's rectitude at trial, the public is encouraged to perform at each possible point of exposure, and the intervals are constantly contracting. Exposure becomes a crucial element in the contemporary management of control, which is now consequently something that is both inclusive and ongoing. Individuals are placed in a flexible condition dependant on their willingness to be and to remain exposed. The other side of this is the panoptic system's capability to close down gaps in this condition of constant exposure. Control is now expanded and stabilized according to the fluidity of the mechanisms employed as well as by the participation of the subject.

GOVERNMENTALITY

This fluidity is as much a condition of the person as it is of the dominant culture. The successful link, according to Foucault, is the result of the internalization of the whims of the state. Labeling this condition "governmentality" allows an analysis to bridge the gap between disciplinary societies like those of the eighteenth and nineteenth centuries and the increasingly pragmatic modes of control enacted around the development of mass communication and the popularization of electronic media. Citizens, simply by the fact of living in the culture they do and being exposed to the norms that govern it through social environments like schools or traditional forms of entertainment like organized sports learn official histories and acceptable ways of interacting with one another. This movement to a less physically determined sense of order has necessarily resulted in modifications in the way people are managed. Once the way people interact with one another is modified, the damage is done. Governmentality, in a nutshell, was a reaction to new modes of living more than it was an enabling element of them. Foucault gave three accounts of what he meant by "governmentality." The first is the one that applies most directly to the study of surveillance and Closed Circuit Television. He said, "The ensemble formed by the institutions, procedures, analyses and reflections, the calculations and tactics that allow the exercise of this very specific albeit complex form of power, which has as its target population, as its principle form of knowledge, political economy, and, as its essential technical means, apparatuses of security."[23] This new form of power involves a give-and-take between security apparatuses and the government that was somewhat absent in previous approaches to security. The demonstration of power through the use of violence is still present—police officers still carry one form of weapon or another and are permitted to use them in specific circumstances—but the increased density and specificity of information on the citizenry that is available to security apparatuses makes the use of violence less and less necessary. The ready availability of information results in a reduction of uncertainty and a more comprehensive form of management. Once the security apparatuses are more aware of the number of citizens, they are in charge of managing and have a clearer picture of their behavior, the need for violent demonstrations of potency abates.

This process of investigation acted out on this "new object" labeled the population does not just redefine the relationship between the individual and the society they are affiliated with. It also modifies the relationship in terms of the total amount of interaction between the two parties. Whereas the relationship between a person and their government might once only have been manifested in a few relatively infrequent events over the course of that individual's life, the intensity of exposure that results in governmentality has turned this connection into one that is more or less constant from birth to death. The preindustrial world might have worked off established demonstrations of power and the ability to act upon the body of the citizen in all sorts of creative and horrifying ways, the internalization of the will of the state inherent in the governmental turn is directly linked to this new understanding of human existence as a process of exchange and modification. The tendency is to think of the movement of information as something that allows the government to carry out actions that make the management of people simpler. This economy of data—the assignment of labels and signifiers to specific citizens to indicate what actions are appropriate on the part of the government in managing them—is a means by which the security services can determine the best managerial approach. Labeling someone a "criminal" or a burden to the state appears at first glance to have some sort of trajectory to it, but the signifier allows an adjustment that enables the government to handle the citizen rather than the other way around. For earlier governments that used violence as a means of control, punishment would appear to have been the best way to handle offenses against the social order. If someone steals, they are imprisoned or beaten, then imprisoned. If someone murders, the state takes their life. But once the society in question has rounded the turn from disciplinary modalities to governmentality, the citizen becomes a unit of exchange, a part of the larger conversation regarding how a society should run as a process. The citizen becomes one side of a relationship that is involved in a constant give-and-take that implies adjustment on the part of the public as well as that of the state. There appears to be a bit more autonomy since the public now has a degree of responsibility that was absent in governing systems that selected punishment (the expressed purpose of executing someone in public was that of inspiring fear of the sovereign or the state) but the inclusion of the citizen in the functioning of the state is restricted, limited to the delivery of information to the state. It is this faux inclusiveness, really, that has the greatest impact on the citizen-power structure relationship. The use of the citizen as a reflection of the will of the state, and the encouragement of thinking of oneself as a component of it rather than its subject, is the opening to governmentality. The establishment of an ongoing relationship, a need for information from the populace that at once cements the link between the citizen and the power structure while still allowing the power structure to frame the dialogue around what citizenship is, is the core of this new system of exchange between the individual and the state. To quote directly from Foucault: "The process, or rather the result of the process, through which the state of justice of the Middle Ages, transformed into the administrative State during the fifteenth and sixteenth centuries, gradually becomes 'governmentalized.' "[24]

What is the shape of this relationship, then? How is it formulated? Foucault was, in fact, a bit more concise in *Discipline and Punish* when he stated that power "is exercised by surveillance rather than ceremonies, by observation rather than commemorative accounts, by comparative measures that have the 'norm' as reference rather than genealogies giving ancestors as points of reference; by 'gaps' rather than by deeds."[25] So much of the language around policing and security these days fits into a dialogue about process or stability. Many police departments adorn their vehicles and, in some cases, their uniforms with the words "Protect and Serve" emphasizing an intractable rooting in the present. The justifications for repressive police actions around popular protests like the 1999 Seattle World Trade Organization summit are invariably phrased as "keeping public order" rather than "executing the will of the State." Bound up in this language and these actions is a declaration of process or of procedure that serves the entire community rather than just defending the primacy of the security services. The stability of the system is not ensured by pageantry like the Diamond Jubilee or the State of the Union speech. It is established and perpetuated by maintaining a constant impression of control—a technology comprised of different mechanisms that not only make the stability of the system a task acted upon by multiple entities (the police, the judiciary, the market, the clinic, the school) but by making this technology and all of the components that contribute to it appear *natural*. What Foucault was driving at in describing this process of ingraining the will of the system was the degree to which this integration makes the mechanisms and the outcome all but invisible. The naturalization of limits, the compulsive need to maintain a degree of invisibility from different areas of the control apparatus are less a matter of fear now than they are an inflicted sense of responsibility.

In a very real way, one could point to these larger exercises like Canada Day, Independence Day in the United States or the "Trooping of the Colour" in the United Kingdom as methods of ignoring the larger apparatus of governmentality. The almost campy nature of the celebrations, the overt simplicity in the national narratives is at once so problematic that it almost begs a fanatical adherence to drown out the inevitable uncertainty that will result from questioning the dogma. The sense of stability and tradition created by these celebrations, however, allows for the more pervasive elements of the system to continue operating with little interference. The more problematic elements of the behavior of the security apparatuses are looped back into larger mythologies. As in the US government's charging of Edward Snowden for leaking classified documents under the Espionage Act,[26] the narrative is that the transgression effects the population as a whole rather than just the power structure. This is, in a very real way, governmentality in action. The competing issues debated are always concerned with who is most aware of how to be a better citizen and never whether the basic assumptions framing the argument are the problem. As such, a truncated vocabulary based on binary right-and-wrong positions perpetuates the basic elements of the system and prevents any real critical investigation. It is also participatory by its very nature and allows the public a feeling of autonomy that is conveniently limited by the acceptable boundaries within which any debate is contained.

All of these reveal a (somewhat) flexible structure of meaning designed to establish and maintain control over a population. The organizing and filtering of information is an element that serves to perpetuate this flexibility and the use of any viable technology (theoretical or otherwise) that organizes or limits the scope of debate adds to the resiliency of the state. The tools the state uses to maintain the norms that are linked to the local culture cannot escape the norms inherent in the culture. We can therefore see a disparity in the way surveillance technologies are used in the United Kingdom and the United States. Where the streets of London are saturated with CCTV cameras and there is little debate regarding the disappearance of privacy, the use of obvious surveillance technologies in the United States is far less pervasive. This may be due to the fact that the US public is largely more apprehensive about surveillance and government oversight. Perhaps because of this, the approach in the United States appears to focus on covert modalities of surveillance like the use of drones[27] rather than lamppost-mounted CCTV cameras. The discrepancy between techniques would appear to follow the greater tendency toward deference to power in the United Kingdom versus the (largely symbolic) deference to personal autonomy in the United States.

In cultural terms, then, the introduction of a technology necessitates a process of implementation on the part of the state followed by a continuous evaluation of its efficacy. The opening requirement of any technology of control is determining which populations it should be used on and establishing some certainty that the population will remain in range of it. The continuing process of governing involves getting to know the lay of the land, so to speak, and the simplest way in which this can be achieved is through surveillance. Populations move about. Landscapes can change in significant ways over time. The degree to which this condition known as "governmentality" is able to take root is determined by the government's ability to permeate the cultural and physical landscapes within its jurisdiction.

Foucault, in writing about the Panopticon, said the purpose of the structure is "to induce in the inmate a state of conscious and permanent visibility that assures the automatic functioning of power."[28] Under ideal circumstances, this knowledge results in an adherence to prescribed social and cultural norms buried so deep in the psyche that they could be referred to as a "reflex." The manifestations of this vary, but the impression is sometimes bewildering. In 2002, my wife and I attended the 128th running of the Kentucky Derby. We were in the infield, where the youthful and hedonistic atmosphere contrasts sharply with the promoted images of upper-class men and women sipping mint juleps and basking quietly in the Kentucky sunshine. Toward the end of the day, a fistfight broke out between two young men. Inward-facing bleachers had been erected at the northeast corner of the field. A number of riot police were seated there in order to keep watch on the crowd. Upon noticing the fight, some forty or so police rose and disembarked in single file, banging their truncheons on their shields as they marched toward the disturbance. The crowd instantly parted, the two drunken pugilists, not having noticed anything other than each other since the start of the fight, were separated, thrown to the ground and handcuffed. The police reformed into a column, picked the offenders up and began to march them back in formation toward the bleachers. As they did so, the crowd around us began to applaud. An older woman exclaimed, "Thank you for protecting us!"

To an extent, that reaction can be chalked up to the bizarre condition of irrational fear that gripped much of the United States shortly after the attack on the World Trade Centre. The idea that two drunken twentysomethings were in any way a threat to the rest of those in attendance was as absurd as the ostentatious display of power by the Louisville Police Department. What I think is important to note, however, is the fact that the immediate response of the crowd, regardless of the absurdity of the circumstances, was to support the security forces. This was not a considered evaluation of the situation—the decision to express some sort of support for the police was almost certainly subconscious and the display of it—the fact that everyone else began to clap along—was equally instinctive. The momentary trauma of witnessing members of the group step outside the prescribed limits of behavior was immediately quelled by seeing the system snap back into a position of authority. The need to thank the police officers for such an absurd expression of force was a predictable component of the need to return to equilibrium. Foucault alludes to how this state of "conscious and permanent visibility that assures the automatic functioning of power" works on a social level as much as it does on a personal one. The response from that crowd at the police display of force is similar to the reassurance that citizens might feel from noticing a CCTV camera installed on a dark train platform. The police quell the outburst in the infield and calm is restored. In the same way, the camera, being visible to all, promises a solution to an event that has not happened yet. Deviance is met with enforced control or the promise of enforced control.

NOTES

1. M. Foucault, *Discipline and Punish: The Birth of the Prison* (Harmondsworth: Penguin, 1979), 192.
2. M. Dean, *Governmentality: Power and Rule in Modern Society* (London: Sage, 1999), 14.
3. M. Foucault, "Governmentality." *The Foucault Effect: Studies in Governmentality* (London: Harvester Wheatsheaf, 1991), 102.
4. Ibid., 99.
5. Ibid., 104.
6. M. Dean, *Governmentality: Power and Rule in Modern Society* (London: Sage, 1999), 19.
7. Ibid., 19.
8. T. Miller, *The Well-Tempered Self: Citizenship, Culture, and the Postmodern Subject* (London: Johns Hopkins University Press, 1993), xiii–xiv.
9. Ibid., xiv.
10. Ibid., 59.
11. M. Foucault, *Discipline and Punish: The Birth of the Prison* (Harmondsworth: Penguin, 1979), 200–201.
12. Ibid., 201.
13. Ibid., 197.
14. Ibid., 204.
15. Ibid., 205.
16. Ibid., 206.
17. S. Graham, *Cities Under Siege: The New Military Urbanism* (Verso: New York, 2011), 149.
18. M.P. McQueen, "How Technology Can Help Trim Auto Insurance." *The Wall Street Journal Online*. June 26, 2008. May 30, 2012.
19. T. Miller, *The Well-Tempered Self: Citizenship, Culture, and the Postmodern Subject* (London: Johns Hopkins University Press, 1993), 12.
20. M. Foucault, *Discipline and Punish: The Birth of the Prison* (Harmondsworth: Penguin, 1979), 206–207.
21. T. Miller, *The Well-Tempered Self: Citizenship, Culture, and the Postmodern Subject* (London: Johns Hopkins University Press, 1993), 34.

22. M. Foucault, *Discipline and Punish: The Birth of the Prison* (Harmondsworth: Penguin, 1979), 48–49.
23. M. Foucault, "Governmentality." *The Foucault Effect* (Chicago: University of Chicago Press, 1991), 102.
24. Ibid., 103.
25. M. Foucault, *Discipline and Punish: The Birth of the Prison* (Harmondsworth: Penguin, 1979), 193.
26. G. Greenwald, "On the Espionage Act charges against Edward Snowden." *The Guardian*. June 22, 2013. Web. July 26, 2015.
27. S. Graham, *Cities Under Siege: The New Military Urbanism* (Verso: New York, 2011), xviii, 119, 363, 365.
28. M. Foucault, *Discipline and Punish: The Birth of the Prison* (Harmondsworth: Penguin, 1979), 201.

Chapter 8

Visibility and Control

CONTROL AND SOCIETY

Deleuze, in tracing the social progression from disciplinary societies—those in which violence and confinement were the main methods of maintaining order—to control societies—those in which the appearance of mobility and some semblance of autonomy are the norm—argued that,

> The various forms of control [. . .] are inseparable variations, forming a system of varying geometry whose language is *digital* (though not necessarily binary). Confinements are *molds*, different moldings, while controls are a *modulation*, like a self-transmuting molding continually changing from one moment to the next, or like a sieve whose mesh varies from one point to another.[1] [italics author's]

This capacity for variation is at the root of surveillance and it informs the general attitude toward mechanisms of control. It is the principle of variation that goes along with these "various forms of control" that, absurdly, gives them a sense of legitimacy. The current procedures acted out on protesters in major cities are a good case in point.

Approaching this phenomenon with an intended focus on Closed Circuit Television, the examples I find most applicable to this line of inquiry are the G20 summits (and the related protests) held in London in 2009 and Toronto in 2010. Although in the media age the power of media to illuminate or obscure events seems normal, to the extent that the reality of the event itself may become less significant than what the media make of it, CCTV adds a new dimension because of its ubiquity. In both instances, though for different reasons, we can see that CCTV played a major role in the management and in the social and political outcome of the summits. This will be dealt with in detail later, but for now it will be sufficient to speak about them in general as examples of a supposedly heightened civic risk. The response to the specter of unruliness, or threat of independent behavior, the protests against them were likely to generate is typically the enforcement of greater degrees of control. Images of police in riot gear (large shields, helmets, balaclavas, batons and tear gas launchers, etc.) are ubiquitous in media clippings and videos from these events. More importantly, they tend to frame the public perception of control systems as something that is *temporary*—something that can be turned on and off.

From the newsreel saturation of the giant turtle costumes sported during the 1999 WTO summit in Seattle to the current ubiquity of images of protesters wearing Guy Fawkes masks, the media representation of various activist campaigns against the Western governments' policies has developed a certain pantomime quality over the last sixteen years or so. The ability to point to a uniform related to deviance enforces the suggestion that there is a proclamation or a conscious performativity in acting against the will of the state. Conversely, the violence inflicted on protesters as well as the appearance and demonstrably cartoonish behavior of the police has folded into a system of repetition that follows Baudrillard's assessments of "integral reality"—the real is hardly visible any longer. More importantly, however, the interchangeability of the images presented of different events establishes both a system of precedent and a temporal memory quality to the entire experience. Images are seen of actions in Toronto or London or New York City or Montreal and the instant assumption is that the situation depicted is temporary and represents a momentary cleansing of the domestic political system rather than a new permanent state of affairs. In many cases, like that of Montreal or New York City, it appears to be how long these things go on that offends those not involved in them more than the specifics of the issue. The disruption in the typically stable system is normally not that difficult to accept—in a way it almost presents itself as a cleansing of sorts—as long as there is a definitive end date to it.

The frustration felt at the length of these spectacles is traceable to this progression as outlined by Deleuze in the quotation given earlier. What the movement from rough demonstrations of power and expressions of rage on the body of a condemned person linked to the disciplinary paradigm of earlier regimes to the more spectral modes of control associated with the contemporary condition will allow for is a knowledge of being watched, yet of not being openly coerced. The persistent presence of the CCTV camera projects this image of an ever-present government and sets the ideal scenario for the internalization of the will of the state that Foucault was outlining.

There is a tendency to sterilize the custodial duties of the state in contemporary Western culture. Prisons are rarely built within municipal boundaries anymore. Executions in countries that still practice them are not public in any meaningful sense (they tend to take place in highly controlled areas with no access to broadcast media if, indeed, they are still enacted at all). All of these elements are swept to the side as the will of the state. The development of these elements that Foucault referred to as governmentality and Deleuze termed the control society is internalized. Deleuze laments that in the integrated world, "Control is short-term and rapidly shifting, but at the same time continuous and unbounded, whereas discipline was long-term, infinite and discontinuous."[2] The emphasis is on the process rather than the event of power. The erection of cameras on street corners is not about visible display but the development of a continuous loop that can be called "security." This need to cover the environment with control events, with continuous expressions of domination, is fallible only in the sense that it is possible to point to its limits. Actually, while I'm on the topic of executions, there is an element of the practice currently employed in the United States that might serve as the ultimate expression of the control society. In the twenty-nine American states that still authorize lethal injections, before the IVs are injected into the condemned person's arms, a required preliminary step is to swab the target area with alcohol. The only logical inference being that the body can only be adequately destroyed in the way specified by the court system. The remote possibility that some rogue super virus might take the life of the condemned before the sodium pentothal, pancuronium bromide, and potassium chloride[3] have the chance to preempt this is too much. The power structure must not only condemn the body, it must destroy it in a way that leaves no possible doubt as to which trauma definitively ended the life. Although the state has long arrogated to itself the power of life and death, the extent to which it now goes to ensure that nothing can intervene to prevent its will being enacted is significant. All events must be closed within the predictable system of control. Like the CCTV feed, the event prescribed must be provable according to its defined limits.

According to Foucault:

> The domain of panopticism is [. . .] that whole lower region, that region of irregular bodies, with their details, their multiple movements, their heterogeneous forces, their spatial relations; what are required are mechanisms that analyse distributions, gaps, series, combinations, and which use instruments that render visible, record, differentiate and compare: a physics of a relational and multiple power, which has its maximum intensity not in the person of the king, but in the bodies that can be individualized by these relations.[4]

It is also important to mention the importance of its range or scope: the degree to which the panoptic system is able to eradicate any blind spot is the degree to which it can be taken seriously. This is what concerns Deleuze when he argues that control societies are "metastable states of a single modulation, a sort of universal transmutation."[5] He notes that the characteristics of the disciplinary mechanism were built from individual projects that were, at least in the initial phases, mutually exclusive. The family, the school, the military, prison and the like were all built according to their own distinct divisions and interruptions. The linkage between them was not designed in any specific way. The movement from discipline to control highlighted the existence of those gaps in influence and demonstrated a need to fill them in. In the quote above, when Foucault identifies the "lower region" as the area of interest, as the necessary focus of a panoptic system, he meant the optimum source of information available in that system. The mapping of all possible bodies is the first necessary step in this determination. The irregular is only definable via the discovery, mapping, and determination of the regular. Bearing this in mind, the use of CCTV systems seems rational. The demarcation of public space as surveilled creates the future crime as something that will have been seen—as something that will have already been captured. The possible offense is already woven into the narrative of control. It loses its final element of unpredictability. The mapping of the territory with video cameras allows the security services to determine what, in the area, is normal and whether what is "normal" needs to be preserved or modified.

MONITORING

Scott McQuire has noted that something as basic as public lighting has been "recognized as an important technique of policing public space since its origins in the 16th century."[6] He also pointed out that the implementation of lighting generated resentment among the population: "Lantern-smashing was a popular act of rebellion against state authority in 19th century Paris."[7] This invasion of light, this act of watching that public lighting initiated, is something that tends to lay the body of the public bare. The resulting feeling of exposure emphasizes this relationship between the condition of being governed and a citizen's sense of ownership of their own bodies. The apparatuses employed by the state to watch over the population, be they gaslight lanterns or CCTV cameras, begin to feel like the control system that observes independently of the will of the individual. The "opening up" of things is the purpose of surveillance in the abstract. The treatment of the urban environment as something that needs monitoring also implies that it needs to be diagnosed and cleansed.

In much the same way that the introduction of public lighting in the sixteenth century may have altered the relationship between citizens and the cities they lived in, it also altered the relationship the state had with the environment it was charged with managing. Foucault pointed out that "the exercise of discipline presupposes a mechanism that coerces by means of observation; an apparatus in which the techniques that make it possible to see induce effects of power, and in which, conversely, the means of coercion make those on whom they are applied clearly visible."[8] What happens when the means of surveillance surpass this need for a specific identification? To what extent can a public continue to limit their understanding of the application of power to instances in which the focus on that public is justified but the characteristics of observation exceed the required specificity involved in witnessing a specific event? When surveillance by means of an apparatus then the consequence is that the state claims a territory as its own. The erection of streetlights as much as the installation of CCTV cameras changed the very landscape of the places people inhabit. The shattering of gaslights in Paris in the nineteenth century suggests that people were already aware of this.

Virilio, writing in the late 1990s, suggested that the expansion of the visual in information was not so much an end to history as an "end of geography."[9] He suggested that "in a world in which obligatory tele-presence is submerging the immediate presence of individuals [. . .] television [. . .] give[s] birth to [. . .] this virtual vision which is supplanting the vision of the real world around us."[10] In other words, the way in which the propagation of the visual amplifies the state's ability to monitor its citizens does not so much amplify its geographic reach as much as it makes geography irrelevant in the practices of surveillance. The population is now visible in a way that requires only the apparatus and a preexisting determination of what is relevant to it. It will, in fact, alter the determination of what individuals constitute in their relationship with the state. The territory of surveillance now follows flows of data and imagery rather than specific geographic areas.[11]

Christopher Nolan's film *The Dark Knight* (2008) provides a good example of how this works. The film follows a standard Batman storyline—a new super villain bent on enormous amounts of destruction emerges and Batman (played by Christian Bale) appears to be the only person who is capable of taking the villain on. What is interesting for the purposes of this text is a small piece of fictional gadgetry offered to Bruce Wayne (aka Batman) by his head techno-wizard, Lucius Fox (played by Morgan Freeman). The need to map an area without the area's inhabitants' knowledge becomes an issue at one point in the film and Fox develops a method of using mobile phone technology to "send out pulses" and report interference patterns to give constant updates on the contours of a physical area. He offers one phone capable of doing this to Wayne in the early stages of the film. Later on, a larger crisis emerges and Wayne modifies the original program to enact these results from every citizen in Gotham City, thereby allowing Batman to map every area of the city regardless of physical barriers. Essentially, the device allows for a constant surveillance on every section of Gotham on anyone who is carrying a cell phone anywhere in the area. The barrier that is provided by physical objects is overcome by a technological tool. What would normally be thought of as geographical properties—concrete, wood, and metal barriers that make up buildings and other man-made structures that block an individual's line of sight—are made transparent. The limits placed on sight are eliminated with this technological tool. Lucius Fox, upon learning of Wayne's modification chastises him: "No one man should have all of this power." Wayne immediately informs Fox of a passcode that will allow him to destroy the system once the immediate danger has been averted. *The Dark Knight* presents a morality tale about the limits of individual power and surveillance and technology makes this excess of agency possible. Wayne encourages Fox to destroy the surveillance system at the end of the story rather than allow the world to become transparent to anyone who has access to that system and, in doing so, appears to return Gotham to a state of equanimity. The ability to see through the physical landscape, to track people beyond their voluntary presence in public (or, at least visible) space is presented as a threat to the freedom of the citizens of Gotham.

What Virilio referred to as "an end of geography" had more to do with a rupture of an understanding of the location of things. Even Foucault's assessment of the progression of confinement—from the family to the school to the factory, and so on—dealt with recognizable, fixed locations. The stability of things has a great deal to do with predictable outcomes and the realization that a subject's movements and their physical presence may become movable elements of information can, at times, give everything a sickeningly supple feel. Lucius Fox's reaction to Batman's cell phone solution comes down to a violation of an assumption regarding privacy. At least, that is the obvious interpretation. It is also likely that the audience relates to Fox's indignation on a more basic level; more than the issue of whether the public should be watched like this, what does this do to the general conceptualization of physical space?

William Bogard states that in the modern era, "[t]erritories [. . .] became *coded as spaces of probability*, and confinement not just a matter of brute restraint but of organizing a whole social machinery in probabilistic terms" [italics author's].[12] This is a crucial point. The purpose of viewing the population as a type of fluid geography is an adjustment. It is a reflection of the need to focus on the possible rather than the historic: to focus on what is likely to happen rather than attempting to retrace what has already happened. Foucault was hinting at this when he stated that "[t]he scarcely sustainable visibility of the monarch is turned into the unavoidable visibility of the subjects."[13] For a contemporary Western public, this visibility is inextricably intertwined with technology. Like the use of mobile phones in *The Dark Knight*, CCTV cameras, systems that monitor online traffic serve as methods to follow what people are doing. More than anything, the CCTV camera converts the landscape before it into a potential location of proof, or a source for accusation and conviction. The situation of being caught in its lens may lead to something, and this is what Bogard is alluding to when he uses the term "spaces of probability." It is the openness of these spaces that makes them problematic. The installation of gaslights in urban areas was the opening gambit in what would, over centuries, be a continuing application of new and viable technologies to control physical space. The focus on technology is a rational and, frankly, predictable response to a desire to manage or monitor public areas.

How does this use of technology to claim space operate? This sustainable visibility, according to Bogard, has morphed into a modality of projection: "It is the model of delinquency, not its 'reality,' that pre-structures the field of monitoring and intervention."[14] The act of viewing the population, then, is not simply that of sitting in front of the monitor and reviewing within range of the camera. The way in which this practice operates is via the application of preexisting assumptions of deviance and it involves an attempt to apply those codified assumptions to the actions witnessed.[15] The repeated justification for an act of surveillance—be it in the case histories discussed earlier in this book or in the official reviews provided by police services after the London or Toronto G20 summits—is the recording and identifying of offenses carried out against the state and, via political reasoning, the population as a whole. A relic of the old monarchic reasoning, *a la* Foucault's analysis in *Discipline and Punish*, the offense against the will of the state is interpreted as an offense against the body of the sovereign.[16] Rooted in this understanding was the idea that the punishment for the offense should be measured according to the damage done to the body of the sovereign. More importantly, the state needed a body to apply this punishment to and it had to be able to defend itself from challenges as to whether the body identified is the right body. In other words, the state needs proof to legitimize the punishment is gives out.

For the moment, it will be enough to assume that the process leading to the identification of a threat is one that is a component of this practice of gathering proof. The state must identify those within a system who would act against the system's interests (or, at least, the state's interests). Government surveillance, in short, is an attempt to buttress the vulnerabilities of a state against whatever elements might threaten its stability. As Foucault once remarked, the act of governing is the "conduct of conduct"[17]: it directs the behavior of the population. As such, surveillance is the evaluation of conduct; it is the catalyst that puts in place the process by which a population is directed and becomes an integral component of the functioning of the state itself. The knowledge that one is being watched, that actions will be noticed by others, is often enough to encourage acceptable behavior (whatever that might mean in each particular circumstance). A good representation of this can be found in Kevin Smith's mumblecore classic film *Clerks* (1994). Around the middle point of the film, the protagonist, Dante, leaves his duties at the convenience store counter for a moment to spend time with his girlfriend. He posts a sign next to the cash register indicating that customers should pay for all items before leaving the store, leave exact change and be honest, and the two lovers stretch out and cuddle on the floor behind the counter. Dante tells her that "Theoretically, people see money on the counter, no one around, they think they're being watched." As the scene continues, customers enter the store, find what they're looking for, carry the items to the counter, read the sign and proceed to leave their money and count out the correct amount of change. The threat of surveillance, of being observed is enough to induce correct behavior.

As Graham Burchell points out, "[t]o govern individuals is to get them to act and to align their particular wills with ends imposed on them through constraining and facilitating models of possible actions."[18] The way in which these alignments come about must be, at least at first, through a demonstration that the government will actually notice if those wills are not aligned with the dominant model. Essentially, in order to "get them to act," one would have to demonstrate that their subsequent actions are being monitored. The public must be convinced that what they do will be known. Beyond that, the model of possible action involves a presupposition on the part of the surveillance system. In other words, parameters must be set prior to the surveillance being enacted. Those watching must know what to watch for. That old adage that "if you've done nothing wrong, you have nothing to fear" stems from this line of reasoning. The belief in the absolute efficacy of the model of behavior allows the system of surveillance to exist.

This prescription of action and the subsequent threat of "checking-up" on the behavior of the population in order to ensure that the guidelines are being actively followed is at the root of what is understood to be surveillance. It is also the fundamental point of departure for every process of governing: the notion that the enactment of any policy on behalf of the government must first have some expectation of coming to the attention of and being monitored by the public. I'm aware that there are innumerable instances of a government conducting surveillance on its own population without consent or admission, but in all of those cases—whether it be the East-German STASI or the "illegal" wiretapping of the American public during the second George W. Bush administration—the procedural action is carried out without transparency but the existence of the practice is acknowledged: It must be to be effective. Control is the fundamental goal of a postindustrial economy and it can only be established by the potential power of surveillance available to the government being known—or at least suspected—by the population it seeks to manage.

NOTES

1. G. Deleuze, *Negotiations* (New York: Columbia University Press, 1995), 178–179.
2. Ibid., 181.
3. In somewhat predictably horrible fashion, the California Department of Corrections and Rehabilitation offers a concise breakdown online that itemizes the major steps between the assignment of a death sentence and the carrying out of the killing: http://www.cdcr.ca.gov/reports_research/lethal_injection.html.
4. M. Foucault, *Discipline and Punish: The Birth of the Prison* (Harmondsworth: Penguin, 1979), 208.
5. G. Deleuze, *Negotiations* (New York: Columbia University Press, 1995), 179.
6. S. McQuire, *The Media City: Media, Architecture and Urban Space* (London: Sage, 2008), 117.
7. Ibid., 129n.
8. M. Foucault, *Discipline and Punish: The Birth of the Prison* (Harmondsworth: Penguin, 1979), 170–171.
9. P. Virilio, *The Information Bomb* (London: Verso, 2005), 9.
10. Ibid., 15.
11. K. Haggerty & R. Ericson, "The New Politics of Surveillance and Visibility" *The New Politics of Surveillance and Visibility* (Toronto: University of Toronto Press, 2006), 11–12.
12. W. Bogard, "Welcome to the Society of Control." *The New Politics of Surveillance and Visibility* (Toronto: University of Toronto Press, 2006), 59.
13. M. Foucault, *Discipline and Punish: The Birth of the Prison* (Harmondsworth: Penguin, 1979), 189.
14. W. Bogard, "Welcome to the Society of Control." *The New Politics of Surveillance and Visibility* (Toronto: University of Toronto Press, 2006), 60.
15. A. Doyle, "An Alternative Current in Surveillance and Control: Broadcasting Surveillance Footage of Crimes." *The New Politics of Surveillance and Visibility* (Toronto: University of Toronto Press, 2006), 207.
16. M. Foucault, *Discipline and Punish: The Birth of the Prison* (Harmondsworth: Penguin, 1979), 49.
17. G. Burchell, C. Gordon, P. Miller, & M. Foucault, *The Foucault Effect: Studies in Governmentality* (London: Harvester Wheatsheaf, 1991), 2.
18. Ibid., 119.

Chapter 9

The Performance of Governing

CONDUCT

In the sense that "government" can be described as a structure that carries out a variety of actions to ensure its own stability, then the reality is that government is traceable to a series of events. Everything from elections to rubbish collection to arresting people reinforces the stability of the government and adds to the public impression of what "government" is. Dean points out that "[g]overnment concerns the shaping of human conduct and acts on the governed as a locus of action and freedom. It therefore entails the possibility that the governed are to some extent capable of acting and thinking otherwise."[1] The process of government, then, is concerned with the management of conduct or the establishment of a doctrine of acceptable action that will, according to Foucault, lead to a subconscious preemption of behavior. This might initially be thought to be the law, though Foucault modified the understanding to something more diffuse: "the calculations and tactics that allow the exercise of this very specific power."[2] Mitchell Dean further explained this by telling his audience to look for these calculations and tactics, "whenever there exists a relatively stable field of correlation of visibilities, mentalities, technologies and agencies, such that they constitute a kind of taken-for-granted point of reference for any form of problematization. In so far as these regimes concern the direction of conduct, they form the object of an analytics of government."[3]

Protest is an interesting element within this dynamic. Even those actions that supposedly challenge the primacy of the government must be enfolded into the narrative of governmental control. A line from the Office of the Independent Police Review Director's (OIPRD) report on the Toronto G20 summit proclaims, "Our Charter of Rights and Freedoms is designed to ensure that everyone in Canada enjoys the same freedoms of assembly and expression."[4] The subsequent sections go on to identify a group adopting a monochromatic (black) uniform and tendency toward the destruction of private property during protests as "Black Bloc."[5] Those identified as Black Bloc are not identified with a cohesive ideological position, though the report roughly assigns them the label "anarchist," but they are said to employ (apparently) recognizable tactics such as throwing rocks at riot police and directly targeting private businesses as places to be vandalized. This scourge on civilization appears to have supernatural powers:

> Another Black Bloc tactic is for participants to embed themselves within an otherwise peaceful group of protesters and inflame them to the extent that some of the peaceful protesters become their "soldiers" or provide cover for them by adopting Black Bloc tactics or actions. People who use Black Bloc tactics are adept at coopting peaceful members of protests to join in their deeds.[6]

This language is reminiscent of the faux stupidity rife in Louis Gasnier's notorious 1936 film *Reefer Madness*, which is famous for the extent to which it is both ignorant of and yet complicit with the very phenomenon it is condemning. In *Reefer Madness*, the use of marijuana is presented as a precursor to exaggerated violent (criminal) behavior, sexual deviance, and madness. Any contact with the drug is depicted as the beginning of a decline into violence, degradation, and inevitable death. The adoption of official language decrying uncontrollable behavior and the specific determination of a group as uncontrollable or irredeemably deviant is similar to the portrayal of drug users as invariably frantic and lawless. Additionally, it betrays the strategy being employed by which it is assumed that anyone who takes to the streets to defend a cause or address a grievance must be very easily led indeed. The logical inference is that the only thing that stands between calm, ordered progress, and a reckless orgy of critical introspection and fiscal oversight is the hysterical organizing of disaffected individuals by those who are savvy enough to manipulate them.

Be that as it may, the inclusion of the act of protesting in the so-called regimes of practices, the encoding of behavior that challenges the primacy of the power structure, allows for minor deviations or for the suppressing of them as though they were some natural function of the system as a whole. In other words, the Canadian Charter of Rights and Freedoms guarantees the right to protest. In line with Herbert Marcuse's theory of "repressive tolerance,"[7] it does not guarantee the fact that those protests will be taken seriously by the state or that the protesters themselves will be treated as though they are full citizens at the time they are protesting. The declaration that the act of protest is something that is tolerated according to predictable dynamics allows sporadic expressions of anger to appear almost as though they are a natural component of the functioning of the system and not a sign that anything is actually wrong. Momentarily tolerating the expression of grievances allows the state to posture as though it is entertaining the grievances of minority opinions while actively ignoring them in practice. To quote Marcuse, "Tolerance is turned from an active into a passive state, from practice to non-practice; laissez faire the constituted authorities. It is the people who tolerate the government, which in turn tolerates opposition within the framework determined by the constituted authorities."[8] Kept in place, the ability for the public to visibly address their grievances allows for an outlet while at the same time keeping the performance of protest out in the open and, indeed, in front of the cameras.

Integral to this practice of allowing conduct that appears to be directed against the state, or the absolute authority of the state, is the requirement that it be monitored. The knowledge that these actions are permitted is one thing, but determining a "regime of practices" involves the assessment of the legitimacy of each of these events. Required, then, is the establishment of a structure that allows the state to monitor the landscape. There are some seventy-eight mentions of CCTV in the text of the OIPRD report on the Toronto summit (curiously, there are only ten in the text of the British House of Commons report on the London 2009 G20 summit[9]). This use of technology, this construction of a structure that records and allows the state to monitor and measure the activity of the population is integral to the efficacy of this "regime of practices." To treat the territory managed by the state as potentially being hostile allows the state to react accordingly in the likely event that it does become hostile.

Foucault's suggestion that "politics is the continuation of war by other means"[10] shifts the line of inquiry from government as a practice of directing conduct to that of a constant effort to assert, establish, and maintain control over the citizenry.[11] The threat of violence carried out by the state as a response to prohibited behavior is, in the end, a condition of perpetual war. This war can be described as a successful one as long as the threat of violence keeps the population at bay. The fragility of this approach might be exemplified by the 2012 student protests in Montreal against rises in tuition fees and government austerity. Though significant violence had been visited on those participating in demonstrations, the protesters were unwilling to back down. The state's equal unwillingness to back down harms the image of the state more than it does the protesters' for this specific reason: The legitimacy of violence used by the state is rooted entirely in its ability to direct or limit the conduct of the population. As Foucault says, "[L]aw is pacification, for beneath the law, war continues to rage in all the mechanisms of power, even in the most regular. War is the motor behind institutions and order."[12] Under optimal circumstances, the state's use of violence pacifies the population and order is reestablished. If it does not, the legitimacy of the state's use of violence can legitimately be called into question. The justification for warfare carried out against the population is that it is effective.

So the door swings both ways. The system of action is traceable, linear enough to reveal the roots of its own processes. This is partly due to the fact that a successful practice would naturally be used again, but also because the demonstrative value of a successful practice must also point to a defined limit of behavior. Foucault, in *Discipline and Punish* pointed out that "[d]iscipline organizes an analytical space."[13] The establishment of rules, of boundaries of behavior, provides a space for the evaluation of public conduct. The key to determining the efficacy of policies and procedures is provided by finding the same results in different situations. In this instance, the camera is invaluable. The OIPRD report justifies nearly every police action in a given setting in the report by citing CCTV footage as the primary evidence. The production of footage on the part of the state creates a new analytical space that allows it to modify and refine procedures. The action captured is framed around the supposedly public but still state-oriented image.

More broadly speaking, the way in which control is maintained is via the flow of information. This flow offers a continual refinement and expansion of successful techniques. Further, as Foucault notes,

> A new demand appears to which discipline must respond: to construct a machine whose effect will be maximized by the concerted articulation of the elementary parts of which it is composed. Discipline is no longer simply an art of distributing bodies, of extracting time from them and accumulating it, but of composing forces in order to obtain an efficient machine.[14]

Strictly speaking, the visibility and announcement of the presence of CCTV cameras is a means of modifying behavior for people who are now aware that an area they might inhabit is under surveillance as well as a way to alert people to the fact that events in that area are now recorded and kept as a record. The desired and necessary result of this process would be control. Even in the collapse of control, or the near collapse, the ability of those components to work together to force equilibrium is essential to the stability of the state. The lifeblood of the systems Foucault is describing is information.

This flow of information necessarily requires that the tools normally used to achieve control in restrictive spaces like prisons become mobile. In a very real way, this enactment of surveillance and the conditions of control is just a transplanting of penal mechanisms from their normal location within the physical limits of the prison into the outside world. Foucault indicated that "[t]he 'theory of the prison' was its constant set of operational instructions.

. . . The prison has always formed part of an active field in which projects, improvements, experiments, theoretical statements, personal evidence and investigations have proliferated."[15] CCTV's establishment as a perpetual feature of the urban landscape in the United Kingdom and, increasingly, in Canada as well indicates that this system of surveillance which has the aim of correction and control is one that has escaped the normal confines of penal applicability. The street has grown eyes, so to speak, and the wiring leads directly back to the seat of power. Canadian attitudes toward surveillance might typically be more reserved than they are in the United Kingdom, but the assertion that a major event like the Toronto G20 might result in increased deviance is enough to justify extending the amount of CCTV surveillance well beyond its previous limits. The assumption that surveillance in the interest of control is something that should *precede* deviance rather than respond to it in a *reactive* sense is just a logical progression from successes observed in the prison. The use of that which appeared to increase control and the viability of new and existing mechanisms of control outside of the prison has to do with a desire to enact the same qualities of control tested and proven in prison across the civilian landscape. These innovations have as their goal the refinement and the preservation of the existing system. With this in mind, it is important to realize that the process of control does not necessarily have to be completely effective. In fact, it is important for the control of deviance to allow for frequent enactments of deviance. To return once more to Foucault, "delinquency, with its specificity, is a result of the system; bit it also becomes a part and an instrument of it. . . . Police surveillance provides the prison with offenders, which the prison transforms into delinquents, the targets and auxiliaries of police supervisors, which regularly send back a certain number of them to prison."[16] Establishing "control" has as much to do with demonstrating a continual process of the management of deviance as it does with identifying it. The process that Foucault is explaining, where deviancy becomes something to be proven and processed via an endless repetition of capture-and-release, provides a demonstration of the need for the police and courts to continue doing what they are doing without providing any real hope of a permanent solution to the deviance itself. It is, in the abstract, a system that continues to offer justification for its own existence by not completing the job it supposedly exists to perform.

Virilio referred to "omnivoyance" as Western Europe's totalitarian ambition and identified the process of enactment as "the formation of [the] whole image by repressing the invisible."[17] If Foucault's assertion that the idea of the prison works as an active field within which different social experiments will be carried out and that the purpose of the process is to repeat those experiments on the rest of the population is applied, the most obvious prerequisite for such a system of experimentation is surveillance. The use of personal data as well as camera surveillance to track the movements and behavior of a population is the logical use of the available technology to establish this condition of "omnivoyance." As much as government "concerns the shaping of human conduct," that shaping has to be enacted and monitored.

PRESENCE

Control hinges on one principle; that those in a position of control have a vested interest in directing the actions of the population they manage.[18] There are a variety of methods by which this can take place: economic programs, the strengthening of security forces (police, military, etc.), the establishment of a government that extends to local councils and legislatures. The way in which any of these methods of control are judged to be working properly, in any instance, is via systems of information that are fed back to the government itself. The logistical problems that go along with the efficacy of any mechanism of control are solved and/or updated via surveillance.

Extreme cases, as always, offer the best examples. This is evident in the 286 pages of the Toronto G20 report. Night shift Incident Commander Superintendent Fenton described the incidents that led to the police assault on protesters in 2010:

> I attended the conference room that was set up as an area for the Chief and Command to view some of the CCTV [closed-circuit television] video being generated. [. . .] The Chief was asking why he could not see police officers in the pictures that he was watching on his screens. Superintendent Ferguson addressed the questions. The Chief appeared to be angry and frustrated in his demeanour and the manner in which he was asking the questions.[19]

While the circumstances described here are rare, if not unique, the frustration at the breakdown of the flow of information is not. As the situation was (supposedly) getting out of hand, the greatest degree of frustration for those in charge came from their inability to get a clear picture of the situation and direct their subordinates accordingly. The logic here is relatively easy to follow; successful directions will depend on the total assessment of the situation. A lack of knowledge will inevitably require guesswork. Guessing is dangerous. At the onset of the 2003 Iraqi invasion, the 24-hour news networks were awash with pundits spewing information regarding deployment patterns, the assessment of the forces that the Western nations would encounter and the like. Nearly all of the prognostications, however, were couched with a final reminder that, inevitably, the "fog of war" would eventually descend and make the flow of information slow (where it wasn't deliberately misleading) and the gathering of accurate data difficult if not impossible.

The compulsion, then, is to attempt to create a network of awareness. The goal of any control system is to anticipate and map out possible trouble areas. This is at the root of any CCTV system. The claiming of territory is about establishing two presences. The first is the most obvious—that of the state. The placement of the camera determines an area as being one that is of interest and that must be acted upon. The second presence is that of the person, of the subject who is incorporated into the surveillance text. The first systematic attempt at marrying these two elements would have been Bentham's Panopticon had it been built. The construction of a confined space, a space that creates the permanent subject out of a space of permanent visibility is the zenith of the control society. Where CCTV breaks with the original scope of the Panopticon, however, is in the removal of the brick-and-mortar limits of the design. In the Panopticon, someone would have to be incarcerated in order to be subject to an ideal level of scrutiny. In other words, they can only be watched after they've done something wrong and been condemned to prison. CCTV goes beyond this limitation by allowing for a permanent establishment of presence outside of the process of incarcerating someone and the physical limits of prison. The person subject to the gaze is put under surveillance no matter what their personal history. The claiming of public space as a state surveillance area circumvents the need to specify a subject. The fact that all territory incorporated within the boundaries of the state is justification enough for such surveillance.

Achille Mbembé and Libby Meintjes looked at the connection between colonialism and space. The process of colonial occupation was one of "seizing, delimiting, and asserting control over a physical geographical area—of writing on the ground a new set of social and spatial relations."[20] This "writing of a new set of social and spatial relations" is the result of the establishment of a surveillance system and the positioning of a CCTV camera in any space is a means of colonizing it. Mbembé and Meintjes pointed out that, under colonial rule, "Space was therefore the raw material of sovereignty and the violence it carried with it. Sovereignty meant occupation."[21] This process of occupation was only made possible by laying claim to space. In the case of traditional colonialism, this was carried out through the injection of military or mercenary forces and the prolonged or permanent installation of those forces. Granted, CCTV is more abstract, but the process is effectively the same. The promise of violence is present in both instances. The colonial government will punish uprisings and the local government will find, arrest, and prosecute anyone caught committing crimes on camera.

It is likely that these two examples are directly related in a lineal sense. Foucault noted a curious product of colonialism—that procedures of control that were often implemented as emergency measures in occupied territories would afterwards often be implemented back home once they'd proven effective. Calling them "boomerang effects," he stated that "A whole series of colonial models was brought back to the West, and the result was that the West could practice something resembling colonization, or an internal colonialism, on itself."[22] Recent news stories and political debates have outlined the willingness of the American authorities to use unmanned drone technology to monitor their own territory. One can only assume that the test subjects for the viability of this new technology have been the numerous Asian and North African countries subjected to Western intervention over the past decade.

The division is, to some extent, beginning to break down. Particularly in the United Kingdom, where the expansion of CCTV surveillance outpaces any other state on the planet, modifications to the existing technology are attempting to make the determination of presence, the absolute ability of the state to identify and simultaneously lay claim to territory, that much more effective:

> Following early experiments with face-recognition software in Newham, Birmingham, Tameside, Manchester, and elsewhere, a shift to digital CCTV, which uses computer algorithms to do automated searches for stipulated people or behaviours, has been gaining momentum. This shift again exemplifies the boomerang effect, as it parallels experiments with face recognition and smart CCTV to pacify urban insurgencies in Iraq.[23]

A significant concern in light of this is the realization that the types of categorizations that are ingrained into the technology that is developed to pacify ostensibly hostile populations is the same as that which is being used to monitor the activity of domestic subjects. In other words, the categories that divide bodies into a binary hostile/safe dynamic in theaters of war must still be active in these technologies.

The identification, then, of a population in need of surveillance is the observation of an entity, a stable population on the administrative landscape that is believed to have a potential for deviance. According to Foucault, this would be an indication of the success of a mechanism of separation. The development of a reusable and re-applicable knowledge allows planning for different lines of confrontation and the development of different strategies for management of the population. In other words, the demarcation of a stable category of citizen (or near-citizen) allows for the development of different techniques that can anticipate and manage that person.[24] This stability, the reliability of knowledge that comes from the categorization comes with a need to monitor and track a category of citizen—you have to keep watching.

VISIBILITY

The mechanisms that force visibility are relatively uniform in the way they function. To quote Kevin Haggerty and Richard Ericson, "[s]urveillance technologies do not monitor people *qua* individuals, but instead operate through processes of disassembling and reassembling. People are broken down into a series of discrete informational flows that are stabilized and captured according to pre-established classificatory criteria. They are then transported to centralized locations to be reassembled and combined in ways that serve institutional agendas."[25] As presence is established information is created. That information then becomes a component of the control mechanism. It can be used to construct individuals outside of their physical presence or to describe a person without their direct input. Making information is a component part of surveillance technologies intended to produce visibility—a disembodied type of visibility that can force presence independently of the actual presence of the subject.

David Lyon points out, however, that "such authoritarian potential, though present for all citizens, is especially likely to be realized in relation to political dissidents, minorities, and the poor."[26] A number of recent examples of the use of CCTV fit directly into the category of surveillance of undesirable elements within the polity. The death of Ian Tomlinson at the hands of London police[27] and the removal of CCTV surveillance powers from local councils in the United Kingdom as a result of the blatant abuse of it[28] indicate the mixing of the contemporary technological medium and the traditional modalities of state control. The death of Ian Tomlinson is the sort of thing that might well have happened one hundred years ago under similar circumstances. What makes the case extraordinary is the open disbelief of the public showed when the authorities said that there were no functioning cameras anywhere near the location of his confrontation with police or of his death.[29] In other words, the difference in this case is that the ubiquity and permanence of CCTV alters the understanding of the properties of state surveillance. The way in which the state conducts its watching of the population is no longer through whispered encounters between government operatives and sympathetic citizens. People are aware that they are being watched. They know how they are being watched. They know the properties of the record created. The record is known and it is transferable. It is, therefore, useless to deny its existence.

One element of this realization is a closure of proximity. A great deal of what has been discussed in this book has had to do with a definitive line between the state and the domestic population. The power structure is stable in that it marks a division between the enactment of the power of the state and the effect it has upon who are under its power. Even though the power is exercised by a handful of clearly definable individuals—police, judges, politicians, and so on—those who wield power are also supposedly subject to that power and the application of the punishment of the state to those who normally participate in the process of meting out punishment adds a sense of legitimacy to the act itself. Minor fluctuations in this power dynamic only serve to reinforce the original perception of power. To go a long way back in history, take the example of the so-called Gunpowder Plot—the plan by a number of conspirators to blow up the British Parliament in 1605 by stockpiling an enormous amount of gunpowder under the building and detonating it while the House was in session. A more recent example is the assassination of John F. Kennedy in 1963. The fact that a group of otherwise capable men came so close to destroying the very symbol of British governmental power and that assassination attempt that was indeed successful failed to bring down either government functions as a testament to the stability of the current formation of the state. Despite this, Bonfire Night is observed every November 5 in the United Kingdom while the American media machine continues to pump out largely speculative productions based on the Kennedy administration and his death in office.

Theatrical as these examples are, they do preserve the image of the state as stable and, to an extent, invulnerable. Pairing that image of the control structure of a society with the realization that the information gathered by the state about the population is gathered directly and visibly—very rarely are CCTV cameras even concealed these days—develops an expectation of efficacy with respect to the way the state gathers information. It also presents a feeling of necessity in the simple ubiquity of the cameras in public places. If they erect so many of them, they must be doing the job, musn't they? This idea has become so prevalent in Britain that people were incredulous that the heart of London's financial district might not be fitted with CCTV surveillance as a matter of course at the time of the G20 summit and that the death of Ian Tomlinson could not have been caught on the system. The contemporary assumption of the absolute stability of the state is intrinsically linked to the known visibility of its population—it has put far too much effort into assuring the public of its existence.

In this instance, the closeness that is facilitated between the public and the state—the understanding that surveillance is not only one way but that the technology in certain circumstances allows the former to watch the latter—exposes a minor reversal of force. The Tomlinson case illustrates how an increase in immediacy and total exposure of the lived environment means that a certain amount of accountability on the part of the state may be demanded. The mapping of the physical world may make it more difficult for the state to deny the existence of an act that would otherwise be deniable due to the lack of a physical record. The trauma of Virilio's observation that "[w]e are not seeing an 'end of history,' but we are seeing an end of geography"[30] is felt in both directions. Neither the public nor the state can deny total visibility any longer.

Nevertheless, the revelation in 2009 that local councils in the United Kingdom were abusing CCTV to settle personal scores flew in the face of this impression. One result of this collapse of the mystique of visibility in the United Kingdom resulted in the government threatening or actually removing CCTV observation powers from the hands of local councils. In 2009, then UK Home Secretary Jacqui Smith announced that local councils were to have their ability to monitor citizens cut drastically. According to *The Times*, this was due to the fact that "Councils have used legislation intended to tackle terrorism and serious crime to deal with minor offences such as dog fouling and littering."[31] Later, in 2012, Local Government Secretary Eric Pickles argued that because some local councils in England had allegedly been using CCTV cameras primarily to record and fine greater numbers of citizens and generate more revenue, the public's confidence in CCTV could be threatened.[32] Ultimately, the use of this medium must remain, if not mysterious, at least presumptively legitimate. The boomerang effect of greater technological surveillance enacted through a justification of order forces the state to pretend that the act of constructing the surveillance apparatus is apolitical (no matter how ridiculous such an assertion may be). The abuse of this power leads to questions being raised regarding proper use and about the vulnerability of citizens under total surveillance, as well as to the mechanisms available to address alleged abuse as revealed in the case of the local councilors who sought to abuse them. David Lyon argues that the ubiquity of CCTV is acceptable simply because we are now living in a "viewer society."[33] The council example would appear to disprove that suggestion. If the simple act of being under surveillance for no good reason were entirely acceptable as a result of constant exposure to the surveillance image, its legitimation would be irrelevant. What can be inferred from the council example is that the threshold for unwarranted surveillance may be linked to an assumed legitimacy of the organization conducting the surveillance—in this case, the Home Office rather than a local council in Merseyside.

This process of "disassembling and reassembling" citizens is still one that results in an awareness on the part of the population. Visibility in the purest sense is a one-way equation. The degree to which a state was previously able to make its population "visible" depended on its ability to extract information from members of the polity that would later prove to be reliable. The introduction of technology as the vehicle of this process allows for a greater scope of awareness, a greater amount of detail and an arguably higher level of reliability with regards to the information captured. It also allows for a process of information gathering that involves passive bodies under surveillance rather than those actively informing or arresting/arrested, detaining/detained, and questioning/questioned. This new passivity results in a greater visibility on the part of the population, but it also requires that the act of surveillance take place in the open.

NOTES

1. M. Dean, *Governmentality: Power and Rule in Modern Society* (London: Sage, 1999), 15.
2. M. Foucault, "Governmentality." *The Foucault Effect* (Chicago: University of Chicago Press, 1991), 102.
3. Ibid., 27.
4. G. McNeilly, *Policing the Right to Protest: G20 Systemic Review Report.* Office of the Independent Police Review Director. 2012. Web. 15.
5. Ibid., 12–13.
6. Ibid.
7. H. Marcuse, "Repressive Tolerance." *Marcuse.org*. August 6, 2012. Web. 30 September 2014.
8. Ibid.
9. House of Commons Home Affairs Committee, *Policing of the G20 Protests: Eighth Report of the Session 2008–2009.* June 29, 2009 (London: The Stationary Office Limited, 2009).
10. M. Foucault, *Society Must Be Defended* (London: Penguin, 2003), 15.
11. Ibid., 16.
12. M. Foucault, *Society Must Be Defended* (London: Penguin, 2003), 50.
13. M. Foucault, *Discipline and Punish: The Birth of the Prison* (Harmondsworth: Penguin, 1979), 143.
14. Ibid., 164.
15. M. Foucault, *Discipline and Punish: The Birth of the Prison* (Harmondsworth: Penguin, 1979), 235.
16. Ibid., 282.
17. P. Virilio, *The Vision Machine* (Bloomington: Indiana University Press, 1994), 33.
18. One of the better supporting works to this point would be Foucault's description of the social body: M. Foucault, *Society Must Be Defended* (London: Penguin, 2003), 88.
19. G. McNeilly, *Policing the Right to Protest: G20 Systemic Review Report.* Office of the Independent Police Review Director. 2012. Web. 98.
20. Mbembé, A. & L. Meintjes (2003). "Necropolitics." *Public Culture.* 15(1), 25.
21. Mbembé, A. & L. Meintjes (2003). "Necropolitics." *Public Culture.* 15(1), 26.
22. M. Foucault, *Society Must Be Defended* (London: Penguin, 2003), 103.
23. S. Graham, *Cities Under Siege: The New Military Urbanism* (Verso: New York, 2011), 114.
24. M. Foucault, *Society Must Be Defended* (London: Penguin, 2003), 208.

25. K. Haggerty, & R. Ericson, "The New Politics of Surveillance and Visibility." *The New Politics of Surveillance and Visibility* (Toronto: University of Toronto Press, 2006), 4.

26. D. Lyon, *The Electronic Eye* (Cambridge: Polity Press, 1994), 88.

27. Ian Tomlinson was a newsagent who was trying to walk home after work during the G20 summit in London on April 1, 2009. In attempting to move through cordoned-off areas of the city in West London he encountered and, apparently, argued with several members of the London Metropolitan Police. An American visitor to the city caught on his own camera footage of a police officer dressed in riot gear knocking Mr. Tomlinson to the ground with his truncheon. Tomlinson was walking away with his hands in his pockets. The officer hit Tomlinson in the back, Tomlinson hit the ground, was helped up by some of the protesters who witnessed the assault, and he stumbled away. Mr. Tomlinson later died in a doorway a few blocks away due to internal haemorrhaging. A good breakdown of the totality of what happened can be found at: Laville, S. and Lewis, P. (2009) "G20 Assault: How Metropolitan Police Tried to Manage a Death" *The Guardian*. April 9, 2009. Web. May 17, 2009.

28. R. Ford, "Council Powers to Spy on the Public Are Cut" *The Times Online*. April 17, 2009. Web. May 17, 2009.

29. P. Lewis, "Police Watchdog Chief Wrong to Say No CCTV in Area of Ian Tomlinson Assault" *The Guardian*. April 14, 2009. Web. May 17, 2009.

30. P. Virilio, *The Information Bomb* (London: Verso, 2005), 9.

31. R. Ford, "Council Powers to Spy on the Public Are Cut" *Times Online*. May 17, 2009. Web. September 2, 2014.

32. S. Adams, "Councils Face Ban on Using 'Spy Cars' and Parking Cameras." *Mirror Online*. September 27, 2013. Web. September 2, 2014.

33. D. Lyon, "9/11, Synopticon, and Scopophilia: Watching and Being Watched," in *The New Politics of Surveillance and Visibility*, ed. K. D. Haggerty & R. V. Ericson (Toronto: University of Toronto Press), 36.

Chapter 10

Practices and the Distancing of Government from the Population

FRAGMENTATION/REPRESENTATION

This is not to deny that such a system relies on preexisting divisions within itself. Foucault's concept of "biopolitics" is an important element to keep in mind here. In essence, the principle of biopolitics emerges when it becomes necessary to reinterpret the population and treat it as a field of knowledge. The complexity of modern societies and the resultant need to manage the health and behavior of the population has meant that treating it as a loose disorganized group of individuals was no longer viable. It necessitated a movement by which people came to be regarded as units of information that could be codified, measured, and managed. In other words, it brought about the development of a relationship with a populace based on the collection of data rather than on one of pure intimidation.[1] This awareness of information as a crucial element in the production of a polity functions on a system of technologies.[2] Be they physically enclosed tools like the prison or the school or open technologies like smart cards, used to make travel around London easier, but also providing a means to monitor individual movements, or voter registration, the itemization of people and the subsequent categorization of all citizens is part of a process of management. What coming into focus in the case of CCTV is an opening up of what were previously believed to be procedural limitations in the method of tracking people. There no longer needs to be some incidental justification—suspicion of involvement in a crime or to enable people to vote in an election, for instance—the subject simply needs to be physically present in a space that is specified as being of interest by the state.

This realization of different technologies of control is a precursor and stabilizing factor in the division of populations. To borrow a quote from Hardt and Negri, "[t]he multitude can only be ruled along internal lines, in production, in exchanges, in culture—in other words, in the biopolitical context of its existence."[3] This specification and preservation of divisions is part of the functioning of a state. It is the mechanism through which control systems are established. The way in which this is accomplished is through systems of identification and stabilization. Government uniforms—for instance, those worn by the English "Bobby" and the formal uniforms worn by British guardsmen when standing posts outside of royal palaces and government buildings—are designed around specific visual pretenses. In these particular cases, the low-riding brim of the helmet/hat is designed to hide the eyebrows which are primary indicators of facial expression. Beyond that, the immediate result of any uniform is to call attention to the emblematic representations rather than the individual. Likewise, the image of a camera in a stationary position calls attention to what cannot be seen immediately; the camera represents the police even though it is likely they will only be concerned about the events transmitted via the camera in a reactive context.

What is crucial to note here is that the immediate recognition of the state must always be as a disembodied entity. Uniforms fulfill this function until the entity representing the state has to become active. However, the initial semiotic impact of that embodiment lessens via the recognition that the agent acting on behalf of the state is in fact human. The beauty of the CCTV camera system is that it is, by definition, an extension of the sovereign/state rather than being simply an agent. It is the body of the state transposed outside of its normal corporeal reality. The barrier of interpretation supposedly disappears through the extension of the body of the state along electric lines. Mirroring McLuhan's image of technological man, the sensory limitations of the state evaporate due to the CCTV camera. No longer is it a matter of trusting one individual's version of events over another—the camera, as an inert and unbiased observer, reveals everything and conceals nothing. The state becomes omnipresent via technology and now has no need to depend—at least in semiotic terms—on anything but itself if it wishes to witness the actions of its subjects.

The power contained in the representation lies in its potential to generate action, however, and the perfect operability of the CCTV camera means that *it is always potentially acting*. Previously, the humanity of the state was the fundamental problem associated with its primacy and control. As all citizens are potential deviants, the use of the human form to represent the will and the actions of the state creates problems from the onset. The representation of the state in the form of a uniform, then, simplifies the initial evaluation of a person when first presented with them. The uniform offers the same semiotic information to the outside world regardless of the idiosyncratic characteristics of the person wearing it. The denial of complexity simplifies the idea of the state as well as that of the citizen by reducing all parties to a binary order of signification; a person is either wearing a uniform and represents the state or they are not and they are a member of the public. If this poverty of detail in representation is a happy coincidence or a matter of careful planning, the formless, featureless beauty of permanent surveillance via a mechanical actor is the zenith at which this binary division between the state and the public is preserved. Those idiosyncratic signifiers that cannot be effectively removed via a draping of signification over an individual like sex or height or skin pigmentation evaporate in a pure representation of the state in the physical simplicity of the camera. Differentiation only exists on one side of the binary division; that of the public.

From the perspective of the state, there is a positive element to this stripping away of essence: It is the ability to implant new meanings. A group of police in riot gear appear to an observer in much the same way that a flock of geese or starlings might; their individuality is swallowed whole by the semiotic construction of a nonhuman flock—a corporeal representation of the state. This veil is lifted in a lack of choreography. It could be argued that a cordon of riot police appear as a unified whole.[4] A disruption of a seemingly natural collection of things can highlight individual members and reduce the overall visual effect of the group. It could further be argued that this is why direct violence against cordons of police officers arises so impulsively. The state is not removed from such a situation. The only benefit of throwing a brick or charging the line is to shatter the unified illusion; to create individuals out of this perceived whole. The flock must be ruptured to shatter the impression of indivisibility. This recognition of human, or at least animal, characteristics behind the uniform is the fundamental problem with such representatives: all humans recognize the potential fallibility of the human. CCTV allows the state to exist outside of this possibility.

It is worth noting that the primary by-product of fragmenting the population—of enacting an individualistic outlook on the part of the population—is the establishment of the pervasive "other." This is what Carl Schmitt referred to as the establishment of "the enemy."[5] The process Schmitt identified seems to permeate the contemporary landscape and would appear to indicate that it is a stock procedure in the perpetuation of control in a modern polity. A tactic generally described as "Stop and Search" in the United Kingdom is a good illustration of this. Though the practice of singling out individuals and searching them in public took place prior to 1984, the establishment that year of the *Police and Criminal Evidence Act* (PACE) specifically permitted the practice if the officer claimed to be looking for, "stolen goods, items for use in property offences, knives, among other things."[6] The key element of the Act was the power it gave police to carry out searches without specific grounds for suspicion. The law in the United Kingdom has been updated a number of times and enshrined in other acts such as the Criminal Justice and Public Order Act (1994) and the Terrorism Act (2000). The fact that these "Stop and Search" practices carried out by the police overwhelmingly target visually identifiable minority populations[7] is a good example of the performativity and the utility of the identified other in the practice of demonstrating police power and agency.[8] The program was described in section 43(1) of the *Terrorism Act of 2000* as:

> A power for a constable to stop and search a person whom he or she reasonably suspects is a terrorist, to discover whether that person has anything in their possession which may constitute evidence they are a terrorist.[9]

That the documentation also stipulates that "Powers to stop and search must be used fairly, responsibly, and in accordance with the Equality Act 2010"[10] does not appear to have prevented the tactic from engendering a significant amount of anger from minority communities in London and elsewhere in the United Kingdom. After the London Riots in August 2011, "Stop and Search" was a regularly cited source of anger by minority communities and one of the key factors that sparked the disturbance.[11]

The identification of the enemy within does indeed harken back to state-sponsored procedures of exclusion and may even in some extreme cases lead as far as genocide. That, however, is the antiquated method of discipline and the true test of a control society is the ability to move those procedures outside of the easy locations of confinement and apply them to the population as a whole. The "stop and search" program in use in the United Kingdom and its ideological relative which began in New York City in 2002 "Stop, Question and Frisk"[12] are a component of this. A curious corollary to this is that, as in CCTV, the visual is the primary form of presentation that engenders bias and open discrimination. "Stop and search"[13] is typically enacted against someone who "looks suspicious," something which, in the abstract, is simply a determination that someone does not conform to the prejudicial understanding of what a person should ideally look like. Of course, additional information might be available in the physical instance where a police officer decides to "stop and search" a person that could arguably play a role in their decision-making as well (overheard conversations, smells that might indicate illegal drug use, etc.). With that in mind, however, it is well documented that individuals who are "stopped and searched" are overwhelmingly members of visual minority communities and, given that information, it is difficult to argue that the primary motivating factors in the decision processes of police officers are visual recognition of a certain "type" of person who is worth searching. In light of this, it is worth considering if the same process of forming judgments when involved in a direct interaction with the public that results in "stop and search" is in any way altered once the method of observation is Closed Circuit Television. If there is at least a passing connection between the appearance of someone and their risk of being searched, is it unreasonable to assume that there would be the same likelihood of being singled out in a crowd displayed on a CCTV monitor? It seems reasonable to suggest that the determination that the officer surveying CCTV feeds is making is likely to follow the same process of evaluation as that of the officer in direct contact with the subjects being singled out and searched in person.

The isolation of purely visual surveillance does not wash away the initial prejudices of a culture or polity no matter how benign the mechanism might appear to be. Gordon's take on this is worth quoting at length:

> Computerization and administrative rationalization begin to make possible for the first time a "real" government of population which, by coordinating appropriate forms of expertise and assessment, is capable of identifying all those individual members of society who can be deemed, by manifesting some combination of a specified range of "factors," to present a significant, albeit involuntary, risk to themselves or to the community.[14]

The degree to which prejudice and false accusation are a probable component of this arrangement is difficult to measure. What can be said with some certainty, however, is that the justification for a system of procedures is that it has proven effective in the past. Depressing as it might be, the extension of the visual scope of the state and the reliability of the accuracy of those visual impressions due to technological advancement requires no improvement in the social elements of control or the inherent biases that may be ingrained in the system of identification already in place. At a basic level, the parameters of potential deviance are established ahead of time and the mechanism by which these elements are identified is in the reactive gaze of surveillance. Those other elements that might have made the procedure dubious in the past are not necessarily cleansed via the introduction of a new apparatus.

Ignoring the element of electronic technology for the moment, the identification of deviance or criminality is something that happens across two specific temporal lines; identification of which behaviors are aberrant, on the one hand, and which specific individuals have been behaving aberrantly on the other.[15] That the borders of these definitions continue to shift is essentially irrelevant in terms of process. The fact that, until very recently, popular protest was legal in Montreal does not have any impact on the fact that it is now outlawed.[16] This outlawing was as a result of the so-called Maple Spring, when Montreal students staged mass demonstrations in 2012 against proposed tuition hikes, resulting in prolonged demonstrations on city streets; other organizations joined to show their solidarity and several weeks of violence between protesters and police followed. The prolonged confrontation generated significant global media coverage and brought the dispute to the attention of communities outside of Quebec and Canada. One consequence was the passage of Bill 78, a provincial law that put very strict limitations on the right to protest in the province. Demonstrations now required advance approval from government offices and those violating the terms of the law were subject to arrest and prosecution. The criminalization of democratic action was a significant change in the social definition of "criminality" for Montrealers and resulted in larger public protests from the general public. It is important to note, however, that the larger protests were the result of what many thought was an unreasonable expansion of the definition of criminal behavior. It was the expansion of behavior the public considered lawful into a "crime" that prompted the larger reaction. The possible inclusion of a greater number of citizens in the category of those engaging in unlawful behavior for actions they felt entitled to perform was a step too far. In many instances, what prompts anger from the public arises from where the security services place the line between unacceptable and acceptable behavior and how they go about enforcing that division.

The event of enforcement is one that naturally begs a public performance from the police. In the case of the Montreal protests, the "enforcement" carried out was a familiar one—the active physical confrontation of the protesters was followed by the arrest of as many of them as possible. The vulgarity of this approach, however, has a habit of appearing heavy-handed to those outside of the conflict while strengthening the resolve of those who are already involved. The use of force in public is a clear indication that one section of society has the option of using violence to achieve its goals whereas the other does not. The uneven nature of power in society is brought into glaring relief and the fear that this might breed resentment among the populace is a reasonable one. Along that line, it becomes clear that the primary attraction of CCTV lies in the fact that it gives the appearance of being in control even though one is in fact not physically controlling anything; the sociocultural symbol of CCTV is the act of viewing along with the potential to direct action against the subject displayed, should the actions of that subject warrant it, but it makes lines of police officers in riot gear unnecessary for that impression to be made. It is not active in the situation it is capturing. The image is typically only used as proof of an event having happened. It is not a mechanism for the active stopping of crimes or even of their prevention in the future. The broad assumption that the act of watching creates or reinforces this biopolitical relationship between the population and the control structure goes much deeper than it might appear at first glance.

The aim of biopolitics is stability. The establishment of a division between the state and the population is crucial to the biopolitical process. It is, however, extremely important to note that the actors in either camp need not be stable—that is, that the individuals identified from one moment to the next as either "state" or "population" do not remain static. Prior to the expansion of mechanical modes of surveillance, the state would have necessarily employed individuals who were to some extent both citizen and member of the disciplinary apparatus—police officers, soldiers, and so on. What matters is that there is always a recognizable division. Police officers, even the thug who killed Ian Tomlinson, are still technically citizens in the abstract. With the introduction of mechanical modes of surveillance, the CCTV camera accomplishes what a uniformed soldier or police officer could never possibly accomplish. The camera, supposedly functioning according to entirely mechanical laws, records the events occurring in front of it whether they are innocuous or relevant. There is no room for bias and thus it is the purest instance of biopolitical division—the production of information independent of individual bias (at least in a symbolic context) allows for the purest exchange of information with the subject. The camera identifies an action done by a member of the public and represents the state's potential violence as a result of mechanical memory. That the subject in front of the camera might be a police officer or another obvious member of the state control system is irrelevant from the perspective of CCTV; it sidesteps the complexities in the semiotic fragmentation and human blind spots that can come with uniforms and other biopolitical marker. All that is before the camera is that which is not the state.

PRACTICES

Foucault's notion of "practices" is a good one to bring in at this point. A "practice," for Foucault, could loosely be defined as the nexus within which reasons for acting, the policy of acting within the limits of a system for its preservation, and the justifications for the state's action, meet and so become a prescription for action.[17] At a basic level, it is the recognition that something has happened, is likely to happen again, and that measures should be in place to deal with this eventuality. A bank is robbed. It is in the interest of the state as well as the citizens that the robbery does not happen again or, if it does, that those who committed the robbery and caught and an example is made of them. The apprehension and detention of bank robbers is therefore a practice.

The point at which the need for action meets prescriptions already mapped out in a polity is the point I am most interested in here. A possible argument is that CCTV represents the expansion of the prison outside of its traditional walls—that surveillance on behalf of either the state or via its emissaries, the police and security forces, is the enactment of a *de facto* assumption of guilt due to the universal potential to commit an offending act. The logical end of this position is the assertion that everyone is presumptively guilty. Slavoj Žižek has referred to this as an element of the "performative efficiency" of surveillance[18]—in essence, establishing a setting of presumptive guilt in relation to anyone found in a given area invariably results in a condition of suspended and perpetual guilt.

Such presumption justifies tactics like "kettling" in response to large-scale protests in the West, the trap into which Ian Tomlinson, in the example given earlier, fell. Tomlinson was attempting to make his way home through an area that had been kettled off by the Metropolitan Police during the 2009 G20 summit in London. His route home led him through an area near the Bank of England populated by protesters demonstrating against the G20. Mr. Tomlinson was able to walk into the area, but was prevented from leaving it as police had sealed off the street he'd planned to walk down. An argument ensued, the police held their ground and an aggravated Mr. Tomlinson turned back in the direction from which he'd come. He was struck from behind by a police constable. The blow knocked him to the ground and caused injuries that would result in his death a short time later. Mr. Tomlinson's case is perhaps not typical in terms of the results of kettling, but it does highlight the rigidity of the practice. The absolute refusal to allow anyone to leave an area regardless of whether or not they are involved in the protest under scrutiny indicates that kettling involves an assumption that a person's location is reason enough to prevent their free movement. Kettling involves the creation of zones of presumed threat and, for the practice to work properly, everyone within that zone must be held in place.

Previous protests, most notably the so-called Battle in Seattle in 1999, indicated to police forces that managing the movement of protesters would be paramount if another multi-event, multi-incident clash between police and protesters was to be avoided. The World Trade Organization conference in Seattle in 1999 was the site of massive anti-globalization protests and resulted in numerous confrontations between protesters and the Seattle Police Department. Protesters disrupted traffic flows and engaged in a number of violent clashes with police officers in many locations. What happened in Seattle made the importance of localizing protesters and limiting their mobility clear and would become a primary concern for security forces at subsequent global trade events.[19]

The establishment of a practice, at least in the purest sense, is the determination of a potential threat to the stability of the state and involves the introduction of a series of procedures that they hope will minimize the threat. In a great number of instances, this involves learning from past mistakes as much as it does anticipating unforeseen events. As such, the approach taken by the Toronto Police Service for the 2010 G20 summit seems to make a kind of macabre sense. Their approach was to carpet the downtown area with CCTV cameras and the creation of emergency holding facilities to house the presumptively guilty in a way that fits within the "performative efficiency" of surveillance.

The production of imagery and the rezoning of the downtown area along security lines created a condition of suspended guilt on the part of anyone who happened to be in the area. The area closest to the Metro Toronto Convention Centre, where the meetings between world leaders would take place, was designated the "Controlled Access Zone." This area utilized classic security preparations; a three-meter-high fence and an enormous number of armed security personnel. The area outside of the Controlled Access Zone, however, was labeled "The Interdiction Zone" and extended several city blocks in all directions.[20] The only hope for anyone who could not escape the confines of the security zone was to somehow blend in—to become part of the scenery of the area. To draw attention to oneself under those circumstances was tantamount to announcing one's guilt.

In light of the G20 summits, the "practices" developed to manage security surrounding the connected protests requires the use of many of the more ethically ambiguous elements of the available surveillance infrastructure. The process of imagining the worst possible scenario provides the justification for virtually any extension of the powers of the state. The default justification is that the stability of the social construct is at stake. The expansion of these practices is really only limited by what the population can imagine. Prior to September 2001, the American 9/11 was unimaginable, but the event itself produced an instant expansion of the idea of what was possible and resulted in a process by which the enacting of virtually limitless powers could be justified. A practice was developed in response to the shift in perceptions. The desire to expand the surveillance capabilities of the state against its own people could be reframed as a need, and a performative efficiency that would typically have been reserved for those thought to be foreign or alien was directed inside the walls.

A practice, then, is an attempt to regain the upper hand. The recognition of the possibility of damage done to the polity requires a degree of advanced planning to nullify the event before it takes place and to properly redress any damage it might do. It is an attempt to build a system that cannot be taken by surprise. The use of technology to remove the possibility of human error in the identification/conviction process is, ultimately, a form of the expansion of the system of control outside of the courtroom and the jail cell and into the sphere of daily life. CCTV is thus more about the expansion of penal practices than it is about the development of new ones. It is an attempt to nullify the occurrence of surprises in the general urban space as much as it is within confined areas of control captured on the monitor.

At root, the production of surveillance systems is a response that comes in tandem with a sovereign/state recognizing that the legitimacy of the existing power structure is based on two things: its monopoly on the "legitimate" use of violence and its ability/willingness to carry that violence out. The idea of "practices" is a way of standardizing if not normalizing such violence—and of demonstrating its legitimacy. Where Žižek described the "performative efficiency" of surveillance as the construction of a universal condition of guilt, the surveillance system is a way of proving that guilt. The record created justifies the violence inflicted.

NOTES

1. M. Dean, *Governmentality: Power and Rule in Modern Society* (London: Sage, 1999), 94.
2. Ibid., 95.
3. M. Hardt, & A. Negri, *Empire* (Cambridge, MA: Harvard University Press, 2000), 344.
4. They certainly have to me in the past. In the aforementioned case of the Kentucky Derby (94), the effect was orchestrated in a very obvious way. During the Toronto G20, I noticed from the balcony of my apartment as well as during my walk out on the streets that the physical comportment of all officers in that gear was relatively linear or uniform. They carried themselves the same way. They approached and bullied peaceful citizens the same way. Whether that was directly conditioned or whether it was some strange subconscious result of the situation is still a mystery to me even though the OIPRD spent a significant amount of time covering that very question in the final report.
5. C. Schmitt, *The Concept of the Political* (Chicago: University of Chicago Press, 1996), 26–29.
6. J. Miller, "Stop and Search in England: A Reformed Tactic or Business as Usual?" *The British Journal of Criminology* 50, no. 5 (2010), 955.
7. Ibid., 956.
8. M. Townsend, "Black People '40 Times More Likely' to Be Stopped and Searched in UK" *Guardian Online*: May 4, 2019. Web. January 14, 2020.
9. *Code of Practice: Stop and Search Under the Terrorism Act 2000* (London: The Stationary Office, 2012), 7.
10. Ibid., 5.
11. R. Prasad, "Reading the Riots: 'Humiliating' Stop and Search a Key Factor in Anger Towards Police." *Guardian Online*. December 6, 2011. Web. September 19, 2014.
12. J. Leland, & C. Moynihan, "Thousands March Silently to Protest Stop-and-Frisk Policies." *New York Times*. June 21, 2012. Web. January 14, 2020.
13. The American term is "stop-and-frisk," which of course adds a delightfully playful property to the idea.

14. G. Burchell, C. Gordon, P. Miller, & M. Foucault, *The Foucault Effect: Studies in Governmentality* (London: Harvester Wheatsheaf, 1991), 45.
15. M. Foucault, *Discipline and Punish: The Birth of the Prison* (Harmondsworth: Penguin, 1979), 282.
16. A. Gabbatt, "Canada Student Protests Erupt into Political Crisis with Mass Arrests." *The Guardian*. May 24, 2012. Web. June 22, 2012.
17. G. Burchell, C. Gordon, P. Miller, & M. Foucault, *The Foucault Effect: Studies in Governmentality* (London: Harvester Wheatsheaf, 1991), 75.
18. S. Žižek, *Violence: Six Sideways Reflections* (London: Profile, 2008), 50.
19. E. Olson, "With Seattle a Vivid Memory, W.T.O. Seeks a New Host City." *New York Times*. January 23, 2001. Web. September 19, 2014.
20. G. McNeilly, *Policing the Right to Protest: G20 Systemic Review Report*. Office of the Independent Police Review Director. 2012. Web. April 24, 2014, iii.

Chapter 11

Camera Surveillance as an Exercise of Power

MULTITUDE

I suppose, in a cynical light, recognition that one is being surveilled is a validation of importance; you are at least somewhat important if you are important enough to watch. Foucault spoke about the relationship between the state, the individual, and the condemned at the beginning of *Discipline and Punish*. This process of individualization, of singling out, as a component of the practice of surveillance, is also a method of initiating a pseudo-connection with the population but one that functions as a process of isolation; the subject is removed from the social world and ingested into a world in which he or she has a symbiotic relationship with the state. The subject now becomes a component in the process of governing; the subject legitimates the process of surveillance by providing a willingly surveilled entity.

However, for Robert Castel: "There is, in fact, no longer a relation of immediacy with a subject *because there is no longer a subject*. What the new preventive policies primarily address is no longer individuals but factors, statistical correlations of heterogeneous elements" [italics author's].[1] The subject here is not the Enlightenment subject identified by Foucault as being in the process of dying. Rather, Castel is arguing that the very notion of the "subject," as an individuated being, has ceased to exist. I would, on the contrary, argue that there is, in fact, still a subject. In the simple act of moving through the contemporary urban environment, the individual is actively converting herself or himself into a subject. The degree to which the surveillance system itemizes individuals as it gathers information makes the construction of the subject inevitable. If it is correct to argue that the CCTV approach to monitoring space adopts a "panoptic" approach, then this will inevitably result in the formation of multiple subjects. The camera, in capturing the images of multitudes of people in front of it turns those people into subjects—objects to be monitored and/or evaluated. This act of monitoring people and turning them into subjects involves a process of applying general rules or assumptions to unique individual human beings, but that process does not necessarily have to dehumanize the people observed. It merely means that subjects are reformed within the frame of surveillance according to predefined categories rather than existing in their own right.

Hardt and Negri argued that the multitude is governed from the inside in a postmodern capitalist system. In *Empire* they assert that the governing of the contemporary Westerner must depend on tacit participation or, at the very least, apathetic consent by the population in question as opposed to outright subjugation through the application of state-sponsored violence.[2] This nuanced approach to the management of the state's subjects is meant to support economic and cultural growth promoted by and fostered by a web of interventions or tactical disengagements with the state. The lessening of direct applications of force on the part of the state against the population should foster a more compliant relationship between the power structure and the citizenry.

This overture toward personal autonomy takes on forms that fit into Deleuze's idea of a "control society":

> It's easy to set up a correspondence between any society and some kind of machine, which isn't to say that their machines determine different kinds of society but that they express the social forms capable of producing them and making use of them. The old sovereign societies worked with simple machines, levers, pulleys, clocks; but recent disciplinary societies were equipped with thermodynamic machines presenting the passive danger of entropy and the active danger of sabotage; control societies function with a third generation of machines with information technology and computers, where the passive danger is noise and the active, piracy and viral contamination.[3]

All of these probable dangers, of course, come from within the culture rather than from without. Under the old superstructure, the disciplinary system existed outside of the remainder of social life; it was the operation of the state and the public would witness the results of these operations, but the mechanisms that brought them about were entirely separate from them. Power was something that had a location and a separate life from the majority of the population and though they could sometimes feel the effects of that power directly, they were not given insight or the opportunity for input into the way power functioned. Where Castel noted the disappearance of the subject, Deleuze, Hardt, and Negri see the emergence of a multitude of subjects. The expansion of the system of identifying subjects results an exponential increase in number rather than the disappearance of subjects because the system of identification requires reusable terms and categories—terms and categories that could feasibly be applied to everyone.

The purpose behind this is relatively simple. With the expansion of the ability of the state to monitor its citizens comes a predictable fear among those surveilled that the process will be abused. The application of abstract modes of evaluation, supposedly non-determinational signifiers that could be applied to anyone,[4] hopefully dampens the fears that come about as a result. Whether this works in practice probably depends on the situation and those involved in the actual gathering of information. Those ugly possibilities, the experience of harassment and dubious arrest that many African-ancestored males experience in the West ("If they've done nothing wrong, they have nothing to fear"), for instance, involve the application of statistical factors that result in the creation and the determination of subjects. These are, for instance, the justifications used for the creation of "stop and search" practices by police forces even though they have clearly resulted in the application of those practices to specific groups within society rather than society as a whole. And it is this process of developing reusable abstract codifications for people that can both simplify the process of surveillance and at the same time trap sections of the population under jargon and codifications that limit their autonomy and agency.

Exercises of power are, however, most effective when they are demonstrated to be "legitimate" according to the mores and standards of the state in question. The production of infallibility in the intelligence the state gathers on its own population is an opportunity to increase demonstrations of the power of the state while maintaining the appearance of legitimacy. Here it is necessary to resurrect Castel's argument. Though the subject has not disappeared, the process of determination, now couched in supposedly technical processes, appears to have a degree of legitimacy that previous modes did not. CCTV surveillance is often carried out in areas that have higher than average crime rates. The connection between crime and poverty or a lack of social structure in a given area is somehow overshadowed by the production of filmed evidence that suggests the population is criminal. The properties or characteristics of the subject are still determined by the properties of the CCTV recording.

Guy Debord examined the social effects of visual culture and an increase in the social fascination with images and spectacle in depth. He called it a "diffuse apparatus of images and ideas that produces and regulates public discourse and opinion."[5] In the process of producing surveillance images, the social impression of what surveillance images mean, or why an area might be under surveillance, is integrated into the viewer's initial impressions of the image. The image has the ability to determine political positions as well as dampen opposition to the dominant social order. The emphasis on images, which gives power a visual property, results in a general acceptance of the reliability of the visual. Programs like *America's Dumbest Criminals*, which aired between 1996 and 2000, and *World's Wildest Police Videos*,[6] which aired between 1998 and 2001, were comprised almost entirely of CCTV footage, make subjects archetypal stooges who deserve the benevolent violence of the state.

America's Dumbest Criminals featured voice-over commentary linked to images of stick-up artists unable to exit jewelry stores after robberies because they were pushing rather than pulling on the exit door or rushing out of a business they'd just robbed only to realize that they'd locked the keys inside the getaway car. The voice-over gleefully pointed out every silly mistake made by the assailant and typically closed each story by telling the audience what the offender was charged with and how long their sentence was upon conviction. *Worlds' Wildest Police Chases* generally involved surveillance footage shot by police helicopters during car chases between police and suspects. The normal end for each story told is a car accident followed by a coordinated assault by police officers and the arrest of the suspects. In both cases, there is absolutely no context apart from the very minimal properties of the surveillance image—normally the image is of the quality you would expect from Closed Circuit Television cameras or shot from a significant distance as is natural when the camera is mounted on the bottom of a helicopter shooting events on the ground—and the voice-over of the television show's presenter alternating between humorous observations and righteous condemnation of the subjects.

Those depicted by these television programs have, as mentioned above, their individuality modified by the "types" or categories that apply to surveillance of subjects. There is a removal of individual histories in that the circumstances that might have led to the chase or the robbery disappear and they simply are labeled as "the criminal" in a repeatable comedy that changes setting but never context. It fundamentally limits the discourse around what could be a complex situation. It also has the effect of depriving the people captured on film of any noncontingent substance. The resulting image only portrays action within confined temporal limitations and effectively eliminates any context from the situation.

A quick look at programs like *America's Dumbest Criminals* supports Debord argument that "the fetishistic appearance of pure objectivity in spectacular relationships conceals their true relationships between classes."[7] It illustrates how the conversion of surveillance imagery into entertainment programming results in a de-contextualization of individual events and a normalization of prejudicial and often class-based roles in American culture. It also supports Hardt and Negri's argument that the class structure, even though it is perpetuated via the very citizens it oppresses, perpetuates itself according to these modes of representation. These television programs on the one hand provide light entertainment, but on the other hand they carry with them properties of inequality and oppression. Prior to the pure exploitation of reality in series like *America's Dumbest Criminals* and the like, the use of the camera as an instrument of policing would have given those policing activities a degree of credibility. Now that they do exist, however, these absurd reality programs afford an enhancement of that credibility in the sense that they convey a universalized portrayal of the population managing itself. The programs suggest no process, no series of steps designed to ensure fairness or accuracy that compensates for unequal degrees of power granted to police.

VIOLENCE

Most CCTV surveillance of a population is supposedly enacted in order to determine when criminal behavior is taking place. The result of that determination, under ideal circumstances, is the arrest of those who've committed the crime and their subsequent prosecution and punishment. Max Weber's contention that the state maintains a monopoly on the legitimate use of violence[8] underlies these systems of representation, systems that the general population cannot, in most circumstances avoid. The production of a system that retroactively justifies the use of violence is crucial to the overall legitimization of the idea of rooting that legitimacy in the state. From a Weberian perspective, CCTV can be seen as a continuation of a process by which the legitimation of acts of physical assault and coercion by the state is determined.

The only thing that separates arrest from assault and kidnapping is a process of justification by the state that legitimates that initial use of violence. The initial talismans are supposed to be the uniform and the badge or object identifying that specific individual as personally affiliated with the state and therefore exempt from some of its professed norms. The result of bad behavior on the part of those who have previously held those positions, however, has resulted in the development of control systems that monitor those who are permitted exceptions in behavior that supposedly support the stability of the society. This overture toward monitoring those who hypothetically embody the state moves the process of governing from faith in separate individuals to the development of an abstract system that supposedly is invulnerable to bias or corruption.

Recently I was talking with a friend of mine who has joined the legal profession. We'd been discussing the amount of time spent trying cases and the material and temporal demands this puts on those involved in the prosecution of disputes and decisions. He's also a bit of a technophile and mentioned that there may be a point where the process of arguing legal cases would fall simply to information being entered into a computer program, processed according to an algorithm developed for the purpose, and the judgment would emerge out of the functioning of that system. My concern that, no matter how careful the production of the process, the architects would necessarily be human and therefore vulnerable to any number of prejudices and unintentional mistakes did not phase him. The fact that the system could be built and subsequently instructed to monitor the validity of its own impulses was enough to convince him that it would be an improvement on the use of an individual judge or jury to decide cases. This belief in the inherent rectitude of mechanical systems is not, of course, confined to my friend. The adoption of any number of mechanical systems in aid of managing a society is essentially based on the same beliefs. The trust in the idea that machines are incapable of bias is so potent that the introduction of a machine into a process as delicate as the determination of guilt or innocence somehow cleanses the outcome of that deliberation. The production of violence by the state is somehow less troublesome when the call to action or the justification for it is run through some sort of technological apparatus.

Scott McQuire has argued that "the presence of a camera has long been accepted as a sign of accession to subjecthood."[9] If this is so then the use of CCTV as a method of both claiming space and justifying state violence by means of the camera begins to look like a logical approach. McQuire's work on media and architecture is particularly useful in that it explores how the meaning of the camera has shifted. He argues that "the camera is no longer experienced as the eye of punishment as it has been for Orwell and Foucault, but has become a means for conducting experiments in self-construction."[10] This compulsion to create representations of the self allows for a decreased sense of violation at the realization that we are being photographed and recorded and, more importantly, adds a new degree of acceptance in the validity and the importance of the image. That these representations are invariably folded into the state's justification process is the reason for the resulting acceptance of the process of surveillance as well as a belief in the rectitude of the judgments made by the state.

In the end, efforts to discourage the population's use of violence are a fundamental component of all governmental systems. The problem is that the methods that comprise government are ones that function reactively. When warnings are made, usually in form of codes of law and penal procedures, regarding the deviance of certain types of conduct, this is not the government in action. Imprisoning people, sending columns of police officers after protesters in an effort to "take back the streets," for instance, are the images that come to mind regarding the government in action. It is crucial to focus on the fact that these are actions made in response to something happening. The efficacy of any governmental act of violence is determined retroactively.

When Foucault argued that "Power cannot be exercised unless a certain economy of discourses of truth functions in, on the basis of, and thanks to, that power,"[11] he was talking about justification. The saturation of the streets of Toronto with CCTV cameras ahead of the 2010 G20 summit, the pandemic of surveillance in London, the erection of cameras connected to experimental facial recognition software at border crossings are all programs that are designed to justify subsequent acts of violence on the part of the state. The process of justification that Foucault described is the gathering of evidence that supports actions against the public. The evidence, presented as true, is accepted as true and the violence carried out is deemed appropriate.

The state therefore maintains the appearance of control via the use of these discourses of truth. It can maintain this appearance of control by judging the legitimacy of its own violence after the fact. The production of evidence, of a record of the acts that justify the state acting against members of the public or that demonstrate the state's observation of its own security forces, almost hints at a degree of equality between the citizen and the members of the security forces. The fallacy of this impression is obvious to anyone who is willing to test the theory, but the repeated justification for the use of CCTV across a number of security forces is that the camera is a tool for ensuring safety and assigning blame where blame is necessary. This demonstration should, in theory, generate approval of both the violent actions of the state and the methods used to gather the evidence in the first place.

If Weber's allegation that the stability of the state depends on its ownership of legitimate versus illegitimate violence is accepted, the critical question becomes how that determination is made. The process of communication is typically framed around a notion of egalitarian exchange. One person speaks, another person listens; one person produces images, the other person views them; and so on. The existence of a power dynamic, however, has an impact on the way communication is received. The mechanisms used by the state to produce evidence will not function in the same way when the camera is turned around. The egregious number of civil rights abuses committed at the Toronto G20 summit are still coming to light, but photographic evidence of police carrying out unwarranted assaults, even evidence produced by the state's own cameras, has done little to effect any substantial punishment for the officers recorded in those images. If the situation is reversed, of course, the image serves as the key element in speedy and effective prosecutions.

For the purposes of this argument, Weber's most important argument is that the state's authority rests in its determination of legitimate versus illegitimate use of violence. While it is true that the determination of legitimacy is what gives a state its stability, that dynamic only comes into play once the state has already defined itself. In order for the claim of legitimacy to be made in the first place, the balance of power must be tilted in favor of the state. As such, the CCTV camera functions as both an emblem of the condition of power in a society and as a process of justification for the practices used to maintain that power.

POSITIONING

Mitchell Dean summarizes Foucault's idea of governmentality as the "conduct of conduct." The ideal conclusion of this process would be what Foucault referred to in his later work as "states of domination."[12] What both Dean and Foucault were really talking about is a stabilization of the relationship between an entity that holds power in a state and a multitude that is both subject to and the guarantor of that power. This idea of "domination" is one that requires two stable conditions: the monopoly on the review of the use of violence—Weber's theoretic—and a system by which the state can monitor the behavior of its own population. In the previous section it was determined that the CCTV camera was, in both an active and a reactive sense, a mechanism for justifying state violence and determining that the flow of interpretation only goes in one direction. The state creates the apparatus for surveillance and consequently controls the perspective. This question of "positioning," or of determining the location of what CCTV surveillance really is, is intrinsically linked to these two properties. The determinacy of legitimacy or illegitimacy depends entirely on its ability to produce and reproduce reliable intelligence about a state's own citizenry.

Colin Gordon points out that "the finitude of the State's power to act is an immediate consequence of the limitation of its power to know."[13] Referring back to the Toronto G20 again, the primary frustration reported at the command center was the result of an inability to generate continuous and accurate information regarding what was happening on the street. While it might appear at first that this was a personal frustration with a feeling of powerlessness on the part of what are normally very powerful people, it is much more likely that the fear emerged from an instinctive recognition that, without accurate information, the carefully structured security system put in place for the summit could not function. In other words, the repressive capacity of the Toronto Police Service was limited to its ability to relay accurate information from the street level back to central command. Central command would then be able to coordinate multiple actors and overwhelm whatever opposition might be bubbling up at that moment.

The dynamic shifts in light of the murder of Ian Tomlinson in London. The saturation of CCTV cameras could be described as constituting a pandemic.

Londoners, as a group, have generally become accustomed to the notion that they are on camera most of the time when moving about the city. The fact that Mr. Tomlinson was attacked near the Bank of England meant that it was obvious to anyone that he would be under police surveillance the whole time he was in the area. Quite apart from the specific reasons to be watching on April 1, on the day of the demonstrations, the government's perpetual fear of terrorist attack would necessitate CCTV coverage of the area around such a significant landmark. It should hardly come as a surprise, then, that when the head of the Independent Police Complaints Commission (IPCC) stated that there was "no CCTV footage" of the events leading to Mr. Tomlinson's death, the announcement was greeted with utter disbelief.[14] Where it happened was enough to convince those outside of the state that the surveillance structure must have been watching.

According to Gordon, "[p]olice science seems to aspire to constitute a kind of governed reality, the sensorium of a Leviathan."[15] This Leviathan may carry out its administrative functions far from the reach of regular citizens, but its capacity to see and to feel the actions of its subjects puts components of it into direct contact with the population whether it is desirable or not. The Tomlinson case is fascinating in this respect as it marks a moment when the saturation coverage of the surveillance system has removed any hope of the state being able plausibly to deny its operation. The burden of total surveillance is the knowledge on the part of those watched that everything has been recorded. Those who were interested in the circumstances surrounding Mr. Tomlinson's death could not have rationally been expected to believe that the assault had taken place in a blind spot. Photos of CCTV cameras were produced almost instantly after the announcement had been made by the IPCC.

Though Stephen Graham notes in a number of passages in his book *Cities Under Siege* that the use of unmanned drones is becoming increasingly common for domestic surveillance, urban environments still rely on methods of tracking that are obvious to the citizens who occupy that space. Part of the reason for this control, of course, is that: "We know that you know that we know." Citizens are aware that they are being monitored and, according to the Benthamite dream, the fact that they are results in better behavior. The flaw here is that the same system that announces itself as capable of tracking all behavior everywhere cannot suddenly deny those capabilities when elements of that system have misbehaved. The door swings both ways. The extension of the corpus of the state in the form of electronic media results in a keen awareness of the capabilities of the state on the part of the citizens. The reaction to the suggestion that there was no CCTV footage was as much personal as it was logical. Anyone who has navigated the streets of London in the twenty-first century knows how hard it is to stay out of sight. Mr. Tomlinson was attacked in broad daylight during a massive demonstration around an international trade summit. There could be no anonymity of place, no gap in the feed under those circumstances.

VISIBILITY/INVISIBILITY

Paralleling Richard Dyer's racial assertions in "White,"[16] the true power in Western culture is to be invisible. Invisibility, from Dyer's perspective, is embodied in the property of looking or being "normal" or typical. In other words, the ideal situation is to appear to be generic enough not to be noticed. The identification of the "other" in a culture—the communication to the population that there is an alien entity that must be rooted out for the good of the rest of the population is a standard political and governmental tactic. The tendency is to point to the extreme examples of this like Germany under the Nazis, the atrocities of the Khmer Rouge or the Rwandan Genocide. Though these are legitimate examples, they exist at the exceptional extreme when identification of the unwanted other spirals into madness. Much more common is the determination of the unwanted other or the other that is tolerated as intrinsic to the functioning of the state. Those who are poor or ideologically opposed to the current state structure are obvious examples of a tolerated but alienated component of the population.

In his research, Dyer was illustrating the intrinsic alienation of non-Caucasian persons in filmic presentations created in white European and North American culture. That being the case, I think it is possible to—hopefully without causing any offense—carry this principle of inevitable identification as a precursor to abuse over to this discussion on state surveillance. The use of CCTV conjures up troubling questions with respect to the use of visual signifiers as a means of determining potential deviance. In the case of large street protests, it would seem as though the determination of targets is relatively straightforward. During the Toronto G20, those reviewing whatever images were available openly admitted to focusing on anyone, "wear[ing] black clothing, balaclavas, scarves, hoodies, ski masks, motorcycle helmets with padding or other concealing items [. . .] carry[ing] backpacks for extra clothing, projectiles, weapons, gas masks and the like."[17] The likelihood of a backpack carrying any of those objects or a scarf simply being worn either as a political statement or as a buttress against the effects of probable teargas use on the part of the police does not matter in this instance. This type of visual identification has to function in an openly prejudicial context. There is no point to it otherwise.

The problem, then, resides in the general perception that one's condition of exclusion in contemporary Western culture is temporary. The mythology of upward mobility in most countries in the West softens the perception of being identified as the unwanted or the undesirable. The horror of being immediately identifiable as undesirable is somehow mitigated when social conditions are framed as transitory. The absurdity of this statement is surely apparent right away: the visual signifier of being black still carries an enormous social burden in the United States regardless of who is sitting in the Oval Office. Referential structures that identify those who are a concern for the state security system still operate on relatively unenlightened schematics—"stop and search" procedures in both Britain and the United States overwhelmingly affect adolescent members of visible minority communities disproportionate to their white peers.

The process of determination, of singling out, is at the root of the process of surveillance. CCTV provides a mechanical detachment that allows for a lukewarm type of deniability on the part of the state. The introduction of the electronic medium gives the appearance of impartiality, but as the review of that footage will inevitably be carried out by a member of the dominant culture, there is little hope that the mechanism can in fact cleanse the interpretation. The act of distancing the social prejudices from the determinations made due to the footage is not unlike the traditional construction of a firing squad: the inclusion of one or more shooters who are unknowingly firing blank cartridges rather than live rounds allows for a disavowal of personal responsibility. The reliance on the cold, unemotional essence of technological recording follows these same lines. The apparatus establishes a distance between the event and the observer.

It is worth noting that, even before the firing squad is assembled, the use of a gun rather than an ax drastically improves the odds that a person will attempt to kill. It has long been understood in military circles that the use of technology that allows the decision to kill to be made from a significant distance results in a higher likelihood that a person will pull the trigger with intent to end the life of another person.[18] The reason I bring this up is simple: Is it possible that the use of the electronic medium allows for the same type of suspension in morality? The use of an apparatus often enables people to do things that they would otherwise find very distasteful or know that others would find distasteful. A bigoted interpretation of the product of a CCTV feed would have to be easier to administer when the person reviewing the feed does not actually have to share the same space as the subjects in question. The removal of the active component of surveilling people would result in a further dehumanization of the subjects.

This is, at a basic level, the point at which the technology of surveillance intersects with Dyer's narrative on race and invisibility. Being visible carries with it its own challenges. The implementation of a system whereby the curse of visibility is enacted through a mechanism that washes away all of the social niceties that are woven into direct human interaction, however, is immeasurably worse. CCTV, in a very real way, allows for the typecasting of every subject created by the recording. It simplifies the act of evaluating a person to the point that individual or considered, lengthy observation of the person is no longer necessary in making determinations about them. It is, therefore, a technology of visibility that removes the human aspect of watching someone that normally required to make determinations.

This question of visibility, then, is both complicated and enhanced when CCTV surveillance is added to the mix. The degree to which technology reduces the humanity of the individual making use of the technology can be substantial. The degree to which a culture can make one group of people extremely visible and another vanish entirely is astonishing.

CONNECTIONS

The problem is that the purity of the mechanism that establishes this visibility can only be evaluated through the interpretation being made by an individual, or a system of individuals, and that the impetus behind the implementation of the mechanism results from evaluation of the subjects of the surveillance equipment, but who are never in charge of its use. The degree to which the interpretation of the events transpiring on screen can vary from the actual experience of the events that the camera records is staggering, yet the accuracy and reliability of the mechanisms that the state employs to control its population is paramount in the justifications it makes for their use. To reveal that the camera was not effectively relating or explaining the details of a situation would call into question the appropriateness of its use.

Dean argues that "If government is to achieve ends, or seeks to realize values, it must use technical means. Those technical means are a condition of governing and often impose limits over what it is possible to do."[19] The technical means that Dean is talking about are not those that involve wires, batteries and lenses, but those that exist in a theoretical light. He means practices of governing and the schematic methods that states will use to manage themselves. From trade policies to traffic laws, the technical means will, however, require some apparatus that allows the state to determine the efficacy of its own policies and infrastructure. The monitoring of trade flows is integral to determining the health of an economy. The use of police to fine motorists caught exceeding speed limits is tracked and recorded. Both of these schematics involve complex recording and information sharing processes that allow different branches of government to keep tabs on the population at all times.

These tools that allow a state to function are enacted in the interest of stabilizing the state—of ensuring that what it claims to be true can be demonstrated as such. The use of the image, of the camera, as a means to carry this out creates an aura of impartiality while still leaving the means of interpretation in the hands of the entity that is most likely to abuse it. I would not go so far as to accuse Nick Hardwick, the chair of the IPCC, of lying to the public when he stated that there was no CCTV footage of the Tomlinson killing. I would, however, suggest that the information he was relating to the public was gathered from police officers—officers who would have had a personal interest in maintaining the public image of the police service and potentially a personal relationship with the officer responsible for Mr. Tomlinson's death.

The monopolization of the means to review footage, of the very determination of the efficacy of a technology as an aid in the establishment of control, seems to preclude the experience of the people under surveillance. However, in a world in which those who were on the street have their own cameras and are able to post photographs of CCTV cameras functioning in the area in which the incident took place immediately after the existence of CCTV footage has been denied, this ownership of the technique might not be as absolute at the state would like it to be. The difficulty for the state is that the technical means of monitoring people that is CCTV, at least for the moment, has to be out in the open. Whereas the sources of human intelligence (i.e., witnesses) are easy enough to lose or to make disappear in chaotic events, the camera is typically erected as a permanent component of the landscape. Its installation is the ultimate expression of the state's confidence in the public's faith in its benevolence.

When this faith erodes, however, the flow of influence can threaten to move in the opposite direction. If it is believed that someone is behind the CCTV camera who is actively watching the feed or that a recording is in progress that will later be able to provide proof of an event, the subject's understanding of the process fits into a larger schematic. Namely, that there is a record of events. It is a record that is not limited to the memory of those who might have performed the acts that have been witnessed by the camera, as was the case in London at the time of the G20 summit. Head of the IPCC, Nick Hardwick would have been able to suggest that the details of Mr. Tomlinson's interaction with police were lost in the chaos of the situation were it not for the presence of a surveillance mechanism giving numerous points of view. This would be the point at which the reason behind one of Bentham's major innovations in the schematic for the Panopticon is more easily understood: It was determined that, though the guard in the central tower would be able to see into every cell at all times, none of those inmates would be able to do the reverse. The stated rationale being that, under the constant threat of surveillance each inmate would naturally become a model prisoner. It was even claimed that, as long as it was assumed that there was a guard in the tower, the tower could in fact be left vacant; the inmates would monitor their own behavior out of uncertainty and fear. Well, now that CCTV has moved the surveillance apparatus outside of the prison walls, the security forces are supposedly under the watchful eye of the tower as well. To suggest that there is no record would be to suggest that records had never been kept—that there was, in fact, never a guard in the tower.

The result, then, is that the state must admit the efficacy of its own surveillance systems or lose the reason it has used to justify using them. The assertion that there is validity in the data collected via CCTV carries with it an obligation to demonstrate efficacy when it is called upon to do so. The fact that Hardwick initially denied the existence of the CCTV footage of Mr. Tomlinson's killing speaks either to the continued dependency on human intelligence even with a surveillance system demonstrably in place or a lack of enthusiasm to turn the cameras around in the other direction (so to speak). The publishing of photographs of very visible CCTV cameras in the area around the Bank of England after Mr. Hardwick made his announcement represented a momentary shift in the normal use of the cameras.[20] That members of the public could demonstrate the state surveillance system would have captured the events of Mr. Tomlinson's and effectively trump the police service's plausible deniability puts the police services in a very difficult position. Either the CCTV system does not actually work and there really is no footage of the attack on Mr. Tomlinson or there is footage and it depicts the bad behavior of a member of the police service. For the purposes of this analysis, the most notable thing about the Tomlinson case is the fact that the public were able to point to the physical evidence of a surveillance structure and challenge a professed lack of knowledge claimed by the government by pointing to state's own surveillance system.

NOTES

1. G. Burchell, C. Gordon, P. Miller, & M. Foucault, *The Foucault Effect: Studies in Governmentality* (London: Harvester Wheatsheaf, 1991), 288.
2. M. Hardt, & A. Negri, *Empire* (Cambridge, MA: Harvard University Press, 2000), 318–319.
3. G. Deleuze, *Negotiations* (New York: Columbia University Press, 1995), 180.
4. On the face of it the absurdity of this suggestion is obvious. Modalities of determination—ways in which people who are charged with monitoring populations—are always culturally biased.
5. M. Hardt, & A. Negri, *Empire* (Cambridge, MA: Harvard University Press, 2000), 321.
6. *World's Wildest Police Videos* was originally produced in the United States by the FOX network but later appeared in Hungary, Sweden, Iceland, the United Kingdom and several other countries. *America's Dumbest Criminals* was also originally produced in the United States, and was also broadcast in Scandanavia, the

United Kingdom, Spain, Australia, and New Zealand. Both programs were promoted to a younger male audience and in both cases enjoyed a significant amount of commercial success during their production runs.

7. G. Debord, *The Society of the Spectacle* (New York: Zone Books, 2004), 19.

8. C. Shearing, "Reflections on the refusal to acknowledge private governments" in *Democracy, Society and the Governance of Security* (Cambridge, UK: Cambridge University Press, 2006), 21–22.

9. S. McQuire, *The Media City: Media, Architecture and Urban Space* (London: Sage, 2008), 195.

10. Ibid.

11. M. Foucault, *Society Must Be Defended* (London: Penguin, 2003), 24.

12. M. Dean, *Governmentality: Power and Rule in Modern Society* (London: Sage, 1999), 35.

13. G. Burchell, C. Gordon, P. Miller, & M. Foucault, *The Foucault Effect: Studies in Governmentality* (London: Harvester Wheatsheaf, 1991), 16.

14. P. Lewis, "Police watchdog chief wrong to say no CCTV in area of Ian Tomlinson assault." *The Guardian.* April 14, 2009. Web. June 28, 2012.

15. G. Burchell, C. Gordon, P. Miller, & M. Foucault, *The Foucault Effect: Studies in Governmentality* (London: Harvester Wheatsheaf, 1991), 10.

16. R. Dyer, "White" *Screen* 24, no. 4 (1988), 44–65.

17. G. McNeilly, *Policing the Right to Protest: G20 Systemic Review Report.* Office of the Independent Police Review Director. 2012. Web. 12.

18. D. Grossman, *On Killing: The Psychological Cost of Learning to Kill in War and Society* (Boston: Back Bay, 1996), 99.

19. M. Dean, *Governmentality: Power and Rule in Modern Society* (London: Sage, 1999), 31.

20. P. Lewis, "Police Watchdog Chief Wrong to Say No CCTV in Area of Ian Tomlinson Assault." *Guardian Online.* April 14, 2009. Web. May 17, 2009.

Conclusion

On July 16, 2015, a man named James McIntyre was shot to death by a member of the Royal Canadian Mounted Police outside a public meeting in Dawson Creek, British Columbia. The meeting had been called as a public hearing around the "Site C" hydroelectric dam project proposed by BC Hydro. The dam would be located on the Peace River in northern British Columbia and would (reportedly) require or result in the flooding of 57,000 acres of land along the Peace River valley. There are a number of groups, both First Nations and environmental, who are vocally opposed to the project. It does not appear that Mr. McIntyre was affiliated with any of them on an official level, but it does appear from his Twitter account (@jaymack9) that he was affiliated in some way with the hacker collective known as Anonymous.[1]

Mr. McIntyre was reported to have been wearing one of the Guy Fawkes Masks popularized by Alan Moore's *V for Vendetta* graphic novel and typically associated with the hacker collective known as Anonymous during the protest. Many of the details of the shooting are still being parsed out. That said, the suggestion that McIntyre was affiliated with Anonymous hasn't been challenged by those sympathetic to the victim or by those who are defending the actions that killed him.

Confirmation that he was a member of the collective came with the subsequent announcement video posted on an Anonymous affiliate/sympathizer's YouTube channel.[2] The announcement is voiced over a partially obscured mobile phone video of McIntyre's shooting. The video announces a new "Op" or "Operation" entitled "OpAnonDown" and promises retaliation for the killing of their "comrade." The video is clearly intended to function as proof of the illegality of the shooting and as justification for the outrage evident in the text of the announcement. Hacks were carried out against the RCMP servers after the video was posted and there were vague allusions to a planned leak of sensitive documents hacked from government servers, but little has come to light at the time of writing.

The video does raise some troubling issues, however. The RCMP officer is clearly a good distance away from McIntyre before McIntyre hits the ground. He appears to only be carrying a knife and whether he's waving it at the RCMP officer or not is unclear. The shooting does appear to be unnecessary and will naturally require an investigation. This is known because the footage was made public by private citizens and, in this instance, it does appear that the ability to create records of police actions can be a deciding factor in questioning the legitimacy of police procedures.

On April 4, 2015, a man named Walter Scott was pulled over for a malfunctioning brake light in Charleston, South Carolina. The owner of the car, Mr. Scott ran away from the police officer, Michael Slager, who then chased him to a vacant lot a short distance away. Subsequent reports have indicated that Mr. Scott owed back payments for child support and may have feared he would be arrested as a result. Whatever the case, the chase took the two men into a vacant lot next to a muffler shop. The police later claimed that Officer Slager, after catching up to the suspect fired his Taser at Mr. Scott but it failed to stop him. The two grappled while the stun gun was still attached to Mr. Scott. Mr. Scott broke free and ran away from Officer Slager. Slager drew his firearm and reportedly fired eight times at Mr. Scott as he ran away. Five of the rounds struck Walter Scott—at least one hitting his heart—and he fell to the ground. He died at the scene.[3]

A bystander named Feidin Santana filmed the confrontation in the vacant lot with his cell phone.[4] After Mr. Scott had fallen to the ground, Officer Slager reportedly radioed that shots had been fired and that "He took my Taser."[5] The video shows the officer holstering his weapon after firing, running back to the site of the original wrestling match, picking a black object up off the ground, walking back over to Scott's body and dropping the object on the ground. The police report indicated that the officers delivered first aid and performed CPR on Mr. Scott however the video taken by the bystander shows that Mr. Scott lay unassisted and handcuffed on the ground for several minutes until another officer attended to him. There was no footage that supported the claim that CPR had been performed.[6] Mr. Scott's family's lawyer forwarded the video of the incident to the *New York Times* (it is unclear how they came to be in possession of it in the first place). The *Times* published the video online. Officer Slager was fired from the police force shortly after and, in June 2015, was formally charged with the murder of Walter Scott.[7] Slager's murder trial ended in a mistrial but he pleaded guilty to violating Mr. Scott's civil rights in 2017. Slager's appeal against his 20 year sentence was denied in April of 2021.[8]

As a final example, a man named Eric Garner was choked to death by New York Police Department officer Daniel Pantaleo on July 17, 2014. He'd been stopped by NYPD officers under suspicion of selling untaxed cigarettes, possession of marijuana, and false impersonation. Mr. Garner refused to be arrested and Pantaleo put him in a chokehold and wrestled him to the ground.[9] Video of the incident was captured by a number of people, but Ramsay Orta's film of the event is the most widely viewed. The video was reproduced and viewed globally and became a central text in the emerging Black Lives Matter movement. It became a particular rallying cry after the grand jury declined to indict Officer Pantaleo in connection to Garner's death.[10] Mr. Orta has claimed that, as a result of being the person who recorded the image, he has been the subject of targeted harassment by the New York Police Department and has had to leave his home in Staten Island.[11] This has also been an issue for Feidin Santana—the witness who filmed the killing of Walter Scott. He now claims to be the target of police harassment and fears walking around his old neighborhood at night.[12]

This is nothing new of course. From Daniel Ellsberg to Edward Snowden, whistleblowers have frequently faced reprisals for releasing information that is damaging to powerful people or organizations. The fact that virtually everyone carries in their pocket or purse the capability of filming any event at any time is, however, relatively recent. The expansion of the camera beyond those (often) large, purpose-built pieces of equipment to the integrated communications devices flippantly called "smart phones" has democratized surveillance to a significant extent. The focus of this book has been the evaluation of CCTV as a component of government prosecutorial power, and this is still a potent element of the structure of power and control in the United Kingdom, Canada, and the United States (among other places). More and more, however, those structures that depended on the lens being pointed away from them are finding themselves subject to the same kind of image-based determinacy because of a private citizen's mobile phone. Clearly, this is progress.

In 2008, UK police announced that the data-gathering infrastructure that allowed London's congestion policies to be implemented—digitally sensed license plates and the digital tracking of moving vehicles—would be shared with MI5 and accessed by counterterrorism personnel. According to Stephen Graham, this program was designed to expand significantly: "UK police and MI5 are also linking a multitude of CCTV systems, originally established for general traffic management, to their Hendon headquarters in order to establish a national system of vehicle tracking based on number plate recognition."[13]

The modification of existing CCTV systems to incorporate facial recognition software has been a goal for security forces for a long time. It received significant enthusiasm after the events of September 11, 2001,[14] when terrorists hijacked commercial airliners and flew them into the World Trade Center in Manhattan and the Pentagon in the District of Columbia. Kelly Gates refers to this as "technostalgia"; a sort of daydreamed revisionism whereby greater efficacy of surveillance tools might have prevented horrible events from taking place.[15] The fact of the matter, however, is that facial recognition software has been stubbornly difficult to produce and deploy with any real efficacy.[16] The dream, however, does not go away.

The use of drones in both domestic and foreign practices continues to increase as well. Their deployment by American forces is admitted to and justified by regular press announcements. Just within the last two days, the Pentagon announced that a drone strike killed an al-Shabaab leader in Somalia.[17] The interface that pilots use to fly the drones is based on the mechanics and the feel of video game console controllers.[18] This movement from a familiar or established format for technology, whether it be in the augmentation of CCTV systems with facial recognition software or in the use of gaming interfaces to carry out contemporary warfare, does indicate something significant. Namely, that the push to further the viability of existing technologies in systems of control and security is natural and, in many instances, rational.

The scope of government surveillance systems that was revealed in leaks by former NSA contractor Edward Snowden and former United States Army intelligence analyst Chelsea Manning add to this overall impression of the eagerness with which governments will pursue technologies that track individuals. The ability for an increasingly networked existence to track individuals in the form of abstractions is significant. The increasing popularity of paying by debit rather than using cash, the increasing popularity of touch cards as a means of paying for the use of public transportation, the scanning and collecting of Internet use by individuals and organizations as well as the well-known tracking capabilities of mobile phones all contribute to this produced galaxy of biographical data. This data is linked to the identities of people and it has power. It can be used to specify someone out of a group. It can be used to develop more coherent profiles of people. It can, like the footage of the CCTV camera, be used as an evidence of wrongdoing and a justification for state action.

It is, however, abstract. The linkage that the information presented is directly connected to a specific person must be accepted by any person who is shown that data. Much like Jonathan Finn's description of the use of fingerprint evidence as a means of identification, at some point someone must tell someone else that there is a direct connection and that second person must believe it.

Video footage seems different from this somehow. It is a natural condition that viewers trust what they see. The data presented in visual forms seems immediately believable and that is the fundamental difference between surveillance data produced by a camera and the data produced by debit cards or Internet search histories. Like the first judge in the case of *R. v. Nikolovski*, the tendency is to believe that viewers do not need someone to interpret video footage or still images for them. It appears to be self-evident. And while a significant amount of the surveillance that the public is subjected to is a by-product of the convenient connectedness that comes with recent technological advances, I think it is likely that it seems innocuous precisely because it is abstract information. The push to incorporate networked systems and the production of images in the practice of surveillance makes sense in this light. It is an attempt to include information that does not intrinsically need to be defended or explained—the image—with information that has to be contextualized as a matter of course—the data.

The image will not go away. Its value as a means of identification and as a demonstration of certainty is woven into Western culture to such an extent that it seems foolish to suggest that it could. It also seems rational to assume that existing technologies will be augmented to allow for greater certainties and predictions on the part of security forces. Drones and facial recognition software have been built off of a familiarity and a faith in the link between visual identification and the management of populations. Those technologies that emerge in the future will likely attempt to extend this same balance between the indexical and the abstract.

With the advent of camera phones, the expansion of online communication into previously unanticipated facets of people's lives, and the continuing debate over privacy in all areas of contemporary Western life, there is a tendency to view the CCTV camera as an artifact of a bygone era. The increased networking in communication as well as the emphasis on data security in most security narratives has the effect of obscuring the importance of CCTV in the overall structure of Western culture. Daily life is still being recorded and, at intervals, those recordings are being used redefine the notion of "public space" and to justify the state's violence on its own citizens. In the abstract, the CCTV camera may appear to be an emblem of the beginning of the state's embodiment in technology. Network surveillance technologies like the FBI's Carnivore program or its successor, NaurusInsight, are far more exotic in that they monitor networked communication, leaving the clumsy meat-and-bone of physical presence where it seemingly belongs—in the past.

As much as it is tempting to think that the business of control or the business of maintaining stability is a process that involves a new, weightless humanity, the ways in which the state manages its citizens still come down to the management of their physical bodies. Those bodies still occupy space and still affect things out in the world physically. The mechanisms might change. The procedure might change. The focus, however, never does. New technological innovations might emerge that allow or even require a reassessment of how power functions, but the purpose behind the power remains the same. Whether the tools that enact control are actually designed to control bodies as well, or this is an accidental by-product of their enactment, the assessment of the efficacy of control regimes lies in the extent to which they do indeed control them. Monitoring all of the digital communication in the world will still only document the direction of physical action taken by the state. It will never eliminate it.

The camera, then, is the point of connection between this emergence of networked culture and the bodies we still, for good or ill, occupy. For the purposes of visual surveillance, the image is the point at which the body becomes part of the maelstrom of information; the endless vortex of swirling data that comprises the population's current attempts to communicate, to organize, to function with each other. The surveillance image can serve as a reminder that, when governments introduce control/domination measures like the USAPATRIOT Act or Canada's recent Bill C-30, the determination of the physical person is still the starting and end point of control strategies. The camera—that seemingly antique method of capturing light reflections off solid objects—seems like a natural conduit between the tangible and the ephemeral.

It is true that we are increasingly identified by bits of data, nonsequential bits of code that attempt to connect abstract systems of communication with tangible persons. The frame for positive identification is still the assertion that a physical presence, a blinking, breathing body is in fact the entity being discussed: fingerprints, DNA, "Do you see that person in this courtroom today?" The photo on a driving license or a passport is a profound confirmation of this: possession of knowledge, being able to list off little tidbits of information on command might satisfy the identification procedure enacted when calling the bank, but permitting a person to move around requires visual confirmation that they are who they say they are. Images are trusted in the purest possible sense. They seem to somehow transcend the inherent subjectivity of abstraction. Indeed, they seem to deny abstraction as a matter of course.

It is this seeming property of being self-evident that makes CCTV so attractive. Relying on the image would almost appear to be obvious—"The camera never lies." It is understood what has happened because the viewer has seen it. It can be proven that it has happened in that the video or photographs can be shown to others. The potential pitfalls regarding the subjectivity of the image and the perceptual gaps related to duplication are typically overlooked. The visual must be trusted—it seemingly stands as the only element of communication that does not require interpretation.

It is, to use a McLuhanite term, this "coolness" of the televised medium that causes concern when it comes to CCTV. The cultural acceptance of the accuracy of any system of representation influences the way it is used as well as how the data it transmits is interpreted. If it is generally agreed that the camera is inert, that it has no inherent biases and if it is capable of transmitting its data without demanding too much input from the initial viewer, the degree to which that data can influence events in the life world is profound. The amount of faith the culture has in the reliability of any system of representation directly impacts upon the interpretation of those representations.

Media have a shaping effect on culture. Culture perpetuates itself through the transfer of ideological, political, and artistic modalities; the residue of previous tenants on a specific physical and temporal plane. Going back as far as Egyptian hieroglyphs, the use of reductive media devices has served to make culture more concrete. No longer was the stability of ideas transferred across time dependant on the individual recipient's reproduction of the data—some multigenerational version of the "telephone game." Over vast expanses of time the process of representing human thought became, seemingly, more resilient. The collective record of thought, interaction, and development is now only as fragile and ephemeral as a Gutenberg bible, a phonographic record, or a 1 Terabyte hard drive.

Problems emerge when it is noted that a change in the stability of information flow and the reliability of information transfer from one brain to the next invariably alters the character of the information itself. McLuhan, Baudrillard and a host of others have written about this extensively. What still has to be evaluated, however, is the way in which perpetual information flow impacts upon modes of governing and, as a direct result, affects the polity's relationship with information. Certainly, the advent of the telegraph, the fax machine and email, and other accelerated modes of information exchange have altered the way in which power systems operate. It is well known, for instance, that the primary organizing method for the Tiananmen Square uprising in 1989 was effected through the exchange of faxed messages. What something elemental in the function of legal process and the management and control of populations like CCTV does is reduce the social and physical plane to a series of functions evaluated and validated or condemned by the dominant power structure.

This is the crux of the argument: that these technologies are woven into the collective consciousness. They have become so ubiquitous as to blend into the background and have a significant impact on the subject's experience of the world. Together, they have massive implications for politics, mechanisms of control, the relationship between an individual or group, and the power structure. They also have a significant impact on the position of television as a cultural and social object and an understanding of the role of technology in day-to-day existence.

The recognition of how central, how integral to the contemporary Western urban landscape the televised image and the process of duplication are is paramount to evaluating the conditions of that space. The integration of surveillance and the process of endless duplication into the management of space is one thing, but the subjective effects of the event and the knowledge of it have a very real effect on any subsequent interaction with the life world.

The image, in its purest form, has become part of the overall process of interacting with space. The representation is now woven into the real to such a degree that evaluating one or the other is the result of a kind of willful blindness. It is a blindness that is born of the privileging of the process rather than its history and, in light of what has been learned about the image and its position in the collective experiential terrain, a need to evaluate how these representations are seen as external to the observer. And how fallible that perception really is.

Much of the support for electronic surveillance hinges on the notion that the possibility of human error is drastically diminished by reducing the number of human intervals in the data-gathering process. The trial judge's exclusion of eyewitness testimony in favor of the CCTV footage of the robbery in the case considered earlier of *R. v. Nikolovski* is a clear example of this. In removing the human element from establishing a record of events, it is assumed, the more reliable the data used to evaluate guilt or innocence will be. This is the governmental version of commodity fetishism: These developments do not spring fully grown out of the ether. Decisions are made regarding the disturbance required to activate motion-sensitive cameras, the placement of the cameras themselves, the quality of the image, the method of the accumulation of data—streaming or time-set still image capture—and the purpose or use that goes along with the information once collected. Add to this problem the notion that the image itself is not entirely reliable from a comprehension standpoint and it is difficult not to question the efficacy of the system.

This is the contribution I've attempted to make with this book. The image appears in most cases to be an artifact without agency—a benign representation that serves as an illustration or an exhibit of the functioning of the state. The power that the image has to direct action and to actively justify it normally gets swallowed up in the details of a case like Nicholas Russell Henry's appeal or *R. v. Nikolovski*. The public normally sees CCTV imagery as a component of a news broadcast or repackaged as entertainment on a live-action television show. The agency that the image has in the functioning of the state is much more significant than appears at first glance. Therefore, the goal of this text is to demonstrate the importance of the image in not only legitimizing but also enabling uses of power by the state. This book is an attempt to highlight and bring to the fore the agency intrinsic in the image—to show how it directs power systems to act and modifies the means of justification for those actions.

Going forward, the goal will be to push the understanding of how the image frames the recipient's relationship with the realities supposedly conveyed.

It will be necessary to evaluate what an interaction with images in place of the real does to the understanding of the physical world and whether the demarcation of such divisions is still practical in any procedural sense. Most importantly, it must be determined whether abstraction allows for greater savagery at the same time as it allows for greater immediacy and scope. The introduction of different technologies has allowed for shocking advances in human capabilities; some of them noble, some of them undeniably barbaric. CCTV, to my mind, represents the zero-level of this merging of electric technology and the fight for dominance of domestic space.

The primary examples I've pointed to here—the two G20 summits in London and Toronto—are convenient, encapsulated instances of this larger issue. The degree to which abstraction is considered part of the basic process of managing or controlling space and populations has a direct impact on the procedures and the tactics that the system of control enacts in attempting to control that space. That the upper ranks of the Toronto Police Department were panicking during the demonstrations appears to come down to the fact that they couldn't survey the entire city landscape. That need to have a representation of all space, of all events, so that nothing escapes their attention, is contingent on both an understanding of the potential of technology and the appropriate uses to which it is put.

The fallout is that the process of governing is now inextricably linked to technological processes. The understanding of how these technologies work is crucial to an understanding of the process of government, the efficacy of government and the resulting relationships the multitude has with power systems and with itself. More than any other technological mechanism, CCTV fractures and realigns the contemporary human across internal, metaphysical and external planes. The televised image is no longer simply a vehicle for transmitting visual conditions from one space to another; the function of the image has been granted a stake in the power structure and its incorporation has changed the shape and character of that power structure. In line with McLuhan's terminology, the process of governing has "cooled."

NOTES

1. S. Bein, "Everything We Know About the Death of an Anonymous 'Comrade' in RCMP Shooting" *Vice*. July 20, 2015. Web. March 27, 2016.
2. anon2world, "Anonymous Operation AnonDown" *YouTube*. July 18, 2015. Web. March 27, 2016.
3. M. Schmidt & M. Apuzzo, "South Carolina Officer Is Charged with Murder of Walter Scott." *New York Times*. April 7, 2015. Web. March 28, 2016.

4. Associated Press, "Walter Scott's Family to Receive $6.5m Settlement after Police Shooting." *The Guardian*. October 9, 2015. Web. March 29, 2016.

5. M. Schmidt & M. Apuzzo, "South Carolina Officer Is Charged with Murder of Walter Scott" *New York Times*. April 7, 2015. Web. March 28, 2016.

6. Ibid.

7. J. Swaine, "Former Police Officer Who Shot Walter Scott Indicted for Murder." *The Guardian*. June 8, 2015. Web. March 29, 2016.

8. J. Lynch & J. Hanna, "A judge declined to toss the federal sentence of ex-officer Michael Slager in fatal Walter Scott shooting." *CNN*. April 20, 2021. Web. April 21, 2021.

9. L. Gambino, "Eric Garner: Grand Jury Declines to Indict NYPD Officer over Chokehold Death." *The Guardian*. December 3, 2014. Web. April 1, 2016.

10. J. Glenza, "Anger Mounts over Failure to Indict New York Police Officer in Chokehold Death." *The Guardian*. December 3, 2014. Web. April 1, 2016.

11. J. Sanburn, "The Witness: One Year after Filming Eric Garner's Fatal Confrontation with Police, Ramsey Orta's Life Has Been Upended." *Time*. No date. Web. April 1, 2016.

12. Ibid.

13. S. Graham, *Cities Under Siege: The New Military Urbanism* (New York: Verso, 2010), 328.

14. K. Gates, *Our Biometric Future: Facial Recognition Technology and the Culture of Surveillance* (New York: New York University Press, 2011), 1.

15. Ibid., 2.

16. Ibid., 5.

17. S. Ackerman, "US Drone Strike Kills Key al-Shabaab Leader in Somalia." *The Guardian*. April 1, 2016. Web. April 3, 2016.

18. S. Graham, *Cities Under Siege: The New Military Urbanism* (New York: Verso, 2010), 214–215.

Bibliography

Ackerman, S. (2016). "US Drone Strike Kills Key al-Shabaab Leader in Somalia." *The Guardian*. 1 April 2016. Web. 3 April 2016.

Adams, R. (2014). "CCTV in Classrooms Turning Teachers into Lab Rats, Union Warns." *The Guardian*. 20 April 2014. Web. 24 April 2014.

Adorno, T. (2003). *The Jargon of Authenticity*. London: Routledge Classics.

Adorno, T., Adorno G. & Tiedmann, R. (2004). *Aesthetic Theory*. London: Continuum Impacts.

Adorno, T. & J. M. Bernstein (2001). *The Culture Industry: Selected Essays on Mass Culture*. London: Routledge Classics.

Anrejevic, M. (2007). *iSpy: Surveillance and Power in the Interactive Era*. Lawrence: University Press of Kansas.

Associated Press. "Walter Scott's Family to Receive $6.5m Settlement after Police Shooting." *The Guardian*. 9 October 2015. Web. 29 March 2016.

Baudrillard, J. (1983). *Simulations*. trans. Paul Foss, Paul Patton and Philip Beitchman. Los Angeles: Semiotext[e].

Baudrillard, J. (1989). *America*. trans. Chris Turner. London: Verso.

Baudrillard, J. (1994). *Simulacra and Simulation*. Ann Arbor: University of Michigan Press.

Baudrillard, J. (1995). *The Gulf War Did Not Take Place*. Bloomington: Indiana University Press.

Baudrillard, J. (1996). *The System of Objects*. London: Verso.

Baudrillard, J. (1999). *The Ecstasy of Communication*. trans. Bernard & Caroline Schutze. Los Angeles: Semiotext[e].

Baudrillard, J. (2005a). *The Conspiracy of Art: Manifestos, Interviews, Essays*. New York: Semiotext(e).

Baudrillard, J. (2005b). *The Intelligence of Evil or the Lucidity Pact*. Oxford: Berg.

Baudrillard, J. (2010). *The Agony of Power*. trans. Ames Hodges. Los Angeles: Semiotext[e].

Baudrillard, J. (2012). *The Spirit of Terrorism*. trans. Chris Terrorism. New York: Verso.

Bein, S. (2015). "Everything We Know About the Death of an Anonymous 'Comrade' in RCMP Shooting." Vice. 20 July 2015. Web. 27 March 2016.

Beller, J. (2006). *The Cinematic Mode of Production*. Hanover, NH: Dartmouth College University Press.

Benjamin, W. (2007). *Reflections: Essays, Aphorisms, Autobiographical Writings*. New York: Schocken Books.

"Birmingham: Police Release Street Attack CCTV—Video." *The Guardian*. 20 January 2014. Web. 24 April 2014.

Bogard, W. (1996). *The Simulation of Surveillance: Hypercontrol in Telematic Societies*. Cambridge: Cambridge University Press.

Bowcott, O. (2008). "CCTV Boom Has Failed to Slash Crime, Say Police." *The Guardian*. 6 May 2008. Web. 25 April 2014.

Bowcott, O. (2011). "Law Against Phone Hacking Is Not Working, Says Civil Liberties Group." *The Guardian*. 4 November 2011. Web. 25 April 2014.

Burchell, G., Gordon, C., Miller, P. & Foucault, M. (1991) *The Foucault Effect: Studies in Governmentality*. London: Harvester Wheatsheaf.

Burghart, D. (2014). "What I've Learned from Two Years Collecting Data on Police Killings." *Gawker*. 22 August 2014. Web. 29 April 2015.

Canadian Press (2011). "Vancouver to Considering Adding More CCTV Cameras." *CTV News Online*. 2 September 2011. Web. 24 April 2014.

Chow, R. (2006). *The Age of the World Target: Self-Referentiality in War, Theory, and Comparative Work*. Durham: Duke University Press.

Code of Practice: Stop and Search Under the Terrorism Act 2000. London: The Stationary Office, 2012.

Coleman, R. (2003). "Images from a Neoliberal City: The State, Surveillance and Social Control." *Critical Criminology*. 12(1). 21–42.

Crary, J. (1992). *Techniques of the Observer: On Vision and Modernity in the Nineteenth Century*. Cambridge: The MIT Press.

Crary, J. (1999). *Suspensions of Perception: Attention, Spectacle and Modern Culture*. Cambridge: The MIT Press.

Crockford, K. & Murray, N. (2011). "The Advent of the Surveillance Society." *Truthout.org*. 8 September 2011. Web. 25 April 2014.

Cross, M. (2009). "Explainer: CCTV." *The Guardian*. 6 November 2009. Web. 24 April 2014.

Davies, C. (2014). "Chris Huhne Ordered to Pay £78,000 Costs for Speeding Case." *Guardian Online*. 9 May, 2014. Web. 26 May, 2015.

Dean, M. (1999). *Governmentality: Power and Rule in Modern Society*. London: Sage.

Debord, G. (2004). *The Society of the Spectacle*. trans. Donald Nicholson-Smith. New York: Zone Books.

Deleuze, G. (1995). *Negotiations*. New York: Columbia University Press.

Deleuze, G. (2004). *The Logic of Sense*. trans. Mark Lester. London: Continuum.

Deleuze, G. & Guattari, F. (2004). *A Thousand Plateaus*. New York: Continuum.

Derrida J. (2004). *Dissemination*. trans. Barbara Johnson. London: Continuum.

Derrida, J. & Stiegler, B. (2002). *Echographies of Television: Filmed Interviews*. Cambridge: Polity Press.

Doctorow, C. (2011). "Why CCTV Has Failed to Deter Criminals." *The Guardian*. 17 August 2011. Web. 24 April 2014.

Durham, M. G. & Kellner, D. M. (2002). *Media and Cultural Studies: Key Works*. London: Blackwell.

Dyer, R. (1988). "White." *Screen*. 24(4). 44–65.

Fabianic, D. (1997). "Television Dramas and Homicide Causation." *Journal of Criminal Justice*. 25(3). 195–203.

Feldman, A. (2005). "On the Actuarial Gaze: From 9/11 to Abu Ghraib." *Cultural Studies*. 19(2). 203–226.

Ferguson, E. (2003). "Ten years on." *The Guardian Online*. 9 February 2003. Web. 16 December 2014.

Finn, J. (2009). *Capturing the Criminal Image: From Mug Shot to Surveillance Society*. Minneapolis: University of Minnesota Press.

Ford, R. (2009). "Council Powers to Spy on the Public Are Cut." *Times Online*. Web. 17 May 2009.

Ford, R. & O'Neill, S. (2009) "Blacks Bear Brunt of Rise in Stop and Search." *Times Online*. Web. 19 June 2009.

Foster, H. (1996). *The Return of the Real: the Avant Garde at the End of the Century*. London: MIT Press.

Foucault, M. (1979). *Discipline and Punish: The Birth of the Prison*. Harmondsworth: Penguin.

Foucault, M. (1994). *The Birth of the Clinic: An Archaeology of Medical Perception*. New York: Vintage.

Foucault, M. (2003). *Society Must Be Defended*. London: Penguin.

Foucault, M. (2004). *The Order of Things: An Archaelogy of the Human Sciences*. London: Routlege Classics.

Foucault, M. (2005). *The Hermeneutics of the Subject: Lectures at the College de France 1981–1982*. trans. Graham Burchell. New York: Picador.

Foucault, M. (2007). *Security, Territory, Population: Lectures at the College de France 1977–78*. trans. Graham Burchell. New York: Palgrave MacMillan.

Foucault, M. (2008). *The Birth of Biopolitics: Lectures at the College de France 1978–79*. trans. Graham Burchell. New York: Palgrave MacMillan.

Foucault, M. (2009). *History of Madness*. New York: Routledge.

Foucualt, M. (2010). *Government of Self and Others: Lectures at the College de France 1982–1983*. trans. Graham Burchell. New York: Palgrave MacMillan.

Fussey, P. (2008). "Beyond Liberty, Beyond Security: The Politics of Public Surveillance." *British Politics*. 3(1). London: Palgrave Macmillan. 120–135.

Gambino, L. (2014). "Eric Garner: Grand Jury Declines to Indict NYPD Officer over Chokehold Death." *The Guardian*. 3 December 2014. Web. 1 April 2016.

Gandy Jr., O. (1993). *The Panoptic Sort: A Political Economy of Personal Information*. Boulder: Westview Press.

Gates, K. (2006). "Identifying the 9/11 'Faces of Terror': The Promise and Problem of Facial Recognition Technology." *Cultural Studies*. 20(4). 417–440.

Gates, K. (2011). *Our Biometric Future: Facial Recognition and the Culture of Surveillance*. New York: New York University Press.

Gheclu, A. N. (2013). "Toronto Tenants Complain of 'Double Standard' over Cameras." *The Star Online*. 11 August 2013. Web. 25 April 2014.

Giroux, H. (2006). *Beyond the Spectacle of Terrorism*. London: Paradigm.

Glassner, B. (1999). *The Culture of Fear: Why Americans are Afraid of the Wrong Things*. New York: Basic.

Glenza, J. (2014). "Anger Mounts over Failure to Indict New York Police Officer in Chokehold Death." *The Guardian*. 3 December 2014. Web. 1 April 2016.

Goodwin, C. (1994). "Professional Vision." *American Anthropologist*. 96(3). 606–633.

Goold, B., Loader, I. & Angélica Thumala. (2013). "The Banality of Security." *British Journal of Criminology*. 53. 977–996.

Graham, S. (2010). *Cities Under Siege: The New Military Urbanism*. London: Verso.

Gras, M. L. (2004). "The Legal Regulation of CCTV in Europe." *Surveillance & Society*. 2(2/3). 216–229.

Greenwald, G. (2013). "On the Espionage Act Charges against Edward Snowden." *The Guardian*. 22 June 2013. Web. 26 July 2015.

Groombridge, N. (2008). "Stars of CCTV? How the Home Office Wasted Millions—A Radical 'Treasury/Audit Commission' View." *Surveillance and Society*. 5(1). 73–80.

Habermas, J. (2005). *Legitimation Crisis*. Boston: Beacon Press.

Haggerty, K. & Ericson, R. (Eds.) (2006). *The New Politics of Surveillance and Visibility*. Toronto: University of Toronto Press.

Hardt, M. & Negri, A. (2000). *Empire*. Cambridge, MA: Harvard University Press.

Harris, D. (2012). *Failed Evidence*. New York: New York University Press.

Hasham, A. (2015). "No Jail for Toronto Police Officer Convicted of G20 Assault." *Toronto Star Online*. 29 Jan 2015. Web. 29 June 2015.

Hersh, S (2005). *Chain of Command: The Road From 9/11 to Abu Ghraib*. New York: Harper Perennial.

Hier, S. (2004). "Risky Space and Dangerous Faces: Urban Surveillance, Social Disorder and CCTV." *Social & Legal Studies*. 13(4). 541–554.

Hier, S. P., Greenberg, J., Walby, Kevin & Lett, D. (2007). "Media, Communication and the Establishment of Public Camera Surveillance Programmes in Canada." *Media, Culture & Society*. 29(5). 727–751.

Hough, A. (2012). "CCTV Police Officer 'Chased Himself' after Being Mistaken for Burglar." *The Telegraph Online*. 7 February 2012. Web. 25 April 2014.

James, A. & Jenks, C. (1996). "Public Perceptions of Childhood Criminality." *The British Journal of Sociology*. 47(2). 315–331.

Joyce, J. (2009). "Police 'Kettle' Tactic Feels the Heat." *BBC News*. British Broadcasting Corporation. 16 April 2009. Web. 24 April 2014.

Kellner, D. (1995). *Media Culture: Cultural Studies, Identity and Politics Between the Modern and the Postmodern*. New York: Routledge.

Kroener, I. (2013). "Caught on Camera: The Media Representation of Video Surveillance in Relation to the 2005 London Underground Bombings." *Surveillance & Society*. 11(1/2). 121–133.

Landler, M. (2007). "Where Little Is Left Outside the Camera's Eye." *New York Times Online*. 8 July 2007. Web. 24 April 2014.

Lash, S. (2006). *Critique of Information*. London: Sage.

Laville, S. & Lewis, P. (2009) "G20 Assault: How Metropolitan Police Tried to Manage a Death." *The Guardian*. 9 April 2009. Web. 17 May 2009.

Lefebvre, H. (2004). "Seen from the Window." in *Rhythmanalysis: Space, Time & Everyday Life*. trans. Stuart Elder. London: Athlone.

Leman-Langlois, S. (2002). "The Myopic Panopticon: The Social Consequences of Policing Through the Lens." *Policing and Society*. 13(1). London: Taylor and Francis. 43–58.

Lewis, P. (2009). "Police Watchdog Chief Wrong to Say No CCTV in Area of Ian Tomlinson Assault." *The Guardian e*. 14 April 2009. Web. 17 May 2009.

Lewis, P. (2011). "You're Being Watched: There's one CCTV Camera for Every 32 People in UK." *The Guardian*. 2 March 2011. Web. 24 April 2014.

Lewis, P. & Topham, L. (2009). "CCTV Shows Arrest of Man Who Died in Custody." *The Guardian*. 1 July 2009. Web. 24 April 2014.

Lohr, S. (2013). "How Surveillance Changes Behavior: A Restaurant Workers Case Study." *The New York Times*. 26 August 2013. Web. 28 April 2014.

Lyon, D. (1994). *The Electronic Eye: The Rise of Surveillance Society*. Cambridge: Polity Press.

Lyon, D. (2004). "Globalizing Surveillance: Comparative and Sociological Perspectives." *International Sociology*. 19(2). 135–149.

MacGregor Wise, J. (2004). "An Immense and Unexpected Field of Action: Webcams, Surveillance and Everyday Life." *Cultural Studies*. 18(2/3). 424–442.

Manning, P. (2008). *The Technology of Policing*. New York: New York University Press.

Marcuse, H. (1965). "Repressive Tolerance." *Marcuse.org*. 6 October, 2004. Web. 2 October, 2014.

Marx, K. (1990). *Capital Vol. 1*. London: Penguin Classics.

Mbembé, A. & Meintjes, L. (2003). "Necropolitics." *Public Culture*. 15(1). 11–40.

McCahill, M. & Norris, C. (2002). *Working Paper No. 3: CCTV in Britain*. Hull: Centre for Criminology and Criminal Justice, School of Comparative and Applied Social Sciences.

McCarthy, T. (2015). "Police Killed More Than Twice as Many People as Reported by US Government." *The Guardian*. 4 March, 2015. Web. 14 July, 2015.

McLeland, S. (2011). "Ted Turner." *The Museum of Broadcast Communications*. 7 May, 2011. Web. 24 April 2014.

McLuhan, E. & W. Terrence Gordon (Eds.) (2005). *Marshall McLuhan Unbound*. Corte Madera, CA: Gingko.

McLuhan, E. & Frank Zingrone (Eds.) (1995). *Essential McLuhan*. Concord, ON: Anansi.

McLuhan, M. (1967). *The Mechanical Bride: Folklore of Industrial Man*. London: Routledge.

McLuhan, M. (2001). *Understanding Media: The Extensions of Man*. London: Routledge.

McLuhan, M. (2011). *The Gutenberg Galaxy*. Toronto: The University of Toronto Press.

McLuhan, S. & Powell, P. (1984) *Marshall McLuhan: The Man and His Message*. Perf. Marshall McLuhan. Canadian Broadcasting Corporation.

McNeilly, Gerry (2012) *Policing the Right to Protest: G20 Systemic Review Report*. Office of the Independent Police Review Director. Web. 24 April 2014.

McQuire, S. (2008). *Media City*. London: Sage.

Medina, J. (2012). "Rodney King Dies at 47; Police Beating Victim Who Asked, 'Can We All Get Along?" *The New York Times Online*. 17 June, 2012. Web. 29 June, 2015.

Merleau-Ponty, M. (2008). *Penomenology of Perception*. London: Routledge.

Miller, J. (2010) "Stop and Search in England: A Reformed Tactic or Business as Usual?" *The British Journal of Criminology*. 50(5). 954–974.

Miller, T. (1993). *The Well-Tempered Self: Citizenship, Culture, and the Postmodern Subject*. London: The Johns Hopkins University Press.

Minton, A. (2012). "CCTV Increases People's Sense of Anxiety." *The Guardian*. 30 October 2012. Web. 24 April 2014.

Monbiot, G. (2004). *The Age of Consent: A Manifesto for a New World Order*. London: Harper Perennial.

Moore, A. (1988). *The Killing Joke*. New York: DC Comics.

Morris, H. (2013). "Defenders of Public Spaces Take Inspiration from Turkish Protests." *The New York Times*. 17 June, 2013. Web. 28 April 2014.

Morris, R. (2004). "Images of Untranslatability in the US War on Terror." *Interventions*. 6(3). 401–423.

"Officers of Parliament—Privacy Commissioners 1977 to Date." *Parliament of Canada*. 6 June, 2014. Web. 17 December, 2014.

Olivier, C. (2013). "Record Homicide Rate in Surrey Prompts Mayor to Appoint Task Force." *The Vancouver Sun*. 18 November 2013. Web. 28 April 2014.

Olson, E. (2001). "With Seattle a Vivid Memory, W.T.O. Seeks a New Host City." New York Times Online. 23 January 2001. Web. 19 September 2014.

Omtzigt, P. (2015). "Draft Resolution: Mass Surveillance." *Committee on Legal Affairs and Human Rights*. Council of Europe. Web.

Orr, D. (2013). "Is Domestic Violence a Private Matter Because There's No CCTV at Home?" *The Guardian*. 13 July 2013. Web. 25 April 2014.

Pagilaro, J. (2013). "Police Recover Bikes and Camera Footage in Slayings of O'She Doyles-White and Kwame Duodu." *The Star Online*. 26 August 2013. Web. 24 April 2014.

Palmer, G. (2003). *Discipline and Liberty: Television and Governance*. Manchester: Manchester University Press.

Parness, N. (2010). "Toronto Police Want to Keep Most G20 Security Cameras." *CTV News*. Bell Media. 15 November, 2010. Web. 20 February, 2014.

Patient, D. (2009). "AA and RAC Raised Concerns Over Use of Cameras Which Automatically Issue Fines." *The Guardian*. Newsquest. 19 February, 2014. Web. 20 February, 2014.

Porter, H. (2012). "Hi-def CCTV Technology Threatens Our Democracy—We Must Act Now." *The Guardian*. 3 October 2012. Web. 28 April 2014.

Prasad, Raekha. (2011). "Reading the Riots: 'Humiliating' Stop and Search a Key Factor in Anger Towards Police." Guardian Online. 6 December 2011. Web. 19 September, 2014.

Press Association (2014). "West Ham's James Tomkins' Trial Delayed after Police Lose CCTV Footage." *The Guardian* 17 April 2014. Web. 24 April 2014.

"Profile: Who Is Vicky Pryce?" ITV Report. *ITV News Online*. 7 March 2013. Web. 26 May, 2015.

"Program Sales and Production Details." *European Media Business and Finance*. Potomac: Access Intelligence LLC. 10 February 1997.

POV (2010). "CCTV Cameras: Do They Deter Crime?" *CBC News Online*. 16 November 2010. Web. 24 April 2014.

Robin, C. (2004). *Fear: The History of a Political Idea*. Oxford: Oxford University Press.

Rosenberg, D. & Friend Harding, S. (Eds.) (2005). *Histories of the Future*. Durham, NC: Duke University Press.

Rowley, S. (2009). "Wrongful Conviction Throws Spotlight on Unreliability of Eyewitness Evidence." *The Guardian*. 18 August 2009. Web. 5 May 2012.

Rutherford, P. (2000). *Endless Propaganda: The Advertising of Public Goods*. Toronto: The University of Toronto Press.

Sanburn, J. (2016). "The Witness: One Year after Filming Eric Garner's Fatal Confrontation with Police, Ramsey Orta's Life Has Been Upended." *Time*. No date. Web. 1 April 2016.

Schmitt, C. (1996). *The Concept of the Political*. Chicago: The University of Chicago Press.

Schmidt M. & Apuzzo, M. (2015) "South Carolina Officer is Charged with Murder of Walter Scott." of Walter Scott." The New York Times. 7 April, 2015. Web. 28 March, 2016.

Schneier, B. (2008). "CCTV Doesn't Keep Us Safe, yet the Cameras Are Everywhere." *The Guardian*. 26 June 2008. Web. 25 April 2014.

Scott, I. (2013). "Ways to Improve Ontario's SIU." *The Star Online*. 10 October 2013. Web. 24 April 2014.

Sengupta, S. (2013). "Privacy Fears Grow as Cities Increase Surveillance." *The New York Times*. 13 October 2013. Web. 28 April 2014.

Shoichet, C. & Friedman, C. (2016). "Walter Scott Case: Michael Slager Released from Jail after Posting Bond." *CNN*. 5 January 2016. Web. 31 March 2016.

Sibley, J. (2010). "Evidence Verité and the Law of Film." *Cardozo Law Review*. 31(4). 1257–1299.

Sinoski, K. & Crawford, T. (2014). "TransLink Pushes for Stiffer Sentences for Attacks on Bus Drivers." *The Vancouver Sun*. 27 March 2014. Web. 28 April 2014.

Spigel, L. & Olsson, J. (2004). *Television after TV: Essays on a Medium in Transition*. Durham, NC: Duke University Press.

Stahl, R. (2006). "Have You Played the War on Terror?" *Critical Media Studies*. 23(2). 112–130.

Stallwood, O. (2013). "Game to Destroy CCTV Cameras: Vandalism or Valid Protest." Shortcuts Blog. *Guardian Oline*. 25 January 2013. Web. 24 April 2014.

Sunshine Press (2010). "Collateral Murder—Wikileaks—Iraq." YouTube. 3 April 2010. Web. 24 July 2014.

Swaine, J. (2015). "Former Police Officer Who Shot Walter Scott Indicted for Murder." *The Guardian*. 8 June 2015. Web. 29 March 2016.

Vallis, M. (2010). "G20: Security Cameras Installed on Nearly Every Corner of Downtown Toronto." Posted Toronto. *National Post*. 3 June 2010. Web. 14 August 2014.

Virilio, P. (1994). *The Vision Machine*. Bloomington: Indiana University Press.

Virilio, P. (2005). *The Information Bomb*. London, Verso.

Virilio, P. (2006). *Speed and Politics*. Trans. Marc Polizzotti. Cambridge: The MIT Press.

Walker, P. (2013). "Chris Huhne and Vicky Pryce Each Jailed for Eight Months." *Guardian Online*. 11 March, 2013. Web. 26 May, 2015.

Winchester, S. (2003). *Krakatoa—The Day the World Exploded: August 27, 1883*. New York: Perennial.

Wood, J. & Dupont, B. (Eds.) (2006) *Democracy, Society and the Governance of Security*. Cambridge: Cambridge University Press.

Yesil, B. (2006). "Watching Ourselves: Video Surveillance, Urban Space and Self-Responsibilization." *Cultural Studies*. 20(4). 400–416.

Zerbisias, A. (2014). "Cop Watch App Records Police-Citizen Interactions." *The Star Online*. 28 January 2014. Web. 25 April 2014.

Zielinski, S. (2006). *Deep Time of the Media: Toward an Archaeology of Hearing and Seeing by Technical Means*. Cambridge, MA: MIT Press.

Zimmer, C. (2015). *Surveillance Cinema*. New York: New York University Press.

Žižek, S. (2002). *Welcome to the Desert of the Real! Five Essays on September 11 and Related Dates*. New York: Verso.

Žižek, S. (2005). *Interrogating the Real: Selected Writings*. London: Continuum.

Žižek, S. (2008). *Violence: Six Sideways Reflections*. London: Profile.

FILMS & TELEVISION SERIES

American Beauty. Dir. Sam Mendes. Perf. Kevin Spacey, Annette Bening, Thora Birch, Wes Bentley. DreamWorks Pictures, 1999.

Baraka. Dir. Ron Fricke. The Samuel Goldwyn Company: 1992.

The Bourne Identity. Dir. Doug Liman. Perf. Franka Potente, Matt Damon, Chris Cooper. Universal Studios: 2002.

Clerks. Dir. Kevin Smith. Perf. Brian O'Halloran, Jeff Anderson, Marilyn Ghigliotti. Buena Visa: 1994.

A Clockwork Orange. Dir. Stanley Kubrick. Perf. Malcolm McDowell, Patrick Magee, Michael Bates. Warner Bros.: 1971.

The Dark Knight. Dir. Christopher Nolan. Perf. Christian Bale, Heath Ledger, Maggie Gyllenhaal, Michael Caine. Warner Bros.: 2008.

Fight Club. Dir. David Fincher. Perf. Brad Pitt, Edward Norton, Helena Bonham Carter. 20th Century Fox: 1999.

JFK. Dir. Oliver Stone. Perf. Kevin Costner, Sissy, Spacek, Gary Oldman, Jack Lemmon. Warner Bros.: 1991.
Koyaanisqatsi. Dir. Godfrey Reggio. Perf. Lou Dobbs, Ted Koppel. New Cinema: 1982.
Lie To Me. Perf. Tim Roth, Kelli Williams, Brendan Hines. 20th Century Fox Television, 2009–2011.
Peeping Tom. Dir. Michael Powell. Perf. Karlheinz Böhm, Anna Massey, Moira Shearer. Anglo-Amalgamated Film Distributors, 1960.
Reefer Madness. Perf. Dorothy Short, Kenneth Craig, Lillian Miles. Dir. Louis Gasnier. New Line Cinema: 1936.
Spaceballs. Dir. Mel Brooks. Perf. Mel Brooks, John Candy, Rick Moranis. Metro-Goldwyn-Mayer: 1987.
True Romance. Dir. Tony Scott. Perf. Christian Slater, Patricia Arquette, Dennis Hopper, Christopher Walken. Warner Bros.: 1993.

ONLINE VIDEOS

anon2world. (2015). "Anonymous Operation AnonDown." YouTube. 18 July 2015. Web. 27 March, 2016.

COURT CASES AND LEGAL TEXTS

Browne v. The Commissioner of Police of the Metropolis. 2014 EWHC 3999 (QB). Case No. HQ11X01233. *High Court of Justice, Queen's Bench Division*. HHJ Coe QC.
Canada (Attorney General) v. Bedford. 2013 SCJ 72. *Supreme Court of Canada*. McLachlin, C.J. and LeBel, Fish, Abella, Rothstein, Cromwell, Moldaver, Karakatsanis and Wagner J.J.
Henry v. HM Advocate. 2012 HCJAC 128. Appeal No.: XC724/11. *High Court of the Justiciary*. Opinion delivered by Lord Brodie.
O'Halloran and Francis v. The United Kingdom. 2007. Application Nos. 15809/02 and 25624/02, Grand Chamber. *European Court of Human Rights*. 29 June 2007. Web. 25 May 2015.
Order F2015-02; Alberta (Justice and Solicitor General). Re: Alberta Justice and Solicitor General. 2015. A.I.P.C.D. No.2. Case File Number F7276. *Alberta Information and Privacy Commissioner*. Teresa Cunningham, Adjudicator. 29 January 2015.
Order MO-2758; Hamilton Police Services Board. 2012. O.I.P.C. No. 138. Appeal No. MA11-392. *Ontario Information and Privacy Commissioner*. Bernard Morrow, Adjudicator. 28 June 2012.
Order PO-3405; Ontario (Ministry of Community Safety and Correctional Services). 2014. O.I.P.C. No. 232. Appeal No. PA13-170. Daphne Loukidelis, Adjudicator. 30 September 2014.

Peck v. United Kingdom. 2003 ECHR 44. Application No. 44647/98. *European Court of Human Rights*. Pelonpää, M. and Bratza, Pastor Ridruejo, Fischbach, Maruste, Pavlovschi, Garlicki, O'Boyle.

Peters v. The Chief Constable of West Yorkshire Police. 2014 EWHC 1458. *Leeds Combined Court*. Blair J.

Petriella v. A.G. 2013 JRC 057. *Jersey Royal Court*. Sir Michael Birt, Kt., Bailiff and Jurats Clapham and Crill.

R. v. Akita. 1999. BCJ 868. *British Columbia Provincial Court (Traffic Division)*. Turley J.P.

R. v. Amer. 2014. BCJ 790. *British Columbia Provincial Court*. G.M. Rideout. Prov. Ct. J.

R. v. Chief Constable of South Yorkshire Police (Respondent) ex parte LS (by his mother and litigation friend JB (FC) (Appellant), R. v. Chief Constable of South Yorkshire Police (Respondent) ex parte Marper (FC) (Appellant) (Consolidated Appeals). 2004 UKHL 39. *House of Lords*. Lord Steyn, Lord Rodger of Earlsferry, Baroness Hale of Richmond, Lords Carswell, Lord Brown of Eaton-under-Heywood.

R. v. Clarke. 1999. BCJ 1545. *British Columbia Provincial Court (Traffic Division)*. Makhdoom J.P.

R. v. Fischer. 1999. BCJ 2421. *British Columbia Provincial Court (Traffic Division)*. Makhdoom J.P.

R. v. Henshaw. 2000. BCJ 1399. *British Columbia Provincial Court (Traffic Division)*. Makhdoom J.P.

R. v. Hodson. 2012. BCJ 2802. *British Columbia Provincial Court*. J.F. Palmer Prov. Ct. J.

R. v. Jackson. 2011. OJ 1974. *Ontario Court of Justice*. F.C. O'Donnell J.

R. v. John. 2010. OJ 4738. *Ontario Superior Court of Justice*. M.A. Code J.

R. v. Kerr. 2000. BCJ 691. *British Columbia Provincial Court (Traffic Division)*. Hughes J.P.

R. v. L. (D.O.). 1993. SCJ 72. *Supreme Court of Canada*. Lamer C.J. and La Forest, L'Heureux-Dubé, Sopinka, Gonthier, Cory, McLachlin, Iacobucci and Major J.J.

R. v. McLetchie. 2011. OJ 1244. *Ontario Superior Court of Justice*. M.A. Code J.

R. v. Mikolajczyk. 2014. MJ 7. *Manitoba Court of Appeal*. F.M. Steel, H.C. Beard and M.M. Monnin JJ.A.

R. v. N.S. 2012. SCJ 72. *Supreme Court of Canada*. McLachlin C.J. and LeBel, Deschamps, Fish, Abella, Rothstein and Cromwell J.J.

R. v. Ng. 1998. BCJ 1716. *British Columbia Provincial Court (Traffic Division)*. Hayes, J.P.

R. v. Nikolovski. 1996. 3 SCR 1197. *Supreme Court of Canada*. Lamer, C.J. and La Forest, L'Heureux-Dubé, Sopinka, Gonthier, Cory, McLachlin, Iacobucci and Major JJ.

R. v Nilsson. 2011. BCJ 2316. *British Columbia Supreme Court*. P.W. Walker J.

R. v. Paruk. 1999. BCJ 2975. *British Columbia Supreme Court*. Bennett J.

R. v. Rockey. 1996. SCJ 114. *Supreme Court of Canada*. Lamer, C.J. and La Forest, L'Heureux-Dubé, Sopinka, Gonthier, Cory, McLachlin, Iacobucci and Major J.J.

R. v. Sharma. 2014. A.J. No. 640. Docket 130113343P1. *Alberta Provincial Court.* A.A. Fradsham Prov. Ct. J.

R. v. Tessling. 2004. 3 S.C.R. 432, *Supreme Court of Canada.* S.C.C. 67.

R. v. Tri-M Systems Inc. 1998. BCJ 2702. *British Columbia Supreme Court.* Brenner J.

R. v. Tsang. 1998. BCJ 1216. *British Columbia Provincial Court (Traffic Division).* Hayes, J.P.

R. v. Villeda. 2014. BCJ 789. *British Columbia Provincial Court.* G.M. Rideout Prov. Ct. J.

R. v. Zunic. 2012. MJ 347. *Manitoba Court of Queen's Bench.* D.J. McCawley J.

Report of an Investigation into Collection and Use of Personal Employee Information without Consent, R.J. Hoffman Holdings Ltd. 2005. Investigation Report P2005-IR-004. *Alberta Information and Privacy Commissioner.* E. Denham (Director, Personal Information Protection Act) and K. Robidoux (Contract Portfolio Officer). 13 May 2005.

Report on the Investigation into Complaint Regarding Collection of Personal Information Re: Edmonton Police Service. 2003. Report F2003-IR-005. A.I.P.C.D. No. 31. Investigation No. 2777. *Alberta Information and Privacy Commissioner.* F. Work, Commissioner. 7 August 2003.

"Testimony Outside of Courtroom—Witness Under 18 or Who Have a Disability." Criminal Code (R.S.C., 1985, c. C-46). *Justice Laws Website.* Government of Canada. 22 May 2015. Web. 24 May 2015.

X v. Scottish Prison Service. Decision 052/2012. Margaret Keyse, Acting Scottish Information Commissioner. Web. www.itspublicknowledge.info.

Index

About the Author

Jeff Heydon teaches in the Communications Studies Department at Wilfrid Laurier University. Trained in media theory and cultural studies, he researches surveillance, violence, new media, and visual culture.

www.ingramcontent.com/pod-product-compliance
Ingram Content Group UK Ltd.
Pitfield, Milton Keynes, MK11 3LW, UK
UKHW012119150926
475560UK00002B/177